The Fountain & the Furnace

THE WAY OF TEARS AND FIRE

Maggie Ross

Paulist Press ◆ New York ◆ Mahwah

Library of Congress Cataloging-in-Publication Data

Ross, Maggie, 1941–
    The fountain and the furnace.

    Bibliography: p.
    1. Crying—Religious aspects—Christianity.   I. Title.
BT805.R67   1986   248   86-21226
ISBN 0-8091-2840-3 (pbk.)

Published by Paulist Press
997 Macarthur Blvd.
Mahwah, N.J. 07430

Printed and bound in the
United States of America

Contents

I
The Fractured Rock
the human condition; tears as the way forward; greater
and lesser, or chosen and not chosen deaths; introduc-
ing gift of tears; tears distinct from "grief work"; cultural matrix of interior death; fear of death; healing the

II
The Hidden Source
groping for God through tears; tears as most profound
opening to and response to the mystery of kenotic love;
security and mythology, technique, magic, wonder;
the child; God as subject instead of object; "active" and
"contemplative"; description of a kenotic person; sal-

III
The Polluted Spring
evil, power and illusion; recent studies of evil: Tuch-

This book is dedicated to

The Right Reverend Paul Moore
Bishop of New York

The Reverend Canon Roswell O Moore
President, Province VIII
and
my Hermit Father

who know. . . .

The Publisher gratefully acknowledges the use of the following materials:

Material from *The Elusive Presence: Toward a New Biblical Theology* by Samuel Terrien, volume twenty-six of the Religious Perspectives Series planned and edited by Ruth Nanda Anshen, copyright © 1978 by Samuel Terrien and Ruth Nanda Anshen, is reprinted by permission of Harper & Row, Publishers, Inc. Excerpts from *Holy the Firm* by Annie Dillard, copyright ©1977 by Annie Dillard, are reprinted by permission of Harper & Row, Publishers, Inc. Quotations from *The Denial of Death* by Ernest Becker, copyright ©1973 by The Free Press, are reprinted by permission of The Free Press, a division of Macmillan, Inc. Material from *The Courage to Be* by Paul Tillich, copyright ©1952 by Paul Tillich, is reprinted by permission of Yale University Press. Material from *People of the Lie*, copyright ©1983 by M. Scott Peck, M.D., is reprinted by permission of Simon & Schuster, Inc. Excerpts from *The Wound of Knowledge* (published in the USA as *Christian Spirituality*) by Rowan Williams, copyright 1980 by Darton, Longman and Todd Ltd., are reprinted by permission of Darton, Longman and Todd. Quotations from "Little Gidding," from *Four Quartets* by T.S. Eliot, copyright 1943 by T.S. Eliot, renewed 1971 by Esme Valerie Eliot, are reprinted by permission of Harcourt Brace Jovanovich, Inc. Material from *Pilgerman*, copyright ©1983 by Russell Hoban, is reprinted by permission of Summit Books, a division of Simon & Schuster, Inc., and by David Higham, Associates Ltd. The "Prayer for Tears" from *Early Irish Lyrics* edited by Gerard Murphy, copyright 1956 by Gerard Murphy, is reprinted by permission of Oxford University Press. Permission to quote from "Humility and Obedience in Monastic Tradition" by Andre Louf, copyright 1983 by *Cistercian Studies*, has been granted by *Cistercian Studies*. The material from the Second Book of Isaac the Syrian which makes up Appendix III is reprinted by permission of Sebastian Brock and Dana Miller, translators. Permission to reprint the excerpt from Robert Anderson's review of *Habits of the Heart* and the excerpt from Kenneth Brigg's article "Salvation: Do We Run After or Wait for It?" has been granted by the *National Catholic Reporter*. The quotations from "Can We Know Spiritual Reality?" by Donald Evans and from "Our Fragile Brothers" by Jim Nieckarz, both of which appeared in *Commonweal*, are reprinted by permission of the Commonweal Foundation. The poem entitled "The Cradle" is reprinted by permission of Bishop John Taylor. Quotations from *The New English Bible*, second edition, copyright 1970, are reprinted by permission of Oxford and Cambridge University Presses. The quotation from *The Brothers Karamazov* by Fydor Dostoyevsky, translated by David Magarshack (Penguin Classics, 1958), copyright ©1958 by David Magarshack, is reprinted by permission of Penguin Books Ltd. Material from *The Luminous Eye* by Sebastian Brock is reprinted by permission of the Centre for Indian and Inter-Religious Studies, Rome. Sebastian Brock's translation of *On Prayer* by John the Solitary is reprinted by permission of *The Journal of Theological Studies*. The translations from Isaac the Syrian by Sebastian Brock and Robert Murray that appeared in *Eastern Churches Review* are reprinted by permission of *Eastern Churches Review*. The excerpt from *The Holy Spirit in the Syrian Baptismal Tradition* by Sebastian Brock is reprinted by permission of the Thurvanisa Prayer House, Kerala, India. The excerpt from Irvin Ephrenpreis's article on T.S. Eliot is reprinted by permission of *The New York Review of Books*, copyright ©1984 by Nyrev, Inc.

My beloved, having become foolish, I cannot bear to guard the mystery in silence: I am turning into a fool, for the sake of the profit of my brethren. For true love is such that it is unable to tarry in the cause of love when it is separated from those whom it loves.[1]

Author's Note

The birth of any book is something of a mystery, and this one is no exception. My original intention was to write a small study of tears as a long-neglected aspect of "spiritual life", and the role they have played, consciously or unconsciously, in the life of one person.

As I began to pull together the notes and ideas of many years' ponderings, conversations, reading, observation, and experience, a dreadful realization came over me of the magnitude, if not the enormity of what I had undertaken.

It appears that tears may be one key to understanding the unity of the bio-psycho-spiritual person; and more: a key to understanding the mutual *kenosis* of the relationship between God and creation; a key as crucial to understanding what a person is as created in the redeeming love of God as is the double helix in understanding the genetic code.

Additionally, I realized that tears could never be understood in the context of the accumulated weight of centuries of controversy, systematizing, insistence on terminology and definition, and the assumption that we can know and form an image of what goes on in another's mind and heart. If I were to write about tears, I had to attempt to restate, as far as possible in common-sense language, what the journey into God is all about.

I realize now, only at the end of writing this book, that I have undertaken a survey of spiritual theology in which the idea of *kenosis* is absolutely central, and in which tears play the crucial role.

What do I mean by this word, *kenosis?*

Let each of you look not only to his own interests, but also to the interests of others. Have this mind among yourselves,

3

which is yours in Christ Jesus, who though he was in the form of God, did not count equality with God a thing to be grasped, but emptied himself, taking the form of a servant, being born in the likeness of men. And being found in human form he humbled himself and became obedient unto death, even death on a cross. (Phil. 2:5–9 RSV)

The "mind" of God, the "mind" of Christ is self-emptying, that is, God willingly limits God's power in order to become engaged in life on earth. And more: God is willing to limit God's power to undergo the ultimate in powerlessness so that the power and glory of God can enter the world. To effect this, Jesus gives up security, status, dominance, reputation.

> He [the author of the hymn in Philippians 2:6ff] discerned in Jesus the type of man who did not yield to the greed of deification through egocentricity. "He emptied himself" . . . Theology is kenotic when it stresses the divine act of divesting oneself of prerogatives. The kenotic theology of the hymnist offers a prelude to the life of the man Jesus. It intimates in parallel fashion the "overshadowing" of the myth of the annunciation, the debasement of the baptism, when Jesus was immersed in the common guilt of the human race, the agony of his temptation to use power in the desert and in the garden, and the taunting of the by-standers who said, before his last gasps of pain, "If thou be the Son of God, save thyself!"
>
> The poet, in effect, sang the presence of the *deus absconditus* at the crucifixion.[2]

In his hymns on the Nativity, St Ephrem (4th c) implicitly acknowledges Mary as the mirror of her Son's divine *kenosis*. Her willing loss of reputation; her physical emptiness in order to receive him, evidence a heart cleaving only to God:

> The Light settled on Mary as on an eye,
> It purified her mind, it cleansed her understanding,
> it washed her thought, it made her virginity shine.[3]

> Your mother's womb has reversed the roles:
> the Establisher of all entered in His richness,
> but came forth poor; the Exalted One entered her,

but came forth meek; the Splendrous One entered her,
but came forth having put on a lowly hue.

The Mighty One entered, and put on insecurity
from her womb: the Provisioner of all entered
—and experienced hunger: He who gives drink to all entered
—and experienced thirst: naked and stripped
there came forth from her He who clothes all.[4]

She is seen as the burning bush that became "empty" in order
to bear the divine flame:

Just as the bush on Horeb bore
God in the flame,
so did Mary bear
Christ in her virginity. . . .

A virgin is pregnant with God,
and a barren woman is pregnant with a virgin,
the son of sterility leaps
at the pregnancy of virginity.[5]

This is only the beginning of a description of *kenosis* and its implications.*

Because of the vastness of this undertaking, the present book
should be regarded as a preliminary study.

I have had to paint with a broad brush. The material is suggestive and not demonstrative. I have attempted to integrate prismatic
and discursive writing because the material necessarily combines
symbolic and discursive thought.

While decoding some of the tradition, it is possible, that because of the necessity of writing in a kind of shorthand of ideas I
have created a code of my own. It may lead readers to respond to
what appears here: to criticise, suggest alternative interpretations,
texts, and, most of all, I would hope, lead them to illuminate this
topic with their own scholarship and personal experience.

The question as to how and why I became interested in this

---

*This tradition has lived on in Eastern Christianity in a far more vital way than
in the West, and has not been confined to christology. For a summary see *The Orthodox Way*, by Father Kallistos Ware, Crestwood, 1980.

particular subject invariably arises, so perhaps a brief comment is in order.

The how has to do with a growing awareness of certain truths about life and death, an awareness that began in early childhood. The why has to do with that major confrontation with despair we all seem to come to at some point in life, the results of which will often determine the character of life's balance.

It would seem that despair now appears earlier than perhaps was the case in the past, and also that it perhaps has become a more conscious, constant, and familiar companion from the very earliest days of awareness.

Or perhaps it is that our awareness of the presence of despair has changed, along with our disavowal of what is unseen, and our growing insistence that mortality is somehow an affront and that the failure of science to "cure" it calls for a lawsuit.

There are signs that this pathological mental and spiritual climate is changing. This book may be one of them.

My own confrontation with these questions came to crisis during my early twenties, a crisis that seemed to sum up all the despair of my past and future and, having fallen through this despair into the hand of God, I became aware of the process through which I was passing. I was enabled to observe certain transformations taking place, and a little of how they were taking place.

This process can perhaps be summed up in three questions which seem to be constants: what do I (or you) want? where do I (or you) hurt? what price am I (are you) willing to pay?

As I listen to the responses, two more questions arise: Why? And, what do I (or you) mean by that?

The answer to the questions, "Why didn't you kill yourself; what made you want to live; how have you found joy?" can be summed up in one word: *tears*.

I am only beginning to understand what the *kenosis* of God and the *kenosis* of human response mean. It is certain that whatever the value of my experience, the process of transformation is a task to which each person must assent in his or her unique way, knowing that there is never an end to these questions, and that the "answer" is the door into the mystery of the love of God.

Feast of the Epiphany, 1986

Acknowledgments

I am more indebted to others for this book than perhaps is usual for an author. On a practical level, I must first of all thank the American Philosophical Society for a grant in 1985 that made possible the major effort toward completing this manuscript.

Additionally, the Rev Kevin Lynch, CSP, Publisher of Paulist Press, through his unfailing support gave me courage to continue what had become a daunting task.

I must also thank Dr Landrum Bolling and his helpful staff for seven valuable weeks in 1985 at the Ecumenical Insitute for Advanced Theological Research, Tantur, Jerusalem.

The Principal, Chapter and community of Pusey House, Oxford, provided me with a totally unexpected *koinonia*, not to mention an anchorhold, thus making the first few months of my stay in Oxford possible. Their steady round of prayer, liturgy, seriousness, hilarity and the occasional discreet airborne delivery of breakfast toast helped keep things in perspective, and suggested that creative innovation and common-sense willingness to see a need and provide for it without fuss have not been entirely lost to the Church and the world.

From an ideational point of view I must thank, in chronological order, the members of the seminars organized by the late Preston G McLean, MD, of which I was privileged to be a member in the years 1966–1972; and the Rev Bruno Barnhart, Cam. OSB, at whose request the primitive form of the ideas in this book was first written down in 1980–1981.

In 1984, in England, France, and Denmark, the following people were willing to listen to the ramblings of an unknown American who landed on their doorsteps, and encouraged the pursuit of this topic in a more significant way than was originally intended: Dr Esther de Waal; the Rev Canon A M Allchin, who named this book; Fr Gregory, CSWG; Sister Jeanette Seager; Dom André Louf, OCSO; Dr Brian McGuire; the Rev Canon W H Vanstone; the Rev Robert Llewelyn; the Rev Canon Michael McLean; Sir Richard Southern, who sponsored my admission to the Bodleian Library and who with Lady Southern made the intercontinental move seem a very good idea; Bishop Kallistos Ware; Sister Sylvia Mary, CSMV; Andrew Louth; the Rev Canon Rowan Williams; and most of all Dr Sebastian Brock, whose idea it was that I return to Oxford; who, in the midst of running his own department took time not only to initiate me into Syrian Christianity, but also to make translations especially for this work; and who, with his wife Helen, have not only opened to me the matchless resources of the University, but also, and much more important, given unstintingly of their comfort, love and prayer.

Finally, there are innumerable people who, through their friendship, good advice, and courage to speak their minds have enabled not only this book but also the living out of the vocation from which it has been drawn. To list them all would require naming virtually every significant human being in my life for the last forty-four years, so I must limit myself to those who have had some concrete connexion with the production of this book: the Rev Dr John Barton; Dr George Bebawi; Père Jacques Bernard; Dr Deborah and Dr Keith Carne; the Rev Sean Caulfield; Community of St Clare, Freeland, Oxford; Community of Ste Marie-du-Mont, Bailleul, France; Pamela Lee Cranston; Bleema Dutre; Joan Evanish; Dr Jim Fleming; Mother Helen, PCC and the Poor Clares of Aptos, California; Nigel Hartley, who proofread the manuscript; Dona Harvey; Susan Harvey; Captain Peter Hunter; Dr William Klassen; the Rev Bill Kirkpatrick; Peter Meadows, who drew the diagram; the Rev Canon Roswell O Moore; Kathryn M Murphy; Dr Donald Nicholl; August O'Conner; Kirsten Pedersen (Soeur Abraham); the Rev H Boone Porter; Penny Read; the Rev Dr Geoffrey Rowell; the Rev Jack Schanhaar; the Rev Donald Schell; Sister Mary Ann Schofield, SM; Archimandrite Sophrony; Liz Specht; Dr Lewis Spitz; Sandol Stoddard; Dr Pardon Tillinghast; Dom Armand Veilleux, OCSO; Sister Benedicta Ward, SLG; Dr Richard Wentz; my agent, Lois Curley, who never lost faith; my Bishop Protector, the Right Rev

Paul Moore of New York, without whose discernment and support my vocation, much less this book, never would have come to any kind of fruition; and finally my family, who have given me their unfailing support no matter how incomprehensible the odd bird who somehow got into the nest.

Often as I was writing these things, my fingers stopped still on the paper, unable to hold the pen in the presence of the delight which fell upon the heart, silencing the senses.[6]

Introduction

At the end of his foreword to Terence Fretheim's *The Suffering of God*, Walter Brueggemann makes the following statement:

> The implications of the study, not drawn by the author, run in two important directions. First, the linkages to the NT and a theology of the cross are important and obvious. Second, it occurs to me that such a way of doing theology not only challenges conventional theology but also conventional cultural assumptions that justify our models of humanness and our practices of political and economic power. The subversive force of this theological assertion extends not only to the religious tradition, but to the derivative forms of social power justified by biblical faith. Western preoccupation with dominance and power is no doubt linked to and derived from our imperial "image of God." Clearly when that discernment of God is challenged, the images which take public form are in deep jeopardy.[7]

I came across Dr Fretheim's work very late in my preparations for this book, but was struck by these words as expressing much of what I hoped to do, although perhaps not in the way Dr Brueggemann envisioned.

It is the subversive element of this vision that requires a restatement of the context and assumptions in which spiritual theology is understood. Thus the need for the first three chapters of the present book on tears, which examine the human condition, the need for a revised understanding of how we relate to God, and a brief look at the problem of evil, power and illusion as it is often experienced in the West today.

The vision of God that is counter to our prevailing attitudes toward dominance is a kenotic one, and since we are meant to be God's image, to mirror God, our response must be a kenotic response. To get from the attitude of dominance to the attitude of kenosis, or the mind of Christ, is an enormous task, and one that only tears can accomplish. Tears are always a sign that we are struggling with power of one sort or another: the loss of ours; the entering of God's.

The next three chapters describe tears proper: how we begin to know them; and their affects and effects; what happens when we allow them.

The last three chapters are an evocation of the kind of understanding that results from entering on the "way" of tears: encounter with elementals; living from the well of nonexperience, which is the well of reality; and finally, putting all of this in practical terms in noncontrolling relationships, life as party and divine play.

I came to the scholarly material in this book backwards. I began my exploration twenty years ago without any idea that I was going to publish. There was my own experience to begin with. Then was added the work I had done in history and theology, psychoanalysis and interdisciplinary studies. There were also several years I spent in a vineyard, farming grapes and running a winery. I became a solitary in the Church. I began to read the desert Fathers and Mothers.

They shed some light, but the method of transmission of their sayings, coupled with their contemporary interpretation, made their essence and *nexus* seem obscure. A complementary, organic vision was lacking. I finally made an intuitive assumption that the sayings about tears had to go with the sayings about fire. The next question was, why did I have this hunch? And then I remembered that these men and women of the wilderness were steeped in scripture.

I went to scripture and found that images of fire and water are virtually inseparable in theophanies both in the Hebrew scriptures and in the New Testament. It was then I began to realize the elemental imagery and vast network of interconnections, the unified vision that had somehow got lost in Christianity very early on.

Somewhere there had to be a writer who lived after New Testament times but whose understanding was in the tradition of semitic Christianity, relatively unscathed by Greek philosophical controversies; one who lived in "nonrefutation" because his or her vision of the God of both Hebrew and New Testament scripture was dazzling enough to transcend the philosophical battles, and dense enough to reflect the awe of one grasped by the glory of God.

There is no question but that my groping toward semitic Christianity and my subsequent meeting with Sebastian Brock, who introduced me to St Ephrem, was divinely inspired.

There are many eloquent writers from the patristic period to the present day, but after working with Ephrem there is little question in my mind that he is the last Christian writer in whom the silence of nonrefutation* and resulting revelation exist in this particular way.

As I read St Ephrem I became convinced that here was the freshness and the intensity that we in the West had gone much farther East to find; here was the worldview that perhaps we in the West had never really understood, or turned on its head, the worldview that so many of the contemporary trends in spirituality seemed to be trying to recover.

Ephrem has been poorly served. He has usually been lumped with the Greek Fathers when, in fact, Syriac spirituality, while not devoid of Greek influence, is entirely "its own thing". Ephrem is one of the Syriac writers least influenced by Greek dualism. His use of imagery, his "luminous eye", his breadth as well as depth, his tightly-packed writing and most of all his insistence on theology done in a matrix of adoration and poetry make him entirely distinct. His view that it is blasphemy to presume that we can contain God in our finite minds, words, and mental images is one that we need to adopt as our own.

Many works attributed to Ephrem are not his. I have quoted only from those thought to be authentic. Additionally, I have in the main stayed with the Syriac writers, although I have occasionally quoted John Climacus, Symeon the New Theologian, and others. For the most part I have left the Greeks alone because one cannot discuss or quote them without getting entangled in major philo-

---

*This phrase is an allusion to Thomas Merton's experience with the reclining Buddhas in Ceylon, and the description of it in *The Asian Journal*. My use of this word refers to Ephrem's *quality of silence*. Ephrem did write several works of refutation, and many of the Hymns of Faith, and the cycle against Heresies are aimed at Arianism. But the hymns invade the heart as adoration, not polemic.

sophical and historical problems. For the same reasons I have been forced to skip over most of the scattered evidence of the tradition of personal *kenosis* that appears in Western writers—the Wesleys, for example.

In Ephrem I find expression of limpid thought that is not only free from these difficulties but in which they seemingly could not appear.

The other Syriac writer I have frequently cited is Isaac the Syrian (7th c). While he knew of and quotes Evagrius, his writing is nonetheless relatively untrammeled by some of the problems associated with his more famous colleague. While making appropriate bows in Evagrius' direction, Isaac has a healthy attitude toward the body and the things of this world.

Isaac is caught historically in a time of wearying controversy, when the price of incautious speech was exile or death. Implicit in his writing is the vision of a God who weeps over the creation that is inherently good, and in which God is unceasingly involved. This vision is not patripassianism,* and in any event transcends philosophical and theological definition.

Isaac has his own problems, however. He has to be read with an eye to rhetoric and even hyperbole. He is not consistent in his terminology. He seems to be writing primarily for monks, whereas Ephrem is writing hymns everyone can sing with all one's heart.

Yet some of Isaac's phenomenology is superb. He is a great, if not the great early writer on tears. His whole work is shot through with the theme like a stream of light. He lacks Ephrem's fine touch and sense of divine play, but in spite of his sometimes severe protestations about the need for physical solitude, and in spite of being entirely cut off even from family members in need, he reveals his tender heart in passages about love for his friends and for the beasts.

I have taken translations from the most reliable sources I can find. Some of these are extremely difficult to locate. Thus I have often cited a book or a translation because it is more generally available. In some cases new translations have been made (such as Dr

---

*For a discussion of patripassianism, see Gerald Vann, OP, *The Sorrow of God and the Pain of Christ*, Acquin Press, London 1947 and 1961, pp. 62ff. See also the first two chapters of *The Suffering of God, op. cit.*, and A.J. Heschel's discussion of the pathos of God in *The Prophets*, Harper and Row, New York 1962, pp. 268 ff.

Brock's) and I have sometimes given more than one reference so that the reader can explore as deeply as he or she likes.

In the appendix are translations by Dr Brock of some very interesting material: parts of the long-lost Book II of Isaac's, which Dr Brock found in the Bodleian Library in 1983, and which he is currently translating with Dana Miller. As far as we know this is the first time this manuscript has been published. There are also translations from the *Liber Graduum*, and a penetrating study of silence by John the Solitary. This is probably the first time these have been made generally available in English. I am very grateful to Dr Brock and to the Oxford University Press (for John the Solitary) for allowing me to use these translations.

John the Solitary brings up a last point: Dom Armand Veilleux asked me: what is the *nexus* of this book? Which I took to mean: what is the connecting link? After some reflection I think it is silence: the quality of silence, the kinds of silence, the uses of silence, the ability to live in the right kind of silence alone and in relationships. In fact, one might even say that salvation is about silence.

But to explain that, it is best to begin.

"Weep! Truly there is no other way than this."[8]

"You must write, 'It is the only way!' "[9]

Foreword

Joy leaps from the heart of God, a fountain springing from the divine center, and ours. This flood, this vast unstemmable tide, carries with it all the flotsam and jetsam of our lives. This source-less source is never-ending Love and the upwelling and spilling over of tears.

God's and ours.

God's first.

God baptizes us with tears.

God loves creation enough to weep over it, to become one of us, to shed tears as a man. As the divine breath still moves over the salted water of creation, so with tears Mercy bathes and mothers us into new life with her life. Into joy.

It is strange, then, that in these latter days we have repudiated our tears, for by doing so we have allowed our selves to be swirled into an eddy as the joyous torrent rushes toward *parousia* in the here and now. We somehow have lost the understanding that the salt of tears is the savor of life; that life salted with tears is salted with fire; that a life laid down upon the altar drenched with tears arcs to meet fire falling from heaven: tears to tears, salt to salt, fire to fire.

The circle is complete, the circuit made, the dance begun.

We need to recover the salt of our life.

We need to recover our understanding of the life-flood of tears, God's and ours, that mothers the fire of our life, that carries us through the passages of death, real death, complete death. We need to understand with our hearts the *kenosis* that is at the heart of the fiery life of the blessed Trinity into which we are taken; the *kenosis* pouring into our frail vessels, opened by willingness for our own

21

kenosis, spilling out their sullied contents with its prodigality, being deluged by Mercy filling us to overflowing.

Thus *kenosis* fills *kenosis*, and fire springs from an altar bathed with tears.

Resurrection is not mere resuscitation, nor is the idea of the immortality of the soul, which enjoys new popularity today, an early Christian doctrine. When we die, we die. All of us. Body, soul, spirit, if you like those distinctions. But God gives us a new life, a greater, a better. And we are prepared for this life with the continual and simultaneous death and resurrection that takes place in our daily round, the mercy of tears feeding the fountain of joy erupting from our tombs.

This is a book about gifts: the gift of tears and the gift of joy. The two are as inseparable as breathing in and out, or bread and wine, or heaven and earth. Indeed, it is the story of the marriage of heaven and earth: our emptiness is filled with tears which, salted with the fire of the Spirit become wine for the wedding of which we are both stewards and vessels.

Our emptiness is filled with the *kenosis* of God's own life.

This is not a book about melancholy, depression, or death, though all three are mentioned by way of differentiating or healing. Nor is it an attempt to make easy the stark and confrontive reality of interior transformation. Rather, it seeks to make inescapable the need to open our selves to a gift which for centuries has been ignored or dismissed as archaic.

The fire in the well of our hearts—ours and God's—springs from deep caverns, and it is my purpose to explore some of them by what darkling light is given. This expedition's purpose is not so much to describe the many vaulted rooms from whose crystalline stalactites tears still drip, giving these living stones their form. Rather it seeks to describe the passages by which these rooms are continually found and left behind.

We live on many levels all at once. Thus it is difficult if not impossible to write about this life without doing violence to it. Today we often have the impression that it is a progress from one stage to another, and waste enormous amounts of precious time and energy examining our selves in the wrong way to find out exactly where we are. Such self-interest brings us instantly back to square one.

We need to read the ancients again and again. We need their wisdom. We need their signposts and roadmaps. We need the light they left behind as we follow them in this divine spelunking.

But we need most of all to recover what they most wanted to teach: that the whole point of the journey into the fiery love of God is *self-forgetfulness*, a self-forgetfulness evolving from a self-awareness that gradually drops away as we become ever more found in the adoration of God in whom we find our true selves. This movement toward completion no longer needs self-reflection, but needs to be aware only of God.

This is true joy: not the emotions, feelings and "experiences" we usually call by those names and contrive, connive, and compete impotently to achieve. We cannot achieve joy. It, too, is a gift, a gift that comes with our evolution toward simplicity in our diversity.

Our fathers and mothers had much to say about tears and fire. We have tended to regard them—the fathers and the mothers as well as the tears and the fire—separately, thereby distorting one or the other. Their sayings are now as a result largely incomprehensible to us, fossilized and encrusted with centuries of spiritual debris: they no longer seem to be living stones.

But these God-parents of ours knew what they were talking about, even though their sayings about tears have come down to us tidily separated from their sayings about fire. To look at tears or fire in this way makes about as much sense as to have six blind men examine and describe an elephant.

"Weep," our forebears said, "until there are channels inscribed in your cheeks."

"If you wish," they also said, rising and stretching out their arms cruciform, "you can become fire." And flame shot from their spread fingers.

But you see, the fire comes because of the salt in the tears. It was there all the time in God's tears and ours. And perhaps it is not too fanciful to imagine these holy women and men saying instead, as they rise from their prostration, "Weep until there are channels inscribed in your face and *then* you can become fire," and we see the tears pouring out their blessing, feeding the fire which now blinds us.

Come, says the Bride, come to the water without price. Come to these tears, God's burning love. Wedded thus, come, let us explore the dazzling dark.

Prelude

The Fountain

When I lived alone in the canyon my only source of water was not the stream which ran along the geological fault that formed it, but a spring high up the ridge opposite.

On old maps it was known as "Boar Spring". Certainly the wild pigs, lions, bobcats, and coyotes knew it, and doubtless it had been sacred to the Native Americans as was the clearing near which my cabin stood.

The spring welled out of a crack in an enormous rock; "knockers", they're called by geologists, these rocks that seem to rise singly out of the earth.

In early autumn before the rains the flow was a mere trickle, but in April it gushed from the rock and into the "box" carved from the rock, down the pipe to the redwood holding tank, where the water erupted from under its conical lid like lava from a volcano.

Developing and maintaining a spring is a delicate business. Springs are mysterious. Sometimes they will give their water in greater abundance if they are cautiously tapped. But beware of digging carelessly, or too deep. Beware of removing sentinel trees. It is no wonder springs often have been thought to have their own spirits: they are life-bearers, who guard their own secrets.

When the optimal amount of water is coming from the tapped rock the work is then to develop a box where the waters can collect to build up enough pressure to start moving through the pipe to a holding tank. The box is usually hollowed out of the rock, and the banks on every side lined with timbers. Then the box is covered to prevent contamination by animals and debris.

You run the overflow pipe down the side to the bottom of the tank so the animals can lick the water from its mouth.

Even then your work is not over. The spring has to be protected and cared for. Branches flung from surrounding trees during storms can damage the box cover. Leaves collect, and some slip into the water. Small insects can clog the screened opening where the water enters the pipe; and occasionally a dying creature will find its last refuge in the box, seeking the cool shade, and icy water to slake its thirst.

The whole system then becomes polluted and must be cleaned out and purified. This is a difficult and smelly task. With the best effort you must wait until much water has flowed before what pours from the fractured rock is again cold and crystalline.

Sometimes I would go to the spring simply to look at it. I never removed the cover without a sense of awe at the sight of the mirroring pool, and of the water welling into the stone box. I would gaze into its depths for long moments before removing any debris. I was careful never to let anything of my own fall into it, but whether or not I actually touched the water I came away cleansed and purified, and went on my way with liquid flames burning in my heart.

I

The breakers of death rolled over me, and the torrents of
oblivion made me afraid. (Psalm 18:4 BCP)

While I felt secure, I said, "I shall never be disturbed."
You, Lord, with your favor, made me strong as the mountains.
(Psalm 30:7 BCP)

The children of a family share in the same flesh and blood;
and so he too shared ours, so that through death he might break
the power of him who had death at his command, that is, the
devil, and might liberate those who, through fear of death, had
all their lifetime been in servitude. (Heb. 2:14–15 RSV)

The Fractured Rock

That the way of tears unlocks the sources of joy is one of those basic paradoxes on which life in God rests. It is founded on another paradox, one of the most fundamental and misunderstood of Christian truths: that in weakness is strength; in seeming folly, wisdom; in giving up self, self is found; in death is life.

The Goodness of Life and Creation

During the first few centuries of Christian history, these basic, life-enhancing paradoxes somehow were turned around so that they became life-denying. The only life worth living was after death, and while it was not encouraged to take one's own life by patent suicide, the so-called ascetic feats of saints of questionable orthodoxy were held up as models to be imitated. Their lives were embroidered with the glosses necessary to drive the point home that the chances of salvation were few for one in love with creation, and that to conform to the will of God—which often seems to us to have been understood as fixed and terrifying—was no less easy than to be stoic in the embrace of an iron maiden.

Sown in the religious revolt of the 16th century were seeds of hope of finding a more merciful God. But Luther's vision was even more quickly turned on its head than early Christian insight, and the heritage of the reformers was, if anything, more grim than what it originally sought to replace.

The counter-reformation reaction to the reformers carried hatred of the creation and mind-numbing passivity to cruel extremes, most notably in the Inquisition and its insistence on spiritual tyranny.

The popular mind tends to seize on one aspect of a movement and magnify it out of proportion, creating a climate for further revolt, so that in the twentieth century what God has named good is no longer called evil. The reasons have not been religious: in fact, God has frequently been thrown out along with manichean piety.

This secular and social revolt has been materialistic and hedonistic, and the lot of the created world has, if anything, become worse. No longer merely disregarded or pushed away, the creation has become subject to exploitation as never before.

This exploitation has been based in part on the idea that nothing is too good for human beings, and this new legacy has persuaded us that if we pull hard enough on our bootstraps, and invent enough technique and technology, that mortality itself—the final embarrassment—really has no place with us.

Along with affirmation of the good (and some not so good) propensities of human beings and the increasing denial of death have come denial of evil and avoidance of discipline named by traditional religion. Discipline is popular, but only as it relates to spiritual hedonism, self-improvement, beauty, money or pleasure.

The basic Christian message has nothing to do with this sort of negativity, especially in terms of exploitation, or with exaltation of the human to the exclusion of everything else.

We are now beginning to see the end of this revolution and a new time of transition. Despair has not been kept at bay. To complicate matters we are in grave danger of destroying all life by contamination if not by nuclear holocaust. These possibilities add an entirely new element to despair, and renew the temptation to life-denying, apocalyptic religion. This sort of religion has a dangerous propensity to become self-fulfilling; and it is quite likely that there would be no recovery from modern forms of annihilation inherent in such religion of despair.

The irony in all of this is that in the Christian tradition of willing powerlessness lies an exaltation of the human person and its maximum growth, perfection and possibility that far exceeds the vision of any secular humanism.

Underneath its paradoxes is a wisdom tradition far more profound than most exegesis would allow, a wisdom tradition which acknowledges that the potential for destruction is already inherent and set in motion by the seizing of power and control over one's own destiny and that of others.

As we will see, this wisdom tradition in no way denies the basic contemporary understanding of the need for self-motivation, self-affirmation, and "taking control of one's life". Part of the problem is that the language of power has become confused. Occasionally this has been deliberate.

We must gain control in order to be able to lose control and be subject to transcendence; while psychological health is unnecessary for knowing God, at the same time we must have a minimal sense of self, no matter how flawed, before we can begin to be able to give it away. We must be at least a little full before we can be empty.

This is all a way of talking about life and death.

Greater and Lesser Death: Chosen and Unchosen

Suicide, the ultimate act of control, is also a paradox. Some psychiatrists consider it a contagious disease. What is often regarded in the popular mind as the act of someone whose life has become so unbearable that death no longer holds any fear is actually quite the opposite.

We die on as many levels as we live.

And at heart, at least in my experience, people seem to contemplate suicide because they are afraid of, or have been discouraged from what have been called the "little deaths", the personal transformations that open us to larger life here and now.

It is of course impossible to generalize. We can't know another's heart as God knows it; we can't know the anguish of a person driven mad by intractable physical or psychic pain. We can't talk with those who are dead, and in no way do I mean to imply that those who commit suicide are "guilty" or "condemned". I am not passing judgment on anyone, and probing into motives, even with the best will and method, can never be more than conjecture.

Life is a gift without obligation. God does not give us life to make us feel guilty. Guilt comes not from God but from our own recognition of how short we have fallen of the vision given each one of us, no matter how obscure that vision is.

Suicide is a mystery, part of the mystery of mortality. People take their own lives for any number of reasons, most of which are quite possibly only vaguely conscious.

But I would like to suggest, perhaps in contradiction to the older tradition, that the "little death" is mortality itself, the death we die whether we choose or no; and that the greater death is in fact the death of *metanoia*, of commitment to being transformed by God, the death we choose, which has often been called the "little" death.

Even more than the denial of the death that is mortality, it is the denial of the death we may choose that leads to suicide, the premature removal of the life of God incarnate in a particular person, and that person's passing on of that life to others—a parenting that has nothing to do with biological fathering or mothering, and one that often goes unrecognized by everyone surrounding that person, or related by blood.

It is the denial of these chosen deaths that leads us to take instead of give, whether that self-killing is on a physical, psychological, or spiritual level. Each death, chosen or rejected, will ineluctably both affect and effect the others. If one rejection follows on another, there is an eliding of life.

Death on every level stems from this reluctance to grow, to pay the price of transcendence in change. This is true for many of us who have contemplated suicide and for many of those who kill themselves physically, or through the slower process beginning with self-deception. And often those who would heal assist in this process by their own refusal to endure what discomfort might be required to support the growth of those given to their care.

This was sadly the case with a young woman who could not summon the strength on her own to stand up to her parents who demanded that she, an artist, be a scientist. They belittled and devalued her extraordinary talent, beyond ignoring the fact that what they were asking was for her to reverse her inherent thought processes.

After her first suicide attempt she did not find support in the medical community to help her make the necessary wrench away from her family. Instead, against all advice, her doctors took the easy way out and sent her home from college. Within six months she was dead.

In this particular case it seemed that the "helpers" literally drove this person to suicide against her deeper desire, increased her sense of being trapped, and used their medical authority to verify outwardly her impression of the impossibility of ever being able to have a life of her own.

They validated her illusion and invalidated her life because of the effort it would have cost them to attempt both to break the social norm of that time by enabling the girl to establish life on her own, or to attempt to open the closed minds of her family.

This woman's death is a dramatic example, but it is repeated each day in small ways in everyone's life. Every time we seek to be confirmed in our illusions, every time we seek justification in order to avoid the pain of choice of growth for our selves and others over whom we might have authority, we are dying a little, and betraying them. To be sure, such choices are not always so clear-cut, but they are presented to us on innumerable occasions. And these choices—especially those involving the abuse of power and authority—add up.

The Cultural Matrix of Interior Death

If we are to look for a cause for suicide of any sort we have only to look at the culture we have created for our selves. We are the culture, and it is we who go along with it, or dig in our heels and decide to change it.

Our culture preys on weakness and celebrates true sloth disguised as activity. It promises the moon but offers us no tools with which to deal with the despair that invariably follows when we find we can't have it.

It tells us what we should want and abandons us when we are left feeling hollow on achieving. It holds up an illusory model of fairness and justice, and laughs at us when this illusion is shattered. This undermining of truth and vision leads often, I suspect, to people being tempted to physical suicide to say as finally as possible that life is their "possession". The Western milieu hints to us that we may have what we can grasp, and if it consistently betrays attempts to live in the ephemeral world created by advertising and propaganda, life is the only thing left to grasp, even if it is only to be taken.

This is opposite to a Christian view: life as possession versus life as an offering; life which disappoints because it is not "fulfilling"

imperfect vs offering; perfect possession

or "fair"; life seen only in terms of self instead of life in the context of the Creator and creation and transfiguration in Christ.

Everything in our secular culture and some aspects of our religious culture push us toward life in terms of self and away from life in Christ, the life of Christ in us. It is often said that suicide is aimed at someone, and it is impossible not to speculate that some suicides are triggered by having so much of the substantial, if unseen reality of life—values, integrity, vision—compromised. The person who opts for the ending of mortal life is perhaps saying that this is the only act of integrity he or she has left.

Our culture rejects the elderly, the sick, the weak, the handicapped. We shove out of sight those we perceive to be unlovely; we isolate them and allow them to isolate themselves. Further, our standards of what is lovely and what is not are not only capricious but also often unrelated to any but a transient taste in the most superficial sort of beauty.

Thus we increase the chance of their suicide by judging and rejecting the people we don't want to be bothered with, at the same time, without realizing it, contributing to our own living death by refusing to die to our superficial ideas of our selves and our world; refusing to enlarge our vision to encompass the beauty and truth hidden in those we reject; refusing to face what these people represent to us: our own aging, our own spiritual and physical illness; our crippled personalities and values; our final mortality.

In short, we take all the freedom, mystery, and salvation—a word that means freedom, being saved from enemies, being brought into an open place of ever-widening perspective and possibility—out of a willingly offered death as the completion of a willingly offered life. We lose the glory, the density, of a focussed, whole life, warts and all, by self-deception, by grasping control of what our senses immediately see and crave, and by shoving what we cannot see or don't want to see further out of sight. By ignoring the potential of focussed offering, and that offering accepted in the sacrifice of Christ, we abandon the invitation to help pull creation through the needle's eye of transfiguration.

This is not a mere theological abstraction but has its expression in our attitude toward all of the creation, for which we are, belatedly and half-heartedly, assuming stewardship. As we strangle the ecology we choke our selves. By denying the long-range, unseen effects of healthy self-denial in the sense of limiting our seemingly insatiable appetites for gadgets—primarily technology that controls— we deny death its meaning, and death's place in resurrection, as gateway, as culminating gift in transforming life.

This denial leads to the unspoken—and, sadly, sometimes spoken—message to those parts and people of the creation whom we reject for the challenge they offer to our debased value system: you are useless. Why don't you do your duty and die quickly with as little nuisance to us as possible?

Thus we deny the density of holiness brought about by their transcendence through their patient living-out of their full mystery. The noise of avoidance deafens our sense of these open hearts, and tunnel vision blinds us to grace pouring through their brokenness. The radiance of the rejected is lost to the world; we deny them the opportunity to pass on to us this holiness, to parent us by their being, to open our eyes to realities beyond the casually sensuous. And in the process we dull the very selves we think we are pampering.

Our supposedly humanistic culture has failed dismally to increase the value of the human person.

Fear and Desire, Death and Control

It is the fear of death—any death, interior or exterior—that keeps us in servitude to self-deception and the devil, who is a liar, and feeds our lies to our selves. We eat these lies because we believe in the illusion of power and control they give us. We must then tell our selves more lies to maintain the illusion.

As we expend more and more energy to support an ever-inflating ego-empire, its interior has already begun to collapse. It is an empire built on fear and the illusion of power cultivated to deny fear. Learning not to fear any death, chosen or unchosen, is the truth that sets us free.

Death will always inspire dread, but it is the dread of a new and unknown life that is resurrection in Christ, not the kind of panic that pushes us further and further into untruth.

Each flight, each lie narrows possibility, narrows vision, drives us farther from salvation. Slavery to the devil leads to interior or physical suicide, which is the narrowest perspective of all, tunnel vision screwed down to the last millimetre. The fantasies generated by this tunnel vision are petulant, vengeful, and paradoxically based on the assumption that the person who is about to exercise the ultimate acts of control on himself or herself will also control the responses of the very people he or she wishes to "punish" by death.

Many people who think about taking their own lives have a fantasy that they will be able to look down and see "all those people"— from whom they have thoroughly isolated themselves—feeling badly about their death. They assume that children they leave will be cared for kindly by these same people injured by this death, that they would be "taught" and from guilt take responsibility.

Other scenarios do not occur—the possibility, for example, that after death there might be nothing but the awful love of God; that the children might not find refuge with the people on whom fantasies have been imposed, and might join the tens of thousands of homeless children driven to prostitution, drugs, and suicide of their own because an authority figure has set them this example. Even if this is not intended by the person who takes his or her own life, there is a constant pressure against which these children must fight for the rest of their lives. Suicide is, indeed, a contagious disease.

The same applies to families in which denial and control of the emotional as well as physical environment predominates. This kind of suicide is also a contagious disease. In American culture we have combined our fantasies of denial into an attitude of control over death that is ludicrous.

Medicine has made marvellous advances in easing difficult lives and prolonging life after serious trauma. But the same technology is also now being used far beyond the point when natural death would have occurred.

Everyone who has been with a person dying without artificial life-prolonging equipment knows that in the natural process of death there is an ineffable moment when the "work is done", when an assent takes place in a way appropriate to the way in which the person has lived.

But sometimes today, even against explicit instructions, people are put on life support systems and left to struggle toward death like a butterfly on a pin, usually because those in charge cannot face mortality. This is more of a form of murder than "pulling the plug".

But this scenario can be reversed. I heard of a man who was dying of an excruciating disease. He had long been estranged from his family, and in spite of all efforts had never been able to reestablish relationship. At the very last moment, the brother from whom he was most alienated decided that reconciliation had to take place. The news was brought to the hospital room, and this very courageous man, knowing he might not last until the brother arrived from halfway across the world, *asked* to undergo the painful procedure of intubation for the sake of his own and his brother's peace; peace that for the survivor is much more deeply effected in life than after one party is dead.

Unfortunately this sort of example is the exception rather than the rule, and in America one is more likely to hear outraged rumblings and threats of lawsuits from a family who have put an aged and terminally ill member on life-support and who has died in spite of efforts to give him or her an "immortality" no one would choose.

Death, Grief Work, and Tears

We have great confusion about death, death of self, and death of self-image; about short-term and long-term goals; about what is real life on this earth in terms of personal growth; about what is good self-discipline and what is malignant control, or the attempt to deny the realities of one's own life or the lives of others. By "realities" I mean what is presented as that is commonly understood, not necessarily what is perceived. An attempt to live in illusion will skew a person's perceptions of the intentions and appearance of his or her surrounding milieu.

Underneath the traditional phrases of Christianity are deep truths that can help sort out these confusions, deep truths about the way human beings work, about the way they are knit together. As we have noted, these insights have been so badly distorted over the centuries that their apparent meaning often seems opposite to what in fact is meant. Additionally, they have been used as slogans to support and justify personal, and worse, spiritual hedonism and the cults of mystique that seem ever with us.

Many of these phrases have acquired negative connotations: "giving up the will", "self-surrender", "self-denial", "repentance", "compunction". These and similar phrases trigger negative reactions because they are understood as life-denying instead of life-re-leasing. There is historical justification for this attitude.

Humility, for example, has been taught as the passive accept-ance of being treated as a nonperson. Such teaching is antithetical to true humility. True humility is related to perceiving the world without our usual egocentric, controlling bias and, further, requires action, whether sweeping money-changers from the temple, oppos-ing a corrupt government, or refusing to abandon one's integrity when pressured by the mob.

True humility is thus reality-oriented, and the way to humil-ity, we are told from very early times, is through tears.

> When grace has begun to open your eyes so that they per-ceive things by means of precise vision, at that time your eyes will begin to shed tears until they wash your cheeks by their very abundance, and the commotion of the senses will be calmed down, willingly being held in check within you. If anyone teaches you otherwise, do not believe him. To ask from the body anything else apart from tears, as an indication, by means of an outward sign, of the apperception of reality, is not permitted to you.[10] Issac the Syrian

Thus it is one thesis of this book that the gift and way of tears is a vital, healing and ambient grace. Tears are healing in themselves and a sign also of healing already at work in our depths, leading to union with God and God in other people, offering hope for real so-lutions to the horrors that beset us.

This very early Christian understanding of the dynamic of the human person in the redeeming love of God is a key to understand-ing how we can become integrated both as individuals and as a global society. I am dealing only with the Christian perspective, but it should be noted that tears as an ancient wisdom tradition is found in almost every major religious tradition.

The way and gift of tears opens the gate of death in this life to resurrection in this life, the chosen deaths and larger life that put mere mortality in perspective. Tears release us from the prison of power and control into the vast love and infinite possibility of God.

The Conspiracy to Murder Tears

Tears have been given a bad name. Most of us are trained from early childhood to think that there is something wrong with weeping, that it is appropriate only in the most constrained circumstances, and as a last resort. We are taught that tears are unseemly, a sign of weakness of character. We are taught to "keep up appearances", to maintain illusions of family invulnerability, and thus take the first step in establishing the lie we come to believe.

There is certainly a place for self-discipline and not inflicting one's every emotion on others, demanding that they empathize with every vagary of our mood, and devouring them whether they do or don't. But not all tears are related to mood and emotion, and the gift of tears makes no demands on others at all, but rather enhances their freedom.

Unfortunately by the time we are able to understand our tears—to distinguish self-pity from other tears, we have forgotten that we are born knowing how to weep in quite a different way—that is, if the memory of weeping has not been entirely lost.

As early as infancy work begins to train the weeping out of us, or to distort it to support delusion, lest our crying disturb the seemingly tranquil veneer of life around us. Perhaps the weeping of a child is too disturbing to adults, awakens too many haunted memories. We begin to hush our infants' crying not to comfort but to quell. Parents become tired of cries and often, in the West, the child is left to cry lest it become "spoilt", or it is scolded for not being more stoic. It may even be punished or physically abused if the tears are too disturbing.

With this quashing comes also the loss of the meaning of tangible embrace: we learn to associate it with "stop crying" or "get control" instead of the reverse. Most of us know of people who stiffen every time they are touched. While it is necessary to learn self-discipline, it is destructive to make our lives and feelings such gods that abandoning control of them—even when we are abandoning control of them to God—becomes a source of guilt.

Even more destructive is the idea that we must be "strong", that is to say, that even in the face of pain or death we may not admit our feelings to our selves or anyone else. This leads us to believe that tears in the embrace of divine compassion are shameful.

But what is true is that by nature it should be given to all of us to weep. Children themselves in being born teach you this. For at the very time that they issue forth from the womb and fall to the earth, they weep and it is this which appears as a sign of life for the mid-wives and the mothers. For if the infant does not weep, one does not say it is living. But in weeping, it shows by this fact what nature brings along as an accompanying necessity of birth, namely the affliction along with the tears. But as our Father, St Symeon the Studite, has also noted, it is with the same weeping that a man ought to pass the present life; with weeping he ought to die in order that in a short time he may desire to be saved and enter into the happy life, since tears of birth are the symbol of tears of our present life here below. No less in fact than food and drink for the body, tears are necessary for the soul. To such a point that he who does not weep each day, I hesitate to say each hour for fear of appearing immoderate, puts to death hunger and loses his soul.[11]

Tears are the sign of the life of the body linked with our life in God. *We have forgotten that the purpose of self-discipline is to foster true spontaneity and freedom.*

Thus we implicitly learn to stand over and against God, to be "strong" instead of "weak", when we should be, in fact, the reverse. To weep, to accept the grace of tears takes the greatest strength, which is to acknowledge what the world calls weakness. That weakness is our greatest strength and the window into joy because it is the window by which the light of God comes in: the window of our tears.

To yield our selves, to hand our selves over to the way of tears even as Jesus handed himself over in the Garden of Gethsemane to pain and suffering inflicted by human wickedness and mortality, can lead only to resurrection.

This does *not* imply non-resistance to evil or injustice, but rather openness to ways of dealing with them beyond our usual narrow human horizons of control.

Regression and Progression

Psychologists have long understood tears to be related to loss of various kinds. Some psychologists (e.g., Rank, Horney) have related grief to separation anxiety; others have spoken of it in terms of attachment. Both these descriptions are part of what I would like to call "grief work", tears that are part of a process that has a beginning, a middle, and an "end", or closure. True, the pain of loss of loved family and friends lingers, but there is a definite movement through the passage to its end.[12]

Further, this grief work is now recognized as being as much a part of the stress of life-changes as mortality. Any major "life event" is understood to have its process of grief work, whether loss of a spouse by divorce, change of job, change of home, winding up a conference where there has been a sense of belonging to a community, or the annual life event known as Christmas.

Tears in grief work are considered "regressive" by many psychologists. They seem to be part of a recognition process: ". . . a curious process of forgetting, remembering, and forgetting again".[13] Tears in grief work are considered regressive because they are a sign of the anxiety caused by loss.

Tears in grief work are a sign that the necessary defense mechanisms that are part of grief work have served their purpose, and that the person is about to go on to a new phase of the grieving process or out of it altogether.

Tears are a sign of change. In this the tears of grief work strongly resemble and possibly are often mixed with the tears that are a gift. In working with people going through grief over loss this possibility must always be kept in mind.

Grief Work Distinct from the Gift and Way of Tears

The art of discernment is very delicate, and is something learned by being open to more than mere trial and error. There are, additionally, two dangers inherent in the discernment of tears which must be kept in mind.

The first is that we are dealing with a mystery, a gift of God, and any distinctions will be artificial. The most mendacious tears have the potential of becoming holy tears, just as every evil act has the energy and potential of being woven by God into the pattern of redemption.

The second danger is that the knowledge of some kinds of tears will turn us in on our selves, so that we add an additional self-con-

sciousness to a human function already problematic in the twentieth
century. Related to this is the human tendency to make an image
out of someone else's description, and feel that this image forms an
absolute criterion, and thus that all tears of such-and-such type must
exactly fit the mold. This is a mistake. Each human being is a unique
creation of God; each unique created being has its own relationship
with God.

There is a definite difference between the tears of "grief work"
and the way of tears. While the latter is related to the grief work
explored by recent research in the area of physical dying and be-
reavement, it is also something quite separate, and at times opposite.

I do not pretend to have read all the books on grief work. The
ones I have read present problems both in the light of Christianity
and in their implicit assumptions.

One of these assumptions seems to be that grief itself is a "problem" to be dealt with, solved, and finally left behind as an unpleasant if necessary passage by which we cope with the loss of loved ones
or our own life at the end of its chronology.

Another problem is the idea of immortality, which is foreign to
Christianity and different from eternal life. The books that talk of
the experiences of people "coming back from the dead" are about
resuscitation, not about resurrection. People who are dead are dead.
The gospels do not relate what Lazarus experienced during the time
he lay stinking in his tomb, a passage quite different from "near
death" experiences. One criterion of death is that one does not recover from it.

Yet another assumption in these books is the assumption of our
culture that anything that doesn't feel good is bad. Grief work, they
imply, is an unpleasant task that must be got through but is eventually to be left behind with a sigh of relief. Their view of what it
is to "feel good" and "feel bad" represents a hedonistic bias.

Our culture insinuates that emotional highs, a sense of power,
and continual pursuit of fleeting pleasure is "feeling good"; that
grief, tears, a sense of loss is "feeling bad", unnatural, the harbinger
of disaster. We somehow have made our feelings moral creatures to
be judged, manipulated, and controlled chemically or by lies. We
are so intent on circumscribing a comfortable little universe that we
forget there is a cosmos out there, that most of creation, consciousness, and experience are beyond our wildest dreams and outside the

trap we are closing on our selves as we kill our selves. We seem intent on filtering any reality through some kind of anaesthesia, if this reality impinges on the fuzzy dreamworld we have come to idealize.

Even as we discuss "feeling good" and "feeling bad" we have to be careful. As Gerald May has written:

> Commenting on the recent spate of books on the creative possibilities of working through depression, grief, dying and so on, a friend of mine said, "It won't be long until there's a bestseller entitled *The Joy of Agony* or a weekend conference on 'How Misery Can Be Fun'." There is a great deal of difference between such superficial attempts to find some psychologically rewarding experience in suffering, and the joy experienced when true spiritual grace allows one to transcend suffering.[14]

There is nothing in orthodox Christianity that says that suffering or pain or depression or death can or should be enjoyable. The way of tears is not "fun", but then "fun" and "not fun" are hardly categories that apply.

The way of tears requires *effort*, as does any discipline; it requires *grace*, which God pours out with great prodigality, though not in push-button response to technique.

May's distinction between willingness and willfulness is crucial here. Willingness opens up; willfulness narrows; willingness enables God to enable us; willfulness prevents God, who is not a rape artist.

Willingness is just that: willingness to be done to, and to do in response; to give up our small ideas for larger ideas; to give up our small will to control for a larger merging of divine and human effort in unimagined possibility.

Willfulness is the juggernaught that careens ever faster on wheels of delusion leading to the last holocaust.

Willingness is not passivity: it takes every bit of energy we can muster to become truly willing, to give up the quiet, desperate search for a felt security in tangible, envy-provoking materialism that bestows a sense of power.

Death on any level is not fun, but running from it causes greater suffering, if not havoc, in our own lives and all lives with which we are intimately connected: all life. But the tears that enable this chosen death of willingness, this more subtle death, are beyond any self-directed psychological reward—indeed, they make us realize how irrelevant the idea of "psychological reward" can be.

Another important difference between grief work and the way of tears is that death is not left behind. While grief work may have an end, we cannot, in the way of tears, return to a sense of omnipotence and immortality.

There often seems to be a hidden message that doing grief work is secretly a way of greater control and power over life through self-improvement. The implication is that when this work is done, death and all its concomitants can be forgotten and life—for the survivors—can continue on an everyday, if higher plane. Because those who have done this work have succeeded in pulling themselves up by their own bootstraps, this message insists, they have become somehow spiritually upwardly mobile.

As we have noted, the gift of tears is a sign of change, of conversion of the heart. These tears, being tears of willingness, are at the opposite end of the continuum from the "regressive" tears of grief work. It might not be too simplistic to suggest that the tears of grief work, being related to anxiety, are tears that are helping us to let go in the sense that whether we will or not our hands are being unclenched.

The tears that are a gift are a sign of *willingness* to let go, of *desire* to let go, and the power of God acting in response to the person's prayer of longing.

Response to Pain

The tears of grief work are a way in which the self progresses through loss and into growth without becoming fragmented or pathological. They provide a safe passage through the perils of adjusting to loss.

The way of tears and the willing tears that are part of that way, on the other hand, are not self-protective. They are tears that wash away our protective defenses and leave us exposed to the fiery mercy of God. These tears are part of the larger process of *kenosis*, of willingly being emptied by God. This process of being emptied by and filled with God bears a striking resemblance in ancient writers to the taking apart and reassembling of the personality in modern psychoanalysis, which is a sometimes useful, if often flawed imitation of what they are talking about.

In grief work, the self is changed willy-nilly through events that affect it from the outside and tears are part of the self-protective process that enables change to take place without destroying whatever sense of self we may have.

The gift of tears is a sign of self-forgetfulness, a willing nakedness, a desire that comes from within to create space for God by letting go conscious pursuit of security, power, attachment.

Grief work always seems to seek mitigation of pain, seek comfort in establishing relationships that will enable new boundaries of self to be established so that the pain is ended. This is right and proper.

The way of tears, while not seeking pain for its own sake, is a willingness to be continually confronted not only by painful truth about one's self, but also seeks to know this truth on a universal level of human suffering. This compassion mirrors the kenotic God's willing interrelatedness and self-limiting power that comes from *choosing* to be related to the creation.

Far from concentrating on a "sense of self", the way of tears quickly proceeds beyond focus on personal self-knowledge to an orientation toward the Other. Because of this self-knowledge, it looks beyond self to know what lies within the heart of humankind.

The Broken Heart of the World

Nor is this concentration on sin alone. It is a willing participation as fellow-sufferer in the tragedies and disasters and "impossible situations" that are part of the human condition. Further, it is a willingness for whatever, a placing of oneself at the disposal of God to be emptied so that one can be used by God as God sees fit. In the mingling of divine and human tears, in the meeting of the kenotic God and the kenotic person, is the ongoing mystery of the Cross and of redemption.

One who has undertaken the way of tears does not seek mitigation from the pain that invariably accompanies and earths this way. Yet this is not morbidity, nor is the pain a subject of interest. In fact, for one who has embarked on this way, pain while felt is not concentrated on, or even, sometimes, noticed. The focus is other-

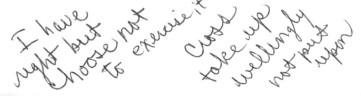

oriented, toward the resurrected, ascended and sovereign Christ who has entered in, and the joy of this vision transcends all "sense" or description (see Chapter VIII). The self is no longer conscious of the need for boundaries because it has been found in the boundless God.

The difference is between adjusting to an unwilling loss and being willing to have something taken away: the illusion of power and control is taken from the first, and willingly given up by the second. Grief work tends to result in once again finding one's balance in the ordinary values of the prevailing culture; the way of tears engages in a grieving process that almost invariably results in being dissociated with, or working against the prevailing culture.

More Than Psychology

But this latter adjustment cannot be grasped or induced by therapy or any other method. Unlike the humanistic psychology of Abraham Maslow on either the "D" level (motivation being deprivation of basic needs of safety, self-esteem, love and status), or the "B" level (motivation at the level of being: truth, beauty, justice etc.), there is no technique or therapy that can manufacture *kenosis*, which is grace in response to desire.[15]

On both of Maslow's levels, pain is transcended by motivation for changing one's condition and values. In the way of tears one's own condition is no longer significant. It is not ignored, but its importance has a very low place in priority. Maslow and the human potential movement are concerned with self-cultivation, which is laudable up to a point, but questionable when it results in narcissism.

The way of tears, by contrast, has the vision of God as its motivation, and concern with the health of the self is disinterested. Indeed, the psychological health or "self-actualization" of people embarked on this way is often quite visible, although it may be expressed in forms that the secular world considers mad. Additionally, as May has shown, it is absurd to try to make a correlation between psychological health and growth into God.

Structures

Both kinds of tears are dealing with powerlessness. The tears of grief work are related to healing a breach in the system of self-supports and identifications. The way of tears is related to abolishing the system, an ongoing commitment to breaking away from preoccupying "needs"—that is, wants which the culture has made to seem to be needs in the interest of control. It does not, of course, deny the basic needs to stay alive.

Rabbi Joseph Soloveitchik has understood this distinction in terms of possibility:

> But while our longings [for one who has died] are a fantasy, since one who has died will never return, longing for the Master of the Universe [from whom one is separated by sin] is realistic, and man is drawn to Him and rushes toward Him with all his strength.[16]

Soloveitchik also points to the importance of memory, of *not* forgetting, common to both Jewish and Christian traditions of salvation:

> "Repentant man," if he wishes to attain this high peak, does not forget his sin or tear out or erase the pages of iniquity from the book of his life. Rather he exists on the spirit of 'my sin is ever before me' (Psalm 51:3). Instead of uprooting the past and erasing the sin, he carries them up with him to heights he could never have dreamed of had he not sinned.[17]

Julian of Norwich has the same insight. "Sin is necessary", she says, and assures us that our worst sins will be honor in heaven.[18]

Soloveitchik says something similar: "For such a person, repentance does not mean a clean break with the past, but rather continuity; for him the Holy One, blessed be He, does not 'overlook sin' but 'bears sin and iniquity.' "[19]

And finally, there is a profound difference in the approach to God, to salvation, between grief work and the way of tears. Grief work and the human potential movement often seem to operate on the premise that humanity has a *right* to salvation. The view of the way of tears is entirely opposite. Donald Nicholl relates this story:

Another man spoke [to Shiva and Parvati who had come down to the world to give salvation] about his sadhana, and the saint told him it would be seven births. In this way everyone asked about getting salvation. The saint told one ten births, another fifteen, others twenty or thirty. Finally, when all were finished, a small, thin, ugly man who had been hiding behind the others came forward. He was shy and afraid but he dared to say, 'Sir, I don't do any sadhana, but I love His creation, and I try not to hurt anyone by my actions, thoughts, or words. Can I get salvation?'

The saint looked at the little man and then scratched his head as if he were in some doubt. The man again bowed to the saint and nervously said, 'Can I, sir?' The saint then said, 'Well, if you go on loving God in the same way, maybe after a thousand births you too will get salvation.'

As soon as the man heard that he could eventually get salvation, he screamed with joy, 'I can get salvation! I can get salvation!' And he began to dance in ecstasy. All of a sudden his body changed into a flame. At the same time the saint and his disciple also changed into flames. All three flames merged into one and disappeared.

Shiva and Parvati were again sitting on the top of Mount Kailasha. Parvati said, 'My Lord, I am very confused. You told the leader, who does such hard austerities, that he would get salvation in three births. Then you told the ugly man that he would get salvation in a thousand births, but you gave it to him instantly.' Shiva said, 'No doubt the first devotee had much devotion and was doing austerities sincerely, but he still had an ego about his sadhana. . . . The other man had so much faith that even a thousand births were very short for him. . . . I did not give him salvation, it was his own faith in my words.'[20]

Dostoyevsky tells the same story:

. . . And when He has done with all of them, then He will summon us: "You too come forth," He will say, "Come forth ye drunkards, come forth ye weak ones, come forth, ye children of shame"! And we shall all come forth, without shame and shall stand before Him. And He will say unto us, "Ye are swine, made in the Image of the Beast and with his mark; but come ye also!" And the wise ones and those of understanding will say,

"Oh Lord, why dost Thou receive these men?" And He will say, "This is why I receive them, oh ye wise, this is why I receive them, oh ye of understanding, that not one of them believed himself to be worthy of this." And He will hold out His hands to us and we shall fall down before Him . . . and we shall weep . . . and we shall understand all things![21]

The Suffering God

The idea of a God who suffers is shocking to the inheritors of a tradition which has understood God as a distanced God, a *deus ex machina*, and the universe as a clockwork universe. But God's willingness to be with creation and within creation and redeeming creation is precisely this commitment to suffer.

In *The Suffering of God*, Terence Fretheim has explored the Hebrew scriptures to remind us that while this God is a transcendent, set-apart, Holy One, this same God has willingly become related to creation with all the suffering such a relationship implies.[22]

This is not a God who ignores the cries of the people; rather, the cries of those who suffer echo the pain of God. This relatedness is especially expressed by the prophets.

The prophetic tradition is particularly concerned with accurate regard, seeing the perversions and illusions of the people for what they are, mourning over them as God mourns. As Fretheim points out, there is a profound sense in which the cry of the prophet is the cry of God.

Fretheim has drawn on Abraham Heschel's[23] discussion of the pathos of God and Soloveitchik understands this as well:

. . . God's departure from man's bosom in the wake of sin. "Mourning the withdrawal is like the mourning over a beloved father and mother." Sooner or later the cloud of mourning will inevitably descend, and then will come fear and loneliness, estrangement, alienation, remoteness and separation; sadness will grow and emptiness will spread in the soul, and man will begin to yearn for the Almighty, and when he apparently sights God's Image from afar, he will begin to run toward it rapidly with all his strength.[24]

An Attitude of Responsibility

It is necessary to understand the distinction between grief work and the way of tears, and the latter especially as related to responsibility and the suffering God.

Part of grief work is to sort out irrational feelings of guilt and responsibility. The right kind of forgetfulness and peace come when a realistic evaluation has taken the place of attempts to retain the illusion of control by claiming responsibility for the death, seeming failure, or life event which is the subject of the grief work.

The commitment to grieve within and for the heart of the world, however, has a different perspective. One who lives in this way takes on a sense of responsibility for all the sin and tragedy in the world, not as an act of power, but as a result of the love of the Christ who has been enabled to live within the space in the heart of such a person, a heart cleansed and emptied by tears.

This sense of responsibility, this sense of oneness with sin and tragedy reflects a very ancient tribal view of the relationship between the individual and the collective, and a very early Christian understanding of the interplay of the individual and the Church as Body of Christ.

In no way is this discussion meant to denigrate psychology. The usefulness of therapy as an aid to the passages of life hardly needs mentioning for an American audience, although in some countries there is still considerable stigma attached to seeking it.

Rather this discussion is a caution against the encroachments of "popular" psychology into religion, and a reminder that there is more than analysis in redemption—and for that matter in analysis, too.[25]

Rituals

Again, it is possible to see the distinction in terms of ritual. There are rituals for grief work, with which we are all familiar, not only the wake and the funeral, but also the goodbye party, the gold watch.

While the Eucharist is the supreme ritual for the way of tears and fire, at the same time it both deepens and becomes useless. This is not to say that the Sacrament is useless! Rather the trappings that surround it, even given the renewed understanding of Presence present in the entire eucharistic liturgy, become a distraction. Why this is so is a mystery. But it possibly has both to do with such a person having tasted the "things of the new world". And—what ritual could express the mingling of our tears with God's?

The Rational Split

Our cultural attitude against tears aggravates what is already in third century Christianity a split between the mind and the heart. It is intensified by the cartesian *hubris* of the past few centuries. "God is, therefore I AM" was replaced by "I think, therefore I am".

Women, who seem to have an instinctive knowledge that the heart has a mind of its own, nonetheless have been as much victims of the resulting competitive rationalism as men. Both men and women have been artificially separated from this knowledge of the heart.

What do we mean by "the heart"? It has been described in numerous ways. For our purposes, it is the center of one's being where we gaze upon the Face of God.

It is very important not to equate the heart and the unconscious. Not only is God *not* the unconscious, as a few psychologists and theologians have suggested, but even psychoanalysts are taking a new look at what is meant by this term we casually toss about.

John Ryle writes of Charles Rycroft:

> The unconscious itself, the heart of psychoanalytic theory, is a logical error: we can be unconscious of what we do or think, but we cannot possess an unconscious—because both consciousness and unconsciousness are attributes of something else.[26]

The knowledge of the heart loses in translation as it is conceptualized, and loses further as it is analyzed. The same is true of more sensory and superficial "experience", or even more, of experience that is evidence of the heart's perception. "The heart has its reasons, which Reason herself does not know," said Pascal, and immediately the dangers inherent in attempting such a book as this become self-evident. Yet it seems worth the risk.

The statement above that women have been equally affected by the rational split as men, has to be qualified by saying that there seems to be a *tendency* in women to experience in an uncritically receptive way, and subsequently to analyze. Men often seem to begin analyzing even while they are receiving experience.

Once a male friend and I were discussing the impact of multiple, rich metaphors after I had used a string of them to discuss an aspect of this book. We then began to discuss the different ways in which we had received these images.

He asked me to go back over the images, one by one, but the impact of receiving them all at once, like viewing the chips in a kaleidescope making a single impression on the observer, was lost.

My friend realized that the analyzer was at work even as he was going through the experience of being affected by the metaphors. In his eagerness to conceptualize, the reception of the experience was cut off before it was complete, and he realized something very important had been missed.

We began to speculate on the nature and process of receptivity as related to rational thought. Subsequently I found myself receiving in both ways, sometimes delaying the analyzing process; sometimes short-circuiting the experience.

Whatever the implications for the need to wait, for male/female receptivity and integration of rational thought processes with "intuition", this situation leads to the tantalizing question—which I have no intention of attempting to answer—whether what is "lost in translation" is not a kind of repression, a kind of avoidance of losing control of experience.

The next question is whether there is a direct relationship between this repression and stress levels. Since women seem more naturally disposed to receiving experience uncritically in its wholeness and postponing analysis, the acquisition of the rational split might possibly take an even greater toll on them than on men.

It may be, too, that this split in women is more easily healed—except in some cases where women have so totally repressed uncritical receptivity that bridging the gap would require breaking down an extensive system of defenses.

There also seems to be a more deeply inherent split in many men than usually found in women. The mind of the heart is initially alien to them.

On the other side of the coin there are also men who are more intuitive than some women, and there are some women who are more split and rationally oriented than men.

This is not a value judgment.

One is not better than the other. I would personally rather have a more "rational" person (man or woman) do business negotiating for me, and a more intuitive person, evaluation. In other words, the propensity (not the sex) suggests that certain people are more suited to certain kinds of tasks. This is hardly a new idea, but it does raise some interesting questions about the language of spiritual theology that has come down to us.

We need to ask how some of these have arisen, and what impact they have. For example, what about the saying, "Put the mind in the heart"? This saying can be very confusing to some women. Is this a saying originating with men? We might assume so because so little of the Ammas' wisdom has come down to us, but there is of course no way to know for sure.

I am not asking an historical question here, but rather suggesting that perhaps we need to look at the literature and traditions of spiritual direction, especially the required authentication of women's spiritual experience by male directors, and attempt to sort out what for our age is appropriate for people with different propensities.

It would seem that these differences tend to disappear after a certain amount of time has been spent in prayer—God seems to do quite a bit of balancing in this area. But there are still questions.

Do women have a tendency to start out more "all of a piece" but learn, necessarily, to temper their intuition with learning how to think in a different way? Is the seeming split in many men related to their necessary differentiation of themselves from their mothers in early childhood? Can we learn to distinguish spiritual theology that might be confusing alternatively to men and women? Can we learn to make such theology complementary, and discern the signs that enough integration has taken place in one or the other so that there is no longer danger of confusion?

If we could answer some of these questions it might be possible to become better spiritual companions for one another; we might more easily be able to sort out the initial task each of us must undertake, and discern the point at which the boundary into a greater unity of person has been crossed.

What do we mean by initial task? For the person who is pre-dominantly intuitive and inclined to find self in self-giving (which can become a trap leading to becoming a victim), the initial task might be to learn how to stand away from this habitual attitude, temper intuition with discursive thought, and discover the way he or she becomes encapsulated by the very gift of self-giving.

For the predominantly rational person the task is oriented more in learning not how not to think, but rather to trust in addition the intuition which has been subordinated or even repressed, and to be-come willing to learn the patience of waiting and self-giving which is the healing of a restless, self-sufficient, and humanly uncommit-ted intellect.

When the initial task is over, then it is perhaps possible to be concerned with finding this same balance in other aspects of daily life, such as reading. Intuitive people need to learn to read philos-ophy, as off-putting and dull as that may seem; and rationally ori-ented people need to learn to read poetry.

If we look at the great writers of spiritual theology from the past we can find both disparity and unity, a certain harmony that de-volves when thinking has been added to intuition, and when intui-tion has supplemented discursive thinking. And it is good to be able to profit from both Lady Julian and Meister Eckhart.

The way and gift of tears crosses sexual differentiation and in-tuitive or rational preference. It is seen in such disparate people as Ephrem the Syrian and Margery Kempe. And while their archaic language may be difficult, and in spite of human evolution, there are still universal constants in the human condition for which this wisdom has both validity and vitality.

What needs to be done to recover it and render it comprehen-sible for today is to attempt to understand the assumptions behind obscure phrases, the interior mechanisms at work, and the passages through which they have traveled.

Power and Empowerment

There is so much confusion about the language of power and empowerment that I will attempt to do some sorting out for the pur-poses of this book.

Perhaps it would be useful to speak of three modes or areas in which the language of power is used. One is political; the second psychological. The third relates the "spiritual" sphere to the other two.

When speaking of "willing powerlessness" in this book I am not speaking of passive acquiescence to tyranny and injustice. Quite the reverse. A contemplative willingness invariably requires a commitment to justice and peace.

All prayer is political, and not to choose is to leave one's choice to be used by someone else, and one's life to be committed by another. What *is* meant in the political sphere by "willing powerlessness" is that action is always accompanied by an open listening and readiness to abandon one's own plans for a greater vision and more compassionate and all-embracing program, listening for the Word which comes from outside the confines of one's own tunnel vision.

Thus the empowerment of the powerless, helping the poor "to count"—Gustavo Gutierrez describes the poor as "those who do not count"—is a primary and ongoing priority of one who follows the Christian way of tears and fire. This commitment is not confined to the third world, racial minorities, or women's rights, but any and every situation in which psychological and spiritual rape and terrorism, as well as physical exploitation, is occurring as it does every day in each of our lives.

On a personal psychological level this book assumes a certain maturity. When I speak of guilt I am assuming the reader knows the difference between neurotic guilt and healthy guilt. When I speak of self-discipline, I am not speaking of pathological repression. When I refer to compassion or empathy, I am not referring to the overwhelming, devouring, ego-flattering inhaling of another's pain but rather what Rowan Williams has described as

> . . . the real alternative to the passionate domination of emotive attachment . . . the educating of a perception and sensibility that is not either defended against the suffering of the world or helplessly submerged in it. This kind of compassion is not simply the visceral feeling of solidarity that often so 'identifies' that the pain of another is felt and feared and at last evaded as if it were one's own (the person too sensitive to contemplate the fact of another's suffering); it is an awareness of another's suffering as *other*. Not every tragedy is *my* tragedy; and that awareness can be an indispensable aspect of authentic compas-

sion. Receptivity to the reality of another's needs is importantly different from the *merging* [previously compared with the Buddhist purging of greedy desire] of another's experience into my own, so that the focus of concern remains essentially myself.[27]

However, this does not preclude participation on a much deeper level:

> . . . the saint is not a mass of quivering sensitivities, but someone who is strong enough to see and feel without deceit or comfort one's own condition and that of others; even someone prepared to risk enormous affective involvement with the world and with person, neither holding back from fear of hurt or loss, nor *using* this involvement to feed and protect the ego.[28]

True communion, true community is not a matter of push-me-pull-you togetherness and destructive dependence relationships but rather what the poet Rilke has described as the meeting of solitudes who know the extravagance of walking unembraced. This acknowledging of otherness is the prerequisite of true union and knowledge of what is meant by the Body of Christ.[29]

How this is related to *apatheia*, *ekstasis*, and *kenosis* as Thunberg has described will, I hope, become clear.[30]

Additionally, in the psychological realm I am assuming that the reader has enough self-knowledge to know that he or she has a self, or an identity, or has some idea of what self-actualization is—whatever language is appropriate to the idea that there is a person embarked on a journey, and who has enough self-knowledge to realize that there is a task to be done.

It is assumed that nothing is completed or finished and that all of us are "little ones", beginners, neophytes no matter how long we have been at it, trying to remember who we are in the love of God.

There is a phrase which today carries a lot of force and which we need to address: "take control of your life". I am understanding this to mean that one is somewhat aware of his or her environment and options and choices. This phrase does *not* mean becoming a petty tyrant in regard to your feelings, or toward other inhabitants of the world, or the biosphere.

This book assumes that the reader knows the difference between these two kinds of restraint. The first I refer to as self-discipline, the second, control.

Finally, in terms of the way of tears which embraces the other two, "power" means the power of God, not an illusory magical power seized by the ego. It means a willing *kenosis* in order to be filled with God, to allow Christ to indwell so that the person does not pray, but Christ prays the person.

Father Zossima said:

> If you are penitent, you love. And if you love you are of God. All things are atoned for, all things saved by love. If I, a sinner, even as you are, am tender with you and have pity on you, how much more will God. Love is such a priceless treasure that you can redeem the whole world by it, and expiate not only your own sins but the sins of others.[31]

We have a lot of redefinition and clarification to do, examining words and assumptions—if not presumptions—we make about the human journey into God; about tears, fire, grief and weeping; about sin, the devil, servitude, compunction, repentance, humility, control, self-control, ascesis, death, union, prayer, and the nature of joy.

To separate this wisdom into concepts, to systematize, to speak even of passages; to discuss physiology apart from psychology or spiritual theology is already to do violence to what is a multi-layered and organic whole. But the knowledge of the heart must be communicated, however haltingly, because the Word will not return empty, and because organized ideas translated into words are the only means we have to communicate. It is no longer possible to live alongside a desert Mother or Father to learn by deeper, nonverbal communication.

As we continue, we need also to be aware of the dangers of the past: of pelagianism, thinking it is all up to us; of gnosticism, thinking there is some secret formula which will liberate us from mortality and created things, and bring us to a well-intentioned narcissism or hedonism; of manicheanism, which calls creation evil; or a kind of reverse manicheanism, which holds suspect any part of life that cannot be empirically experimented upon or analyzed.

Lastly, tears have nothing to do with melancholy. Grief work can be diffuse; the way of tears has a single focus.

Such mourning [says Irénée Hausherr, referring to grief work] has nothing to do with ascetic *penthos* except perhaps as an enemy, through the sadness and *accedia* which it inspires or accompanies.[32]

Dostoyevsky's Zossima is not quite so categorical, and speaks of the relationship between the two:

Be not comforted. Consolation is not what you need. Weep and be not consoled, but weep. Only every time you weep be sure to remember that your little son is one of the angels of God, that he looks down from there at you and sees you, and rejoices at your tears, and *points at them to the Lord God;* and a long while yet will you keep that great mother's grief. But it will turn in the end into quiet joy, and your bitter tears *will be only tears of tender sorrow that purifies the heart and delivers it from sin.*[33]

I will exalt you, O Lord, because you have lifted me up
and have not let my enemies triumph over me.

O Lord my God I cried out to you, and you restored me
to health . . .

You have turned my wailing into dancing; you have put
off my sack-cloth and clothed me with joy. (Psalm 30 BCP)

He brought me out into an open place; he rescued me because he delighted in me. (Psalm 18 BCP)

O worship the Lord in the beauty of holiness!
Bow down before him, his glory proclaim;
With gold of obedience, and increase of lowliness,
Kneel and adore him, the Lord is his name![34]

As our Savior spent three days and three nights in the
depths of the earth, so your first rising from the water represented the first day and your first immersion represented the
first night. At night a man cannot see, but in the day he walks
in the light. So when you were immersed in the water it was
like night for you, and you could not see, but when you rose
again it was like coming into broad daylight. In the same instant
you died and were born again; the saving water was both your
tomb and your mother.[35]

Under a radically different world view, the chief problem
of contemporary theology remains what it was for the ancient
Hebrews and the early Christians. From presence, remembered and anticipated, they received their interpretation of historical existence. From presence, they learned an uneasy
equilibrium between their past and their future, and they obtained at once their condemnation and their liberation to live.
Presence, as well as its modes, is at the root of the theological
problem of revelation.[36]

The Hidden Source

Who is this God who will take a mother's tears and turn them to baptismal waters that cleanse and purify creation?

Who is this God who can undam the paralyzing tears of sorrow and make them tributary to the River of Life?

We grope through our tears for tears of light, as one groping for a hidden spring. And when we find the fountain of Mercy we are swept from tears for our selves only, and shed them as God's Mercy for creation.

How can we come to understand this God who responds to tears? How can we begin to perceive without getting bound by our own words and images?

How can we understand that the way of tears is both the most profound opening to, and the most profound response to the mystery of kenotic love?

We need a new model for the way God works within creation and the human person. The scholastic and post-scholastic divisions are too neat, too tidy, and presume to confine the Spirit. They limit to what is visible and conscious the work that is invisible and must remain so, lest we assume responsibility for what has been wrought out of sight and thus fall into *hubris*.

St Ephrem's approach serves as a much-needed antidote to that tradition of theologizing which seeks to provide theological definitions, Greek *horoi*, or boundaries. To Ephrem, theological definitions are not only potentially dangerous, but they can also be actually blasphemous. They can be dangerous because, by providing 'boundaries', they are likely to have a deadening and fossilizing effect on people's conception of the subject of en-

quiry, which is, after all, none other than the human experience
of God. Dogmatic 'definitions' can, moreover, in Ephrem's eye,
be actually blasphemous when these definitions touch upon
some aspect of God's Being, for by trying to 'define' God one is
in effect attempting to contain the uncontainable, to limit the
limitless. . . .

Ephrem's radically different approach is by way of paradox
and symbolism, and for this purpose poetry proves a far more
suitable vehicle than prose, seeing that poetry is much better capable of sustaining the essential dynamism and fluidity. . . .

The philosophical approach seeks to identify and locate this
central point, in other words, to define it, set boundaries to it.
The symbolic approach, on the other hand, attempts no such
thing: rather it will provide a series of paradoxical pairs of op-
posites, placing them at opposite points around the circumference of the circle; the central point is left undefined, but
something of its nature and whereabouts can be inferred by join-
ing up the various opposite points, the different paradoxes on the
circle's circumference. The former procedure can be seen as providing a static understanding of the centre point, while the later
offers an understanding that remains essentially dynamic in
character.[37]

On the other side of the coin, mythology, too, can be a trap
from which it is difficult to escape. I am using the word "mythology" in a popular, not scholarly sense. It is tempting—and easier—
to live within a mythology that gives a sense of control over life, the
divine, and the ferment of images within our selves than to life
turned outward in faith.

At the same time, mythology can be invaluable in helping us
to become aware of greater depths and truths than we can express
verbally, just as scholastic and linguistic methods can help us when
we do try to express what we have encountered in those depths. We
do not need to use those categories, but knowing that they exist can
help us think clearly.

To steer a course between systematic, scholastic categories on
the one hand, and closed mythological worlds—again, in the popular sense of mythological—on the other requires constant vigilance
over our intentions, and awareness of the implications of our chosen
interpretive mythology and thought systems.

Mythology and History

Most of us who are not biblical scholars think of a divine pan-theon—Greek, Roman, Tibetan, Native American—when we hear or use the word "mythology". Sometimes the inhabitants of my-thology are those seemingly absurd and capricious gods and god-desses who mirror and explain the absurd and capricious behavior of their human counterparts. Sometimes they reflect understanding of nature and the relationship of humans to nature; sometimes an understanding of the deepest human fears and hopes.

Whatever our mythological affinity, we need to understand that mythology is operative on several levels.

On the most superficial level we understand Greek mythology, for example, in the context of Greek history and culture, and use that mythology in turn to understand its context.

Then we might begin to comprehend mythology as a way of communicating human relationship with what is unseen or tran-scendent which cannot be communicated in any other way. My-thology on this level is often used in religion, but there is the concomitant danger that the communicating symbol may close the system.

Or, we might become interested in how mythologies evolve, and begin to see that mythology in this sense is often tied to a cy-clical sense of nature and human action.

At this point we may fall into a confusion: on the one hand, nature *seems* to be cyclical, with a constantly predictable movement of sun and stars, agricultural seasons, birth and death—all linked to certain parts of the year. We insist on the security of these notions even though we know on another level that what seems to be cyclical is in fact suffused with constantly-appearing uniqueness, and grad-ual evolution.

The danger here is that in our desire for security we opt for the illusion instead of the unknown we know to be true.

Additionally, we need to remember that mythology as *com-munication* exists within every religion: the danger is that the my-thology *becomes* the religion, substituting human concepts for what is beyond concept.

It is important to remember that the uniqueness of the Judeo-Christian religion is its break with mythology as a closed system of cyclical nature religion, and its insistence on God's acting cooperatively with people in history.

There is a fundamental shift in receiving what is presented from a mythological "reinterpretation" according to set and given patterns, to trust. There is a great leap made from resting in the knowledge of the predictable to acknowledging that not only does God act in history: God *inter*acts in history. This enables us to go forward in faith not because we have received certain auspicious signs, but because we know that the only sign given is that of Jonas, of the mercy of God somehow incorporating our triumphs and follies in the warp of Love that will bring all the universe to final perfection, although we cannot presume to know what that perfection is.

This unknowing is also part of faith, yet it is always our inclination to counter the uncertainty of faith, the allowing God the freedom to be God, with a secure closed mythology. And like Jonah, in the small world in which we trap our selves, we are not willing for God to show those we do not like the same mercy shown us.

If we were to say we know what is God's idea of final perfection, of *apokatastasis*—even given the revelation of God incarnate in history in Christ—then we return to looking at God's relationship with the universe in a way that begets a closed system.

It is easier to deny God freedom than to admit our own powerlessness.

This innate tendency of ours to create closed systems is more subtle and pervasive than we have any idea. It colors every aspect of our lives. Our desire seems always to be secure and to know exactly where we stand, not only with God and God's action in history, but also in the events of everyday life.

Thus in this book I am giving the word "mythology" a special meaning: the tendency to make predictable and static the dynamic and open-ended life in God.

Again: while the use of symbolism is the only way we can begin to comprehend what is nonverbal, at the same time there is often the desire to mistake the symbol for what it symbolizes. It is true that in religion this is not always so clear-cut: The symbol is in some way *part of* what it symbolizes, a transmitter of what it symbolizes, even at times an incarnation of what it symbolizes.

And yet it must not be mistaken for the *whole* of what is symbolized, because in the case of the divine *there is in fact no object but rather divinity* **consenting** *to live within limits understandable and accessible to us.*

Ephrem understands this perfectly:

> Loving is the Lord who Himself put on our names—
> right down to the mustard seed was He abased in the parable.
> He gave us His names, He received from us our names;
> His names did not make Him any the greater,
> whereas our names made Him small.
> Blessed is the person who has spread Your fair name, Lord,
> over his own name, and adorned with Your names his own
>   names.

> The foolish man saw only what belongs to us
> and imagined that what originated from us referred to God.

> [Dr Brock continues:] It is essential not to misunderstand the character of God's 'borrowed names'. These names which He condescends to put on are designed to draw humanity upwards: only human arrogance and folly uses them to drag God down to the human level.[38]

Thus it is possible to understand how even the Eucharist can become an idol. To mistake symbols in this way, to become entrapped in the mythology thus created, is to make an image that does not enhance life in God but limits it.

To be caught into and pass through the symbol into much wider life, as with the right use of icons, is to participate sacramentally in the life of God's salvation and transfiguration in creation.

> In biblical faith, human beings discern that presence is a surging which soon vanishes and leaves in its disappearance an absence that has been overcome. It is neither absolute nor eternal, but elusive and fragile, even and especially when human beings seek to prolong it in the form of cultus. The collective act of worship seems to be both the indispensable vehicle of presence and its destroyer. Presence dilutes itself into its own illusion whenever it is confused with a spatial or temporal location. When presence is "guaranteed" to human senses or reason, it is no longer real presence. The proprietary sight of the glory de-

stroys the vision, whether in the temple of Zion or in the eucharistic body.

It is when presence escapes man's grasp that it surges, survives, or returns. It is also when human beings meet in social responsibility that presence, once vanished, is heard. "The god comes when those in love recognize one another." [Euripides, Helen, 560] In biblical faith, presence eludes but does not delude. The hearing of the name, which is obedience to the will and the decision to live now for an eternal future, becomes the proleptic vision of the glory.[39]

In the latter part of this century there is for us an additional peril: we have begun to explore the way symbols operate within the human psyche, and we have thus created a new opportunity for mythology. Additionally, we have tended to mythologize scientific method, and while empirical method has deepened our understanding both of our selves, and the texts and liturgies associated with Christianity, there is at the same time the ongoing temptation to say to our selves that we now know how both God and humans work, and particularly how God works within us.

We are tempted to say that we know through textual criticism exactly what a particular passage means in its entirety and implication; that we are certain of the impact of, say, a certain liturgy on the growth of a congregation. We want to convince our selves that we are in control of cause and effect.

Thus in order to allow God to move us into ever-greater spaciousness, away from the slavery of fear that drives us into our closed, "safe" systems and tunnel vision, we have to embrace insecurity in faith and go beyond our favorite images, helpful as they may have been. It may be that they, too, are transformed, but we cannot know that ahead of time.

If we idolize either textual criticism, or psychological interpretation, or "ascetical" hermeneutic, one to the exclusion of the others, then we make a closed system. We use sayings designed to help us look at God to look at our selves, and thus make gods of our selves; we want to "prove" to our selves that something is happening in our interaction with God. When this happens in worship, we may feel cozy and comfortable and good about our selves, but what we are doing is not, in fact, worship.

It is because of these tendencies to make closed systems that we are all "pagan", all struggling endlessly to become Christian. To be Christian implicitly means that one has faith in God's co-operative action in history. Thus a controlled world is antithetical. It leaves no room for God's action, and God's freedom.

The desire to control is "original sin".

The attitude of trust that Zossima recommended to the grieving mother is not the fatalism of *insha'allah* or James 5, nor the *laissez-faire* of the hedonist, but something expectant. This attitude of expectancy, however, is, again, without image. It is not "waiting for something" but rather waiting on God, just as God waits on us. This does not mean non-action but rather a ground-note to action—listening constantly for a "word" that might indicate direction, or, when creativity seems exhausted, waiting in silence for the opening of new possibility that will become manifest as we are willing to be broken out of our closed circles.

Magic

The Hebrew scriptures show us a God who is a life-giver, a God who is a verb through which love is poured out on the creation, which is part of the verb I AM. The scriptures also show us a people in awe, a people who know they are receivers of life, are the "thou" of this love. They are a people who are called to respond, to decide, to act, but always in the context of this loving awe.

Slowly, slowly, however, a change begins to come about. The sense of being "thou" is lost. This is the sense of wonder at God's self-*kenosis* expressed in the rabbinical question, how does God become so dense as to be able to dwell between the cherubim of the ark? Such questions are lost in law and ritual, which have grasped precedence and become closed mythologies. God is no longer a subject but an object (not even a "thou") of sacrifice.

The story of Gideon's sacrifice illustrates such a transition. Gideon sees God, and instead of simply standing in adoration and praise, his thought immediately turns to himself, his safety, and making the "appropriate sacrifice". In contemporary terms, he turns to his technology. He is not so oriented toward God that he is willing to forget himself because his thought turns ever toward himself. (Judges 6:13ff)

However, this transition is not a clearcut demarcation line:

Gideon's tendency to look at himself to see how he is doing, and to test what he is seeing is present from the "beginning". Gideon puts God to the empirical test just as Adam and Eve had done.

> Man is so much like God that he wants to ape the Deity, attempt to force the barriers of his finitude, evade the limitations of his humanity, snatch power, and even use violence in order to achieve his own brand of what he calls "the good." Above all he desires to acquire the dimensions of eternity and to seize infinity in time. He wants to be exactly like God and therefore to be immortal. He eats the fruit of the tree of the knowledge of all things, "from good to evil." *The irony of man's godlikeness is that man is so close to the divine status that he snatches divinity and immediately discovers his alienation, the brokenness of his selfhood, the loss of his own humanity, and a cosmic loneliness. Lusting for immortality, he merely confirms his mortality.*[40]

The key stories are theophanies, self-revelations of God which almost invariably contain images of water and fire in some guise. And at the moment of revelation, the relationship between the divine and human is once again rightly ordered.

The more we turn to an empirical approach to God, the more we seek to control; and the more we seek to control, the closer we come to magic.

In this wider sense, magic is more prevalent in popular religion than we care to admit. We are outraged when God does not seem to respond to *our* prayer, when God does not seem to make things go according to *our* plan. It rarely occurs to us that in this seeming refusal God is perhaps leading us, offering us greater possibility, giving us the opportunity to be led into a wider place, into a salvific experience, out of bondage from our tunnel vision, and into a larger life and freedom.

The gospel analogy of a child's approach to God has been abused and twisted. Whether the references refer to Christian neophytes or children in fact is not really important here. What is important is attitude.

It is not the unquestioning, immature, "blind" approach that is often wished on us. Children aren't like that. They're full of wonder, yes, but the wonder leads them to question, and the questions to greater wonder.

This is a far cry from the sort of spiritual frontal lobotomy that much "childhood" spirituality has wished on us. If God wanted us to shut off our minds, God would have created us differently. We cannot use the image of the child to abrogate responsibility and to seek security in religion. To be a child is to be perpetually in a state of adventure, exploration and insecurity.

> Over the swaying parapet of my arm
> Your sentinel eyes lean gazing. Hugely alert
> In the soft unfinished clay of your infant face,
> They drink light from this candle on the tree.
> Drinking, not pondering, each bright thing you see,
> You make it yours without analysis,
> And, stopping down the aperture of thought
> To a fine pinhole, you are filled with flame.
>
> Give me for Christmas, then, your kind of seeing,
> Not studying candles—angel, manger, star—
> But staring as at a portrait, God's I guess,
> That shocks and holds the eye, till all my being,
> Gathered, intent and still as now you are,
> Breathes out its wonder in a wordless yes.[41]

Faith provides security, but *it is the security to live within insecurity*, and is the opposite of control and magic.

We have to remember that childhood is an *analogy*. There is a tendency to make a mythology out of childhood, and thus lock ourselves into a closed circle of immaturity. There is no question that we are to become mature Christians, but with a true maturity that never loses the awe, the questing, the venturing. This is an *evolved* maturity, an *evolved* simplicity, which denies nothing and embraces everything; is willing to be done to, and to take both responsibility and consequence.

Technique and Freedom

The idea of waiting is implicit in the idea of the neophyte or the child. It is implicit when we listen to another. But it can, like everything else in our repertoire, be manipulative.

If, for example, we encounter hostility and respond with hostility we have pretty much shut the door on a different response. If, however, we respond with understanding and kindness, we open the option for the other person to respond differently: we make a spaciousness for possibility.

Perhaps this act will enable the other person to leave off hostility; perhaps not. Today this sort of self-discipline is taught as a stress-reducing technique, a management technique, to service personnel who deal with the public to help them control the public. There are obvious right uses of these techniques to control people: they are welcome tools when used to defuse a life and death situation at 47,000 feet altitude in a tightly-packed jumbo.

But there are also possibilities for abuse. And there is a profound difference between acting in order to achieve a pre-determined end, and an attitude of the heart.

The discernment here is the leaving open of possibility; the person who genuinely wishes to help another out of a cycle of hostility does not have a stereotyped image of what the person might become or even if the person will accept the help. The helper leaves the freedom for the other to continue hostility. The helper does not take away freedom to choose or establish control. The helper opens options, but not obligations.

A person using a mere technique will continue to use it until the desired result is obtained, or the effort appears hopeless. But the same techniques that can prevent panic on an airplane can be used to deceive and deflect a drive towards relieving injustice.

Technology has both hurt and helped us. It has increased our propensity to try to manipulate our selves and God, but it also has made us more aware of the ways and means of becoming gently focussed, open, and willing to be transformed. Technology and technique must not be mistaken either for the grace of God or the experience of God. The runner runs according to a training program, but does not mistake the daily workout for the process of assimilation and integration that takes place out of sight. Attitude, exercise, and neurology combine to develop muscles in a particular way and the stamina necessary to win a marathon. But the workout is not mistaken for the race.

A golfer hits innumerable golf balls onto the driving range and in practice rounds, but these efforts are not mistaken for the instinctive movements that gradually develop, nor is a practice round mistaken for a tournament. While the golfer might indulge in a winning fantasy during a practice round that helps the process of hitting the ball successfully, there is a clear distinction between the process and the goal.

Such clearly perceived distinctions are not always sought (and sometimes are not possible) in understanding and working toward willingness. People are sometimes so anxious to experience God in prayer that they mistake the technique they have been taught (or the body's response to the technique) for the encounter they seek. Frequently the realization comes that it is not, but there is always the odd person who wants the experience instead of God.

For example, one common technique taught today is "breath prayer". This is a very ancient aid to prayer, and it is true that the exercise can itself merge into prayer. But when combined with physical stillness and a repeated phrase it can induce very pleasant sensations of timelessness and physical lightness.*

In their enthusiasm some people mistake these sensations for an experience of God—which in one sense, of course, it is, since our being sustained from moment to moment in life is an experience of God. But the fact that this sensation leads to self-reflection indicates it must be allowed to slip by while the person praying focusses beyond it. Some people are tempted to seek sensation and not go beyond it. On some occasions this can be quite appropriate: it is good to know techniques that can bring interior calm. But technique should be acknowledged as such, and not debased to something magical.

> A person's new and exhilarating experience of him/herself as spirit is often mistakenly assumed to be a visitation by the Holy Spirit, and an eruption from the emotional unconscious or a psychic invasion from another human being is mistakenly seen as a visitation by the devil. . . .
>
> This constriction is, in my view, a distortion of a legitimate pastoral caution which goes back to St Paul, whom I hear saying something like this: "Don't be egotistically preoccupied with spiritual phenomena such as visions or tongues or prophecies or

---

*For an exposition of the form of concentration known as hypnosis, which coinheres with other phases of consciousness, see the works of Milton Erikson, MD.

ascents to the third heaven. What matters is your openness to the Holy Spirit of love, your being *lived by God in Christ.*"[42]

To illustrate from another angle: a child wants to "grow up" and engages not only in the seeking described above but also in imitative behavior, what is perceived as being "grown up" behavior. But the child has no image of how it will look as an adult, or how it looks to an adult, or what it will become, any more than the parent can predict for it.

This fact of unknowing, and the constant surprises growing children present, can be one of the most profoundly delightful experiences of being around young people. How much less satisfying if we could look at an infant and know what the adult would be; how much poorer we would be if our own fantasies, always narrow in comparison to the unimaginable result, were in fact the determining factors.

When we move from these examples to growth into God we have consciously to add the element of grace, which is operative, if unacknowledged. And not only grace, but also a deliberate rejection of static images of what we should become. While we may glean from scripture and self-knowledge certain hints as to the way in which each of us ought to grow, we have always to remember that these are projections from our limited perspective, and that to lock them into a fixed stereotype is to impose a suicidal spiritual tyranny. All of us know the experience of an unfolding concept: "I thought I knew what peace (or love or joy or detachment or humility) was until. . . ." If we choose to lock our selves into a particular concept we prohibit further growth, or at least make it very difficult.

The history of religion is full of the follies that result from such stereotyping, and the absolutizing of these stereotypes. The creation of a closed mythology is especially anomalous in Christianity, which is supposed to be life in the freedom and play of the Spirit.

We need to understand that while role models are important they are only models, not molds. While we can discern what needs change and growth in our selves, we cannot effect that growth by technique. We can engage in exercises that will help us learn disengagement from push-me-pull-you relationships; we can learn various ways of meditation and focussed stillness, but we must not mistake these activities either for the growth process or for the grace to which we consciously try to open our selves, and which is operative out of our sight.

It takes a constant, delicate discernment to find and keep one's balance, to keep technique from developing into pelagianism, mythology and magic. The criteria of discernment are not that difficult: what is enabling to open us to willingness is useful; what lures us to reflect constantly on our experience and construct a secure system is perilous.

What opens us to continually new, unprojected, unforeseeable possibility, the willingness to live in the insecure security of faith, is valuable. The opposite is lethal.

What is difficult is to insist on being honest with one's self in applying the criteria. The possibilities for self-delusion are legion.

Subject and Object

There is another peril attached to technique of any sort and that is the inherent tendency we have already noted to make God (or our selves) into an object. This proclivity, particularly in regard to God, becomes more and more apparent in Christianity as it moves West, and as doctrine becomes increasingly subject to propositional thinking. While I do not intend to devalue the need for doctrine, it, too, has tended to become systematized mythology, and the catalyst for the very power struggles and institutionalization Jesus knew to be destructive to growth in God.

In the Hebrew scriptures there is a pronounced vision of God, who cannot be object, pouring out God's own life, power, love, on to the creation. The human response to this is not speculation but praise and awe directed toward the divinity-who-cannot-be-object, who is wholly intimate as well as wholly other. One has the feeling, moreover, that for all of the abyss between the Creator and the created, there is no sharp distinction as to where I AM begins and ends because the nature of I AM is kenotic, poured out, pervasive, sustaining.

This vision is in sharp contrast to another view, that of a capricious deity whose wrath is easily aroused, who must be placated by legalism and slaughter. This god is not the God of Sinai, the God who in rabbinical tradition says to the people: do not rejoice at your exodus, for my people have drowned in the sea.

Even the oppressors of the people are beloved. It is unfortunate that this wrathful god has found such popularity, and yet perhaps it is another example of secure mythology replacing the insecurity of faith. It is easier, more reassuring, more conducive to justifying earthly power structures, to be able to say the choices, effects, and punishments are clearcut, than to wait on Mercy.

And it is more reassuring to treat God as object. Today we think nothing of the language of approach to God, which objectifies. "I" am the subject of the sentence and God is the object. "Do I believe in God?" "How do I relate to God?" "How do I experience God?"

It is as if there is a mental image of standing over and against God who is an object for consideration. Perhaps this tendency is one of the reasons for the prohibition of images in the decalogue. Yet how many of us as children picture God as an old man with a long white beard, sitting boringly on a gilded throne up there somewhere? And it would seem that many of us carry some more subliminal image of God as object, even as a more evolved understanding replaces the one wished on us as children. It is not necessary for children or adults to be taught in this way.

The tendency to make God object occurs in the most unlikely places. Even as Paul Tillich attempted to reconcile existentialism and Christianity and demolish some of the idols of the past, he objectified God almost as an existentialist projection. Tillich rightly proclaims that the Church stands for the "God who transcends the God of the religions". But that is not all:

> without sacrificing its concrete symbols can mediate a courage which takes doubt and meaninglessness into itself. It is the Church under the Cross which alone can do this, the Church which preaches the Crucified who cried to God who remained his God after the God of confidence had left him in the darkness of doubt and meaninglessness. To be as a part in such a church is to receive a courage to be *in which one cannot lose one's self* and in which one receives one's world. . . . [itals. mine]

The Lutheran courage returns but not supported by the faith in a judging and forgiving God. It returns in terms of the absolute faith which says Yes although there is no special power that conquers guilt. The courage to take the anxiety of meaninglessness on oneself is the boundary line up to which the courage to be can go. Beyond it is mere non-being. Within it all forms of courage are re-established in the power of God above the God of theism. The courage to be is rooted in the God who appears when God has disappeared in the anxiety of doubt.[43]

There is a problem with this statement, but to better understand what Tillich says, here first is Ernest Becker:

What singles out Tillich's cogitations about the New Being is that there is no nonsense here. Tillich means that man has to have the "courage to be" himself, to stand on his own feet, to face up to the eternal contradictions of the real world. The bold goal of this kind of courage is to absorb into one's own being the maximum amount of nonbeing. As a being, as an extension of all of Being, man has an organismic impulsion: to take into his own organization the maximum amount of the problematic of life. His daily life, then, becomes truly a duty of cosmic proportions, and his courage to face the anxiety of meaninglessness becomes a true cosmic heroism. No longer does one do as God wills, set over against some imaginary figure in heaven. Rather, in one's own person he tries to achieve what the creative powers of emergent Being have themselves so far achieved with lower forms of life: the overcoming of that which would negate life. The problem of meaninglessness is the form in which nonbeing poses itself in our time; then, says Tillich, the task of conscious beings at the height of their evolutionary destiny is to meet and vanquish this new emergent obstacle to sentient life. *In this kind of ontology of immanence of the New Being, what we are describing is not a creature who is transformed and who transforms the world in turn in some miraculous ways, but rather a creature who takes more of the world into himself and develops new forms of courage and endurance.* It is not very different from the Athenian ideal as expressed in Oedipus or from what it meant to Kant to be a man. At least, this is the ideal for a new kind of man; it shows why Tillich's myth of being *"truly centered on one's own energies"* is a radical one. It points to all the evasions of centredness in man: always being part of something or someone else, sheltering one's self in alien powers. Transference, even after we admit its necessary and ideal dimensions, reflects some universal betrayal of *man's own powers*, which is why he is always submerged by the large structures of society. He contributes to the very things that enslave him. The critique of guru therapies also comes to rest here: you

can't talk about an idea of freedom in the same breath that you
willingly give it up. This fact turned Koestler against the East,
just as it also led Tillich to argue so penetratingly that Eastern
mysticism is not for Western man. . . . Tillich's point is that
mystical experience seems to be near to perfect faith but is not.
Mysticism *lacks precisely the element of skepticism, and skepticism is a
more radical experience, a more manly confrontation of potential meaninglessness.* Even more, we must not forget that much of the time,
mysticism, as popularly practised, is fused with a sense of magical omnipotence: it is actually a manic defense and a denial of
creatureliness.[44]

Both Tillich and Becker appeal to what is popularly known as
"the best" in the human person. There are few people who would
deny that courage in the face of meaninglessness and despair is not
laudable, and certainly the idea of the taking of nonbeing into one's
self is very close to what we have been describing. In the faith that
is security with insecurity, we don't have to like the sense that we
are free-falling: we just have to say yes.

Thirty years after Tillich published *The Courage To Be* we see
all around us the myth of the macho person, man or woman, the one
who is unrelated, unconnected, and who can solve the problems by
sheer dint of brute force of will. This is a travesty of what Tillich
was talking about, but this is the sort of life it can result in. Tillich
would doubtless be horrified.

Overvaluing the self, undervaluing everything else, Americans have overdosed on the language of radical individualism,
undermining their capacity to conceive and articulate, much less
act upon, the common good. Individualism . . . has grown can-
cerous, eating at the vitals of our social ecology. Leaving us ill-
equipped to confront "structures of power and interdependence
in a technologically complex society dominated by giant cor-
porations and an increasingly powerful state," the hero worship
of the self has become an invitation for the self to "twist slowly
in the wind."

If we are not to succumb to the "extreme fragmentation" of
the modern world—not to ignore the "extreme threat" it poses
to our very individuation—then a new level of social integration
is required. Indeed, the straitjacket of the self-militant militates
against the kind of collective self-awareness that would restore

public involvement and responsibility to the place of privilege in the American psyche. Arguing that we are doomed if we don't, the authors concentrate their hopes—along with their analysis—on the restoration of those sentiments and practices—"habits of the heart," in de Tocqueville's phrase—that would bring about renewal of community and commitment.[45]

There are other major problems with Tillich's New Being.

1. The kind of theology in which Tillich is engaging is the sort Ephrem would call "blasphemous". He is treating God as object. Granted, he is speaking to an audience disillusioned with traditional popular Christianity, but Tillich is trying to create a new awe and wonder out of meaninglessness, heroism, and doubt.

All of these are necessary to true faith, but not in such a way that they focus on self. His specific statement that the self is not lost is not merely a protest against Hindu absorption or Marxist collectivism, but a positive thrusting toward and elevation of the great me, whether he realizes it or not. He does not distinguish between self and self-image, and that the loss of the latter is necessary for the recovery of the former, and the taking of meaninglessness into one's self. Otherwise the heroism becomes an ego-trip.

2. He does not see God as kenotic, and certainly not interrelated enough with human beings so that *together* the "will of God" is discerned. God is not willful and neither, as God's image, should humans be. Tillich seems to see God as a willful God.

3. Cosmic heroism is futile unless it is seen as an expression of the indwelling Christ. As we shall see, this indwelling is hardly an excuse to abandon responsibility. Quite the reverse. But there is little human beings can do on their own. The evidence of "evolutionary destiny" which he shares with Teilhard de Chardin has hardly proved out in fact. Tillich wrote during a time of great optimism and protest against rigid conformism in America. It would be interesting to see if he would have held this view after the crises of the sixties, especially the Vietnam war.

4. Our view of the interrelatedness of God and humankind in no way denies creativity, but creativity is not a form of either rebellion or submission. It is co-creating with God.

5. Tillich seems to deny any kind of supporting grace; there seems to be no vision of a God whose life interpenetrates the uni-

verse and keeps it going moment by moment by sheer kenotic love.

6. The idea of being centered and the point about evasions of centeredness are good, but, if Becker is right, Tillich's remedy becomes self-centered instead of becoming the power of God. As we noted earlier, the destiny of the human race is far more glorious than humanism ever imagined. Yet in the same breath we must note that we need humanism too, and we do indeed need "new forms of courage and endurance". There is nothing "magical" about the idea of transfiguration and deification. Becker misunderstands this, and perhaps Tillich does as well.

7. Transference as a "betrayal of man's own powers" is true if it is transference to an object. But God is not an object. Further, in order to be true to our own powers we must know their limits and be willing for "the Writer" (see Chapter V) to put in the divine two cents' worth. This means a human being must make every effort but at the same time constantly listening for the Word.

8. Tillich is struggling with *angst*, even as we are. Yet, as we will see, despair is not alien to the kind of Christianity this book is about. It is possible to fall through despair into the hand of God, instead of despairing from the illusions of control.

9. The word "mysticism" should be thrown out completely not only because it is a word that has lost its meaning, but also because it is a word that tends to set knowledge of God apart in some elitist category. Tillich misunderstands that to be truly one with God involves radical skepticism, and an embrace not of potential but *actual* meaninglessness. He is accurate in his assessment of "popular mysticism", and it is doubtless this to which he is referring.

10. This is a very one-sided sort of theology, human-centered; pelagian, holding proudly on to guilt; allowing little room for the meaning of the cross: the forgiving God, grace, receptivity, interdependence, and love, even love beyond emotion. Ironically, the passage that follows what is quoted above approaches authentic "mysticism" as we shall see in Chapter VIII.

If we must speak about God in subject-object terms—and, with Ephrem, I am very much against doing so—the grammar of God's relationship with creation has to be reversed. *God* is the subject, and we are the object—but not object: we are "thou". And yet this view, too, is incomplete. Because of the kenotic nature of divine love there is a continual outpouring and sustaining and even longing that draws us into the fluid tetragrammaton, whose precise meaning in terms of tense and being still escapes translators. God's life by God's choice is continually bound up with creation: I will be for you what I will be.

Over and against this idea of God as object is a God who knows and participates in the life of creation as pervasively as the energy that binds particles into atoms, and atoms into matter. The Hebrew scriptures try to show this intimacy in a God who laughs and weeps, a God whose glory is a word implying weight, or, better, density. And this very glory is kenotic: God is willing to be given over in Name; to participate in history; to dwell between the cherubim of the Ark; to become an infant; to laugh and weep and to be crucified.

God's kenosis is God's potency. And God incarnate in Jesus is *willing to be made object* by the creation in order to overcome the abyss between subject and object, and thus destroy death and the fear of death. God's total *kenosis* in death is the potent act that reveals this glory, this willing, gathered density, available to us, and celebrated as resurrection.

It is the fear of death—either mortality or vulnerability—that causes objectification, because to be named "thou" by God, or to dare to name God "thou", is risking total exposure.

As the image of God, as mirror, we must learn to know that *our kenosis is our potency.*

Our unwillingness to share this kenotic glory, our desire to grasp and control is the basic flaw in us. Like a fault in the earth there is an ontological slippage that groans and shifts under the tension of the density of this glory offered us, and our unwillingness to receive it. We push against this glory with our preference for the treadmill of illusion, especially the desire to have safe limits. And being limited by our fear, we cannot receive the life of Christ who is willing to dwell in us in mutual *kenosis.* We cannot become open to possibility and potential, to healing and transfiguration, until this fracture in our selves is brought to light, until the water of life—our tears and God's—begins to trickle, and then gush from the stony rock of our heart. It is split to reveal not only a hidden Source but, because of the willing exposure of its flaw, it is deemed worthy to become a living stone of the city of God.

For us to participate in the *kenosis* of God, which is our calling as God's image, means that we must give up all that we conceal from our selves and others: it means *to be willing to be emptied*. This is not a conscious process; nor can we empty our selves. It is not the same as meditative stillness, which is an exercise to help us become willing. We may feel empty, but feeling has little to do with being empty.

This kind of emptying is the result of trusting dependence on divine mercy. It involves tears to release the lust for power, the poison in our hearts, to open them so that the oil of the Spirit's anointing may light fire upon the earth.

There is no one moment when we know we have become empty. Like its sister, humility, this emptying precludes self-reflection. It is not something "achieved"; it is a process that does not end. It is not a "state" because the relationship of God and creation, God and us, is dynamic. The idea of interior stillness as *stasis* is part of the stoic inheritance, some of which is not only non-Christian but anti-Christian. Interior stillness itself is dynamic, and comes to be only with great longing and struggle to want nothing else, not even the stillness itself, in order to know God alone.

This is not an impossible task. Our only task—a task that "costs not less than everything"—is to seek willingness. God's love will do the rest. Even as we struggle to be still, love seeks to enter and transform. But as we are changed we realize that our continuing rebirth itself demands further willingness, and finally *a willingness for whatever*.

This radical willingness will, if we are faithful to it, shatter every idea we have about our selves; about our interior growth and transformation; about living a Christian life; about contemplation and our relationship to the world; about God.

Active and Contemplative

In the West we have made some very artificial distinctions about "contemplative life" and "the world". Life in God is not divinely sanctioned navel-gazing. God may and probably will ask anything of us. The process of being emptied turns us inside out so that we are other-oriented; we no longer pray but are prayed. Leaving our selves open to God for "whatever" enables God to use our lives—which are part of God's—as God will, to pour Mercy through us, though we may have no sense of this happening.

We become an integral part of what Paul has glimpsed:

> For I reckon that the sufferings we now endure bear no comparison with the splendour, as yet unrevealed, which is in store for us. For the created universe waits with eager expectation for God's sons to be revealed. It was made the victim of frustration, not by its own choice, but because of him who made it so; yet always there was hope, because the universe itself is to be freed from the shackles of mortality and enter upon the liberty and splendour of the children of God. Up to the present, we know, the whole created universe groans in all its parts as if in the pangs of childbirth. Not only so but even we, to whom the Spirit is given as firstfruits of the harvest to come, are groaning inwardly while we wait for God to make us his sons and set our whole body free . . .
>
> In the same way the Spirit comes to the aid of our weakness. We do not even know how we ought to pray, but through our inarticulate groans the Spirit himself is pleading for us, and God who searches our inmost being knows what the Spirit means, because he pleads for God's people in God's way. . . . (Rom 8:18–24; 26–27 NEB)

An "activist" may find herself a contemplative; a "contemplative" may find himself thrust into the midst of a maelstrom of injustice to witness to nonviolent transformation of the system, an action that can come *only* from interior emptying. It cannot be taught.

None of the so-called traditional stereotypes of exterior living-out of these ideals really matters. One learns that solitude has very little to do on the deepest level with exterior solitude, and a great deal to do with remaining unentangled, which is *not* the same as uncommitted. To remain compassionate and involved, yet unentangled, requires total commitment to kenotic life, complete freedom from the pursuit of self-glorification. One learns that activism is hollow without the dynamic given in solitude and contemplation, and indeed that activity itself frequently goes wrong if that solitude and contemplation is not present in the still-prayer of the heart.

This stillness is a commitment to the working of God in simplicity of life without seeming purpose except this willingness for whatever. Again, "simplicity" is an inward characteristic and has little to do with outward material expression: one can be wealthy and simple—although it is difficult. It is the inward orientation that matters.

We come to learn that it is only those who are unconcerned with "paying dues", who are able to risk without involving others, who are free to act with integrity. And they find they *must* act when called, whether it is the prayer of being, or finding oneself in a police state witnessing to the impotence of tyranny, laughing at, and helping others to laugh at—and therefore neutralize—the rule of fear.

This willingness for whatever demands acute discernment and obedience to the divine task. Since a call often may be obscure, there must be willingness to risk disregarding "what people think", and yet not act without the aid of the counsel of those who have no agendas of their own, but who themselves seek willingness for whatever, who know the workings of the Spirit in themselves and others.

Much has been made of obedience in the past, obedience to earthly superiors. There is a profound rationale behind this idea, yet today there are few in positions of leadership who are free, kenotic, and apolitical enough to warrant such obedience. I am not advocating that everyone kick over the traces, nor am I advocating anarchy in the churches.

Gustavo Gutierrez has said that the truly poor are those who do not count. Not to count, in institutional terms is to be set free. It may mean that one is not listened to; it may mean that one is generally ignored, or it may seem so. This is not to denigrate all institutions by implication: it is simply to say that a person who does not have to answer to others' power is free to proclaim that the emperor has no clothes on. This is not an abrogation of power but an assumption of responsibility. Such a person will not have to worry about jeopardizing others' livelihood or reputation. We may be concerned only with our own *kenosis*.

Such a person may be a member of an institution, but has given up any aspirations to wield power over others, even though he or she may end up in a leadership position. This is a poverty that makes all rich, and enables a confrontiveness in love that leads to justice and peace.

It is almost a truism that those who have power have sought it, and often those who have weak characters seek it most. Few have asked for and received a "heart skilled to listen" (I Kings 3:9)—and Solomon was not a very good ruler. Fewer have the integrity that sets self-glorification aside. To find a truly kenotic person in a hierarchy is, and probably always has been, a rarity.

An institution can be a vehicle for God's power only insofar as its leadership and members function in a kenotic attitude. God's love is not impeded by anything, but power in the name of God is possible only by *kenosis*. Those who have chosen not to count in the sense of seeking power have, in Christian institutions, the added responsibility of maintaining a kenotic witness to those who have chosen to follow another way.

We in the West have had thrust on us an idea of obedience which not only is not the obedience of the early Church and the desert, but also has been an excuse for spiritual and political tyranny. The obedience of the early church and the desert is one of mutual discernment, made with prayer, fasting, and hesitancy. Particularly in the desert, the mothers and fathers were loath to give directives. They would rather teach by example, and so aware were they of the human condition and their own sins, that instead of judging they would rather have an opportunity to forgive.

> There was at that time a meeting at Scetis about a brother who had sinned. The Fathers spoke, but Abba Pior kept silence. Later, he got up and went out; he took a sack, filled it with sand and carried it on his shoulder. He put a little sand also into a small bag which he carried in front of him. When the Fathers asked him what this meant he said, 'In this sack which contains much sand, are my sins which are many; I have put them behind me so as not to be troubled about them and so as not to weep; and see here are the little sins of my brother which are in front of me and I spend my time judging them. This is not right, I ought rather to carry my sins in front of me and concern myself with them, begging God to forgive me for them.'
> The Fathers stood up and said, 'Truly, this is the way of salvation.'[46]

Truly this is the way not only to salvation but genuine peace in the world! (See Chapter IX.)

This attitude of forgiveness does not mean there will not be times when obedience will have to be simply that: an order obeyed even though it seems mistaken (but not morally wrong). At the same time, if we listen, God may demand that we act counter to what is expected of us in terms of playing society's game, whether it be "religious" or secular.

To merely understand this is itself subversive in Brueggemann's sense, and is to fly in the face of established stereotypes. It is only those who are willing to be emptied, who disregard reputation, who seek *kenosis* to be filled with God's wisdom and mercy, turned outward, turned inside out, who will be free enough and humble enough to obey in this way. Not that they will be in any sense "perfect": *kenosis* does not bestow omniscience, and the possibility for falling into subtle traps of willfulness becomes greater.

But as long as the person is willing, mistakes become less significant because the kenotic person is in continual repentance, has no stake in maintaining the error to save face, and knows that nothing is wasted. The kenotic person knows too that the most hideous fault, by Mercy, can be part of the final perfection of all things. Such a person will weep in compunction, and his or her tears light fires of transfiguration.

The "will" of God is not, any more than the "will" we exercise, a rigid, negative, unchangeable and repressive force. The will of God is not a railroad track on to which we must squeeze our lives or perish in eternal damnation. The will of God is not static any more than is the dynamic creation shot through with that same divine Love. We are, each one of us, invited to live in and radiate the divine glory, to realize our potential to become, as our uniquely created, divinely imaged selves, part of that density of light, no matter how fallen we are; no matter how impossible it may seem.

We are asked only to be willing and to trust that it is so, and know that with each person's willingness more than our own self is being transformed and transfigured.

Salvation as Possibility

We have mentioned salvation as possibility in passing, but it is now time to take a closer look. It is part of the response to the question, what does mutual kenotic willingness mean in practical terms, and, more specifically, what can we begin to understand from scripture?

The idea of salvation we encounter in the Hebrew scriptures is one of being brought from a narrow into an open space; of being brought from slavery into freedom. After the founding of the City of David, a vulnerable promontory below the present-day Old City of Jerusalem, it is also associated with being saved from defeat by enemies who may lay siege from the surrounding hills.

To be encompassed in the literal form of manoeuverings of troops and peoples, or in the personal forms of fragmentation, illness, or ego-inflation, is to have possibility limited and to be trapped. In Jesus' ministry we see the thread of possibility running through both his words and his actions. The beatitudes are wisdom sayings that explore possibility hidden in what is ostensibly negative human experience.

The sayings about the rich point out the mistaken notion that riches are a sign of favor from God: thus the disciples' astonishment at the saying that for the rich to enter the kingdom of heaven is more difficult than to put a camel through the eye of a needle, whether that eye is the narrow gate of Jerusalem, or a sewing tool. What Jesus is trying to point out is that the problem is not riches *per se* but rather the power, trappings, and illusion that accompany riches.

So, too, with the Rich Young Man: Jesus is not suggesting he give up his material wealth so much as the sycophants, preference, and self-serving nature that comes with being at the top of the heap.

It is not so much that we are possessed by our possessions as ensnared by the illusion they give us of power over our own fate. Great wealth does not create possibility so much as it limits it. Literature has always played on our fantasies about the rich, yet few people in the world are as limited as the rich in what they can plan or do. Especially in these days of terrorism and kidnapping, they must always be concerned about the effect of their plans and actions on their wealth.

Isaac sums up the problems all of us have with our "wealth", with what is often known as "the world", as distinct from the creation, and whose characteristics are known as "the passions":

> These are: love of riches; the gathering of possessions; fattening up the body, giving rise to the tendency toward carnal

desire; love of honour, which is the source of envy; the exercise
of position of power; pride and the trappings of authority; outward elegance; glory among men, which is the cause of resentment; fear for the body.[47]

Note that these passions not only induce the illusion of power
and status, security and even immortality in the person who possesses—or is possessed—by them, but that they also provoke envy
and resentment in others. And at their root is "bodily fear", that is,
the fear of death. Thus a malignant cycle is begun. Isaac is writing
for monks; thus celibacy is highly prized, and his comment on the
body should not be taken to mean that sexuality is bad. In Chapter
VII we shall see what the Syrian tradition has to say about virginity,
which is far different from the technical concept we have today.

Thus when we are rich in the things of this world—those passions Isaac describes—we are trapped. If we aspire to power or are
born to it, we are even more imprisoned.

In Jesus' ministry we also see possibility restored with physical
health. When the blind are enabled to see, their world becomes im-
measurably larger. When the man with the withered hand is healed,
his restored dexterity opens a new range of activity. The woman
healed from haemorrhage and the lepers made clean are not only free
from disease but also free from ostracism, and made part of human
society again.

When Jesus sends to John in prison (Mt. 11:5; Lk. 7:22) he is
not only pointing to the fulfillment of Isaiah's prophecy, but also
saying that the prophecy itself is pointing to physical signs of a
deeper restored possibility: freedom from the narrow vision in
which we become entrapped in our sin, especially from the root sin
of taking increasing control.

And freedom most of all from the trap of fear, the fear that
drives us to acquiring a facade of illusion behind which to hide from
death.

> Take no part in the barren deeds of darkness, but show
> them up for what they are. The things they do in secret it would
> be shameful even to mention. But everything, when once the
> light has shown it up, is illumined, and everything thus illu-
> mined is all light. . . .
> Finally, then find your strength in the Lord, in *his* mighty

power. Put on all the armour which *God* provides, so that you may be able to stand firm against the devices of the devil. For our fight is not against human foes, but against cosmic powers, against the authorities and potentates of this dark world, against the superhuman forces of evil in the heavens. Therefore take up God's armour; then you will be able to stand your ground when things are at their worst, to complete every task and still to stand. Stand firm, I say. Fasten on the belt of truth; for coat of mail put on integrity; let the shoes on your feet be the gospel of peace, to give you firm footing; and, with all these, take up the great shield of faith, with which you will be able to quench all the flaming arrows of the evil one. Take salvation for helmet; for sword, take that which the Spirit gives you—the words that come from God. Give yourselves wholly to prayer and entreaty; pray on every occasion in the power of the Spirit. To this end keep watch and persevere, always interceding for all God's people. . . . (Eph. 5:11–14; 6:10–19, itals. mine.)*

The relationship between *kenosis* and salvation cannot be over-emphasized. It flies in the face of virtually every secular and some religious attitudes to which our culture has conditioned us. It flies in the face of the inheritance of the idea that the will of God is a narrow, rigid channel to which we have to conform or suffer eternal damnation. It flies in the face, even, of popular ideas of "liberation theology" which all seem quickly to degenerate into another mythology, another closed system, by insisting on a particular political philosophy.

What if the promise of God to make all things—even political systems—new is true? Shall we narrow God's role by insisting on any extant system?

Mutual kenotic willingness is not only the relationship between God and humankind, but also the relationship between people, in cooperation, in co-creation. *The degree to which a person is willing to be emptied out and thus filled with God is the degree to which possibility is opened.*

This kind of living requires a courage to be that surpasses Til-

---

*For a discussion of the character of the Powers—Paul's word for what we must be emptied of—see *Naming the Powers* by Walter Wink, Fortress Press, Philadelphia 1984.

lich's existential heroism, which in the end is a kind of willfulness because it is standing over and against, and thus creating a kind of security. In willingness to be emptied out there is no standing over and against, nor is there any expectation or naming of what one will be filled with. It is this unknowing that is often mislabeled as meaninglessness, whether in fact that is what Tillich meant or not.

In some of the most often quoted texts from the lives of holy men and women, we read that they were so conformed to the will of God that God could not say "no" to them. This idea, misunderstood invincibly or deliberately, has been used to justify everything from spiritual tyranny to the requisite productivity of miracles for canonization in the Roman Church. The absurdity of this sort of push-button mythology of saints having "power" to "intercede" and persuade God to change his/her inexorable mind could not be more contrary to what real sanctity is.

Saints are saints because God has been poured out into them, and through them. They have been willing to be emptied so that God can fill them, so that Christ can live in them and work through them. Saints have not wrested holiness out of their lives like pulling a sword from a stone. They have struggled to be willing, but it is God's life that has been poured into them and through them, and it is God's power that has enabled them to be willing.

Thus it is not that their prayer "persuades" the deity to "relent" but rather that Christ lives so powerfully in the earthly life—and now resurrected life—bestowed on the saint that the saint's willingness and God's "will" cannot help being one because they have met in *kenosis*.

Perhaps the focus on certain saints to "achieve" certain desires in our lives was originally a way toward self-emptying: first, the petitioner would focus on the saint. Second, in focussing in this way, a certain element of self-forgetfulness came about. Third, the petitioner in turning the matter over to the saint would be in essence letting go of the matter and thus broadening vision.

This in no way denigrates miracles but rather is meant to show how our willingness is vital for God's will to be done. Thus the importance of the uniqueness of each of God's creations: God's will is co-creation, and diversity, too, increases possibility and thus movement toward salvation. In other words, if we open to possibility by letting go our own fixed ideas of how things ought to be; if we can let go insisting on uniformity and conformity; if we open our vision; if we can refrain from grasping and narrowing the vision God has given us, then we become empty so that God's poured-out life can fill us. We are called to act, but to act in a listening way so that God can make possibility ours.

Oddly enough, we all experience this on an ordinary level every day, whether we acknowledge God's life pouring into us or not. As I write this book, as any writer writes any book, there is always the sense of the mysteriousness of words appearing out of silence and emptiness. A scientist going over data experiences "insight" coming not so much out of the data itself as a new and fresh set of connexions suddenly "emerging", often, if not always, the whole being more than the sum of its parts.

Each of us experiences these moments many times each day, though most go unnoticed *and should not be noticed* except in terms of wonder and thanksgiving, and except as they encourage us in our struggles toward willingness.

Yet the simplicity of this daily experience is buried under the avalanche of cultural imperatives about taking control, satisfying cravings, and winning. There are even books distorting some of the ideas derivative from *kenosis*.

For example, I heard of one called *Winning Through Letting Go.** This newest magic formula suggests letting go of what is upsetting in order to achieve a desired goal. The fallacy in this sort of thinking is that the desired goal, no matter how selfish, is the best possibility. Thus you can trap your man, girls, by letting go of the fact that you want him so much. This will make him desire you!

Trap or be trapped by one's limited, proximate, illusion-coated desire? Perhaps this *is* the right man. But what about his freedom? What about the powerful illusion created by pheromones and other aspects of our physical makeup that tend to cloud perspective?

And most of all, why does the question have to be posed in terms of win/lose at all? Especially in terms of relationship, this attitude implicitly sets up a power struggle in which someone is going to get hurt. There is no space or silence in such a relationship. There is no solitude or listening—and *hearing*—the other because one is too

*Literally "heard". My impression of this book comes from hearing the author talk about it. The example given is hers.

busy listening for the next manoeuver to which one will have to respond.

Life *is* about power, but not that kind. The kind of power Christianity is about is life-enhancing. The sorts of power that control others are life-denying. Thus when the girl rightly lets go her inordinate desire for the man, she does so *not* to manipulate him into fulfilling her wish for power over him, but to set both him and herself free to possibility, *without predetermining the outcome.*

God gives us this freedom: who are we to take it away from one another? And as God gives us this freedom, so too the kenotic willingness of God is there in both the brokenness and the grace with which to pick up the pieces.

If the girl makes a mistake, if she insists on her own desire and catches the man, and too late realizes that she has in fact entrapped herself, there is still the willingness of God waiting for her willingness to let go her win/lose attitude. And no one can say, or has the right to dictate, what that possibility will be, or it ceases to be possibility. If the girl faithfully follows this course, the only sure outcome is that the relationship will cease being a devouring and limiting one.

There is always uncertainty in freedom, but there is always the certainty of God's redemptive love creating new possibility out of our most horrendous messes, if only we can be willing to allow this redemption to occur.

In this light, what do we mean when we say, "Thy will be done"? It means many things, but one is that we step out of ordinary time into sacred time. And we encounter sacred time at the bottom of the tears which have loosened our grip on power.

Creation as Organism

Kenosis, willingness to be emptied, possibility, freedom—all are enemies to fear, illusions of omnipotence, the security of closed systems, and the kind of mythology that creates those systems.

To put this more positively, to admit the kenotic nature of God is to admit also the kenotic nature of the divine image. As it is not possible to know God—in the sense of intense intimacy of Hebrew Scripture—so it is not possible to know the image as object.

In other words, to objectify humans, to put them in slots or categories, to give praise or blame according to the fulfillment of our expectations, to accord worth on the basis of tangible achievement is to attempt to control them, to limit their possibility. This process is operative on every level of consciousness and society, and encouraged not least by the increasing technological need to contain information about people in numerical bits.

While technology can increase possibility in projects such as space exploration or writing this book, its application to humans tends to decrease possibility. When technological methods are applied in human relationships and personal growth an even more insidious limitation of possibility occurs. A mild example is the analysand who begins to dream to order for a psychoanalyst; an extreme example is brainwashing. We will look at this idea of limiting more closely in the next chapter.

To look at God, people, or creation as object is to assume a static situation. The assumption is that who or what is being made object is unchanging and unchangeable. God, of course, is God, and "unchangeable"—whatever theologians mean by that—but *not* static. "Constancy" might be a better word, or Lady Julian's "courteous".

Kenosis is a dynamic word. It implies unending self-emptying and out-pouring. For creation, it implies continual change on whatever level: in biology, the unpredictable uniqueness of each organism in its individual makeup, while remaining tied to atomic, genetic, cultural antecedents.

Terrifying as it may seem, creation is affected and effected on every level by choice. Thus in time-not-time, choices have infinite reverberation and implication, from the enormous choices attached to nuclear war, to the small, daily, liminal internal choices which add up to a bigger choice and direction for the individual and for the group. It has been well said that we create God, that we shape the whole of reality, however infinitesimally, by the choices we make. Even God's own being is still unfolding, and in this kenotic sense we are co-created with God.

Physics can help illustrate the love of God sustaining creation, invisibly melding together the whole in a fluid economy. Energy is the pervasive constant of creation. It takes many forms depending on speed, density, gravity. Electrons responding to instructions in a microchip form the patterns of dots with which the thermal printer forms the words of this book.

Differently-moving particles form atoms, whose structure makes up the density of the solid table on which the printer is situated; other impulses stimulate my fingers to press the keys, and receive out of silence the thoughts to be expressed. The same energy pervades every rock and shrub on the planet; the light that shines on it; the solar wind through which it travels; the stars from which light travels over eons to reach eyes gazing at the night sky; the "dark matter" that makes up the bulk of the universe.

But this is only a feeble analogy. More pervasive is this love of God, more than we could ever imagine, and gives to each creature not only the energy for mortal life, but, as we are willing, as we understand the relationship between the energy of life and the willingness to be poured-out-through, an increasing capacity for this love.

While the love of God is unlimited, we in our creatureliness are limited by the amounts we can bear to have poured through us, the weight of glory we can be enabled to sustain on the fragile fault which that love, as we are willing, justifies, brings into alignment, into union, so that the slippage and tension decrease. If we are unwilling, the reverse occurs: our fault cannot sustain the simple love that creates our existence each moment.

Ancient cultures understood the creation, and later the human family, as a single organism. It was understood that there is at work in the universe an economy of love, just as there is an economy of energy. Each person participates in this economy whether or not he or she knows it. Thus the burden and contribution of the individual is the burden and contribution of the group and vice versa: the burden and contribution of the group is that of the individual.

These ideas live on in the knowledge of the coinherence of the human race and the created universe. We are beginning to become aware once again of the fragility, the balance, that hangs on the smallest choices of each of us, and the direction other organisms unpredictably take, whether or not this can be construed as "choice"— and I think it can. We have been wrong in valuing our selves above the rest of creation of which we are caretakers and which our choices

most affect. If our choices are not kenotic—as they have not been—
then we are doomed to extinction.

The vineyard is a whole organism: vines, soil, water table, air
flow, and innumerable other variables. It is not simply a matter of
harvesting fruit each year: one has to care for the land as well as the
vines, the soil's aeration not less than the vines' pruning. Christ is
not merely the Vine: Christ is the whole Vineyard, with each aspect
dependent on the rest.

Early Christian theology recognized the perilous task and privilege of each human creature to participate in the redemption—or
not—of creation: its transfiguration; its being brought to the final
perfection we cannot know in our finite minds. In the West particularly we have lost this vision of the terrible power bestowed on the
image of God by this proffered role. But it is a power that demands
self-emptying so that the power at work is not the limited vision of
humankind, but the limitless power of God's vision of creation,
which can come to be by cooperative kenotic choice.

It will not be imposed by God.

The Name and the Shekinah

The glory of the kenotic God is that this God is also the God
of "might, majesty, dominion, power"—every descriptive word and
phrase human language has been able to devise to communicate awe
of the Mercy who is above all and in all, limitless in power and potential, who is Lord. It is this magnificence who willingly enters the
creation and cooperates with its choices; it is the all-powerful who
bestows possibility; it is the omniscient who chooses to give us freedom; it is the One above all concept and reason who becomes object
for our sake.

The rabbinical tradition places this awe in the Name of God,
the tetragrammaton so sacred that it cannot, must not be pronounced: it is in this name that God willingly gives power to the
creature to name and thus wield power, a power to make earth tremble. The words for Lord which came to be used in the place of the
Unpronounceable Name is masculine; the word signifying the kenotic God—light, wisdom, presence, is feminine: *Shekinah*.

There is as great a mystery in the relationship of the Name and the Presence; the density of glory and the Presence, as in the Persons of the blessed Trinity. Indeed, that the Trinitarian understanding has roots in the relationship of *YHWH*, *Kavod*, and *Shekinah* is a tantalizing suggestion too complex to be explored here. But what we need to mention is that at the Fall, the *Shekinah* was shattered, and that part of the redemptive process is the recovering of these fragments of divine light to full density of glory.

There are many legends and parables expressing this idea in both rabbinic and Christian tradition, but it is essential here to say only that the recovery of this density of glory is accomplished not by God's *fiat* of omnipotence but by human *fiat*, willingness—like Mary's—to have that glory poured through us. Each of us enables or blocks this light as we will and as we are willing.

The God who meets us in willing *kenosis*, in tears, embraces all grieving and all glory in the single Word of our salvation.

III

The cords of hell entangled me, and the snares of death were set for me. (Psalm 18:5 BCP)

Then you hid your face, and I was filled with fear. (Psalm 30:8 BCP)

There is a voice of rebellion deep in the heart of the wicked, there is no fear of God before his eyes.
He flatters himself in his own eyes that his hateful sin will not be found out.
The words of his mouth are wicked and deceitful, he has left off acting wisely and doing good.
He thinks up wickedness on his own bed and has set himself up in no good way; he does not abhor that which is evil. (Psalm 36:1–4 BCP)

We walk about like a shadow, and in vain we are in turmoil; we heap up riches and cannot tell who will gather them. (Psalm 39:7 BCP)

He has scattered the proud in their conceit. (Luke 1:49 BCP)

Cease not, wet eyes,
His mercies to entreat;
To cry for vengeance
Sin doth never cease.[48]

Persistence in error is the problem. Practitioners of government continue down the wrong road as if in thrall to some Merlin with magic power to direct their steps.[49]

A leader of the peace movement asked the advice of Senator George Norris . . . Much the same opinion in different circumstances was pronounced by General Eisenhower . . . "Everyone is too cautious, too fearful, too lazy, and too ambitious (personally)." Odd and notable is the appearance of lazy in both catalogues.[50]

Evil people hate the light because it reveals themselves to themselves. They hate goodness because it reveals their badness; they hate love because it reveals their laziness. They will destroy the light, the goodness, the love, in order to avoid the pain of such self-awareness.[51]

Utterly dedicated to preserving their self-image of perfection, they are unceasingly engaged in the effort to maintain the appearance of moral purity. They worry about this a great deal. They are acutely sensitive to social norms and what others might think of them . . . the words "image," "appearance," and "outwardly" are crucial to understanding the morality of the evil. While they seem to lack any motivation to *be* good, they intensely desire to appear good. Their "goodness" is all on a level of pretense. It is, in effect, a lie.[52]

The reader will be struck by the extraordinary willfulness of evil people. They are men and women of obviously strong will, determined to have their own way. There is a remarkable power in the manner in which they attempt to control others.[53]

If we are to study the nature of human evil, it is doubtful how clearly we will be able to separate *them* from *us;* it will most likely be our own natures we are examining.[54]

. . . so that through death he might break the power of those who, through fear of death, had all their lifetime been in servitude. (Heb. 2:15 NEB)

The pharisee represents natural perfection, finally humanistic and secular. The publican illustrates the truly Christian attitude, that of repentance, which is never within man's capacity but always the fruit of free election, and a marvel of grace.

There is always the danger of contamination between these two ways. To express and describe itself Christian experience will constantly have recourse to the vocabulary of humanistic perfection, the only one available. Even when making every effort to purify and, so to speak, bend to a contrary sense the scheme that this vocabulary expresses, the Christian will appear sometimes to adopt it. . . . It expresses an essential tension, which is not only inscribed in the words but reflects an inclination of the human heart—the most insidious temptations perhaps of every soul truly seeking the face of God. . . .

Obedience, asceticism, even prayer can be directed away from the living God and made to serve an ideal of perfection not differing essentially from a secular ethic. They then become works of man and his stronghold, a rampart he erects against others and sometimes against God. In such a "system of justice," repentance, if it remains at all, becomes a single exercise alongside others. But it is no longer the miracle of grace that entirely transforms man, the threshold across which he begins to be born into a new existence—making him completely free in the desires of the Holy Spirit.[55]

The Polluted Spring

In Chapter I, I suggested that the "greater" death is the "chosen" death: learning to live beyond fear and the desire for security on every level.

In Chapter II, I attempted to suggest some ways in which we succumb to the constant temptation to make our lives closed, safe systems in order to reduce our levels of fear and satisfy the desire for control. I have suggested that control is in reality that mysterious ontological "something gone wrong", "original sin", and is intimately related not only to fear of mortality but also to the greater fear of letting go control of what is seen and felt, exteriorly and interiorly, of human perfectionism which represents ourselves to ourselves in a reassuring way. Fear thus becomes a refuge.

I would now like to continue this background study of the trap from which tears are the release by discussing some ways, often unnoticed, in which evil specifically manifests itself today.

Recent Studies of Evil

Our culture is fascinated with evil.

Magic, horror and violence are best-sellers in literature, film, and religion. Books abound on the occult, as do books that discuss evil in secular and religious terms. Two popular authors in this area are Barbara Tuchman and M Scott Peck, MD.

Tuchman's *The March of Folly* is written from an entirely secular point of view. It is a collection of historical anecdotes showing the tendency of individuals and governments not only to act against their own self-interest, but to persist in folly even after it has become evident, and even after they have been warned that their action is leading toward destruction.

Ms Tuchman is a humanist. She believes in the glory of human reason and nothing outside it. She dismisses multiplex Christianity as superstition in a single sentence: "With the advent of Christianity, personal responsibility was given back to the external and super-natural, at the command of God and the Devil."

While this is not the place to discuss whether an historian whose fundamental perception of a religion is opposite to its theol-ogy, and who refuses to explore this theology, is selling prejudice as history, her contemptuous brief analysis—which few historians, secular or religious, would accept—obviates her arriving at any con-clusion except one of entropy.

With the exclusion of any possibility beyond *immediately acces-sible* human consciousness, that is, what can be explained by reason and perhaps a modicum of psychology, she excludes hope for any new insight into bettering the performance of governments and in-dividuals who continue on in "wooden-headedness". She seems to deny the mysterious, the sense of awe found in scientific, artistic, and religious endeavor. And her conclusion, which borders on cyn-icism, is that "We can only muddle on as we have done in those same three or four thousand years, through patches of brilliance and de-cline, great endeavor and shadow."[56]

Ms Tuchman's closed system thus prevents her attempting to approach the question "why": *why* are politicians seemingly "in thrall to some Merlin with magic power"? Beyond this she does not care to go. She does not attempt to tackle either the fundamental causes of folly, or possible alternatives. We might ask why she does not make this attempt: one suspects that the system she has built for herself is too fragile to withstand the challenge from sapiential knowledge which admits of wisdom beyond discursive thought, and would oblige her to face the fact that she is not in the absolute con-trol her illusory universe would suggest.

Further, even a brief examination of Christian literature would show that her perception of abandoned responsibility is entirely in error.

Her conclusion is unacceptable. We are now in a nuclear age. There is little, if any, room for "muddling". One muddle with a multiple warhead and the end of life on this earth will be upon us.

Dr Peck's books attempt to take a closer look at human folly, but his religion and his God look suspiciously like Tuchman's closed humanist system.

His examination of evil cites laziness, control, fear, deception, and scapegoating as some of its causes. He attempts to examine growth and evil in a scientific way. His descriptions are graphic and, in superficial ways, precise. Yet he, too, seems dedicated to the power of science and reason even while admitting their limitations. He is convinced of the possibility of studying evil and researching an approach to its healing. At the same time he admits that in exorcism there is a 5% unknown; the rest can be explained by psychological dynamics.[57] Thus he is pleading both science and mystery.

One can admire Dr Peck's attempt to explore in a rational way a problem that by his own definition is confusing. It is not surprising, therefore, that he seems to have fallen into some of the very traps he has described.

One of the first is that, while admitting the mystery, his exploration is definitely loaded in favor of a scientific approach. It is questionable if evil allows itself to be thus studied unless there is a deliberate attempt to deceive the investigator. The conclusions Dr Peck has drawn from two exorcisms in which he was involved belie the subtlety of evil he has exposed in the first section of his book.

The second problem is that while acknowledging the mystery of evil he wishes to wrest control of it, making it subject to human healing and scientific method, even though he acknowledges that in the end, in the exorcisms, it is the patient who chooses healing and God who heals. There seems to be a contradiction here.

A third problem is that, perhaps for clarity's sake, much of the book is in "we-they" language, objectifying the patients, those subject to evil, as if there were some clear-cut distinctions between those who are evil and those who are not, those who are sick and those who are well, as if we know completely God's idea of perfection for the human person. I submit that even though we have the example of Jesus the Christ we do not have this knowledge. God conceals even while revealing. What is more, there is no agreement amongst psychiatrists as to norms of "health".

At the same time it should be noted that one is not required to give up hard-won "health" for the sake of religion and vocation, although God's emptying-out of us may require it to take some astonishing turns.

A fourth problem becomes evident in *The Road Less Traveled:* Dr Peck makes a distinction between ordinary laziness and the laziness that is the dynamic behind evil. This seems to me a false distinction. It seems to rest on the assumption that "I", the "healer", who am good, can heal the object, which is evil; that I am not subject to laziness, and that by a great deal of energy evil can be conquered.

Although on p. 215 of *People of the Lie* he does say, "If we are to study the nature of human evil, it is doubtful how clearly we will be able to separate *them* from *us;* it will most likely be our own natures we are examining," he seems reluctant elsewhere to lose "scientific" detachment from evil by acknowledging the role of necessarily healing from one's own wounds. While he readily admits he has learned from his own experience, he still gives an impression of reluctance to own the evil inherent and operative in each of us.

Kenneth Briggs has summed up nicely the difference between Peck's and May's approaches:

> At the heart of Peck's appeal is the contention that we can attain what he calls spiritual growth if we try hard enough, if we love ourselves and others as "an act of will". It is a paean to self-achievement and the work ethic. . . .
>
> May says we must give up trying to control our destinies and desist from self-will if we are to satisfy our spiritual hunger. . . .
>
> May rejects the claims that life in the spirit is contiguous with mental health or stages of growth. We may know God in spite of emotional distress and apart from psychological maturity. The idea that we must have a strong sense of selfhood before we can "give it up" strikes him as absurd. It is to deny that we are utterly dependent on God, who can touch us anywhere under any conditions.
>
> Peck essentially repeats the creed of self-reliance, adding a religious dimension, albeit a rather unorthodox one. Religion is the outgrowth of depth psychology. "To put it plainly," he says, "our unconscious is God." And God "wants us to become himself". Grace is available if we want it. Nowhere is the word prayer even mentioned. . . .
>
> Such words comfort many of us who want our selfhood kept intact while receiving spiritual bonuses. Perhaps that's the

reason the book is so popular. In the name of sacrifice and discipline, nothing basically is sacrificed. . . .

[May] says no to the obsession with self as the answer to the call of the Gospel. It has the audacity, in our individualistic, self-centered society, to ask us to stop all that striving and be willing to listen.

"In the face of such a heavy cultural push toward solidity of self-image," May writes, "the message of contemplative traditions is decidedly unpleasant." These traditions, Eastern and Western, both maintain that to have any hope of satisfying spiritual longing, the importance of self-image must steadily be decreased. One must "become as a little child", full of appreciation, but lacking in comprehension and mastery. Notions such as this, of giving up and self-surrender, rub harshly against the grain of modern society, but the contemplatives go even further. They proclaim with a conviction that can be absolutely frightening, that self-image must truly die.[58]

We do not grow into God by pitting our willfulness against the willfulness of evil.

However, Peck does make an observation which touches on one of the major thrusts of this book:

Ernest Becker, in his final work, *Escape from Evil* (Macmillan, 1965), pointed out the essential role of scapegoating in the genesis of human evil. He erred, I believe, in focusing exclusively on the fear of death as the sole motive for such scapegoating. Indeed, I think the fear of self-criticism is the more potent motive. Although Becker did not make the point, *he might have equated the fear of self-criticism with the fear of death.*[59]

There is one problem with Peck's description, however: that is the implied self-judgment in the use of the word, "self-criticism". Self-exposure is one thing; self-criticism quite another. Self-criticism can make us feel very good about our selves. Self-exposure in the light of God is Other-oriented. This is the chosen death. Self-criticism is just another form of control.

Control fosters a sense of omnipotence and invulnerability: it seems to me that this is what is at the root of sin and evil. It pits my will against God's self-emptying love. Peck's desire to heal evil is admirable, but he seems to have created a diabolically closed system.

Redemption, salvation, health are all related to possibility, and while psychology can help open our eyes to certain options, it is in its own way a system subtly closed by the limitations in each person involved in the process. Additionally, Peck does not differentiate between sin and evil, nor does he seem familiar with the idea of the *value* of sin, the *felix culpa*. Contrast Peck with Louf:

> In its first moment this prayer still bursts from the depth of distress. It exposes its wretchedness. It calls for help, or implores pardon. But the more it overruns the heart with its incessant flow, the more it appeases and reconciles itself, so to say, with sin. Or rather, *it ends by turning its gaze away from its own weakness to look solely on the face of mercy.* Repentance sweetly stirs then in humble and discrete joy, in loving fear, finally, in thanksgiving. The sin is not denied, nor excused, but it rebounds in pardon. There where sin had abounded, grace ceased not abounding all the more (see Rom. 5, 20). All that sin had undone, grace restored more marvelously yet. If prayer retains a vestige of sin and wretchedness it is henceforth a case of a happy fault, a *felix culpa*, guilt assumed and swallowed up by love. Prayer is then close to becoming ceaseless thanksgiving.[60]

I would like to suggest that what is most essential to healing our own evil and to come to repentance is to acknowledge that we must wait on and be attentive to possibility outside our control, whether this is acknowledged as "creativity" in Tuchman's purely secular perception; "higher power" to use a theologically neutral word, or the Christian understanding of grace, the life and love of God that pervades all creation.

Far from permitting abrogation of responsibility to choose, choice in Christianity is mandated; the responsibility each of us bears should leave us full of dread.

While the idea of possibility has appeared in both secular and religious mythologies, it is uniquely expressed in Christianity, which is the only major religion in which a kenotic God acts in history, in which humans are invited to co-create in mutual *kenosis* with this God who weaves our sins, mistakes, and follies into a pattern, and thus offers us salvation *contingent on our willingness to have it.*

The strait place of tears is the pain of acknowledgment of our ontological desire to control and *is itself* the fire of the love poured through us when we relinquish that control. (See Chapter IV)

Evil as Continuum

To find our way out of entropy and folly requires first that we look within our selves for the sources of evil. We tend to see terrorism, for example, as something "they" do to us, like the hijacking of an airliner. We fail to see, refuse to admit, that each time we do not keep our word, each time we betray another, each time we make a promise that belies our intention (hidden agendas), we commit an act of terrorism on another person's sense of trust and reality as surely as if we had fired a gun or thrown a bomb.

Terrorism is not the exclusive territory of extremist political groups: terrorism is the deliberate removal of another's sense of being earthed, the ground on which he or she has a right to stand as a human being worthy of love and respect. Each time we challenge another's sense of reality as an act of willful deceit, each time we commit our selves and personal lives to expediency at the expense of truth in order to manipulate and control, we commit an act of terrorism.

The deliberate violation by control, the deliberate taking away of another's sense of reality of life by deceit, intimidation, devaluation, belittling or other means, of his or her accurate perception, for the purpose of self-gratification of the desire to control, is rape. And often rape on this psycho-spiritual level, because it is so subtle, and so hard to pin down—especially when one's peers are being equally raped and thus terrified of acknowledging and supporting one another in such a situation—can often be more damaging and harder to heal than physical rape.

Each of us does this innumerable times in our lives. Each time the habit becomes more deeply ingrained, so that our word depreciates in value, and we do not deserve the trust we demand. Breaking our word becomes a way of life to the point that often today it seems that it is assumed beforehand that a verbal or written contract is dependent not on trust but on expediency.

Isaiah speaks of "your covenant with sheol":

Who is it that the prophet hopes to teach,
to whom will what they hear make sense?
Are they babes new weaned, just taken from the breast?
It is all harsh cries and raucous shouts,
'A little more here, a little there!'
So it will be with barbarous speech and strange tongue
that this people will hear God speaking,
this people to whom he once said
'This is true rest; let the exhausted have rest.
This is repose', and they refused to listen.
Now to them the word of the Lord will be
harsh cries and raucous shouts,
'A little more here, a little there!'—
and so, as they walk, they will stumble backwards,
they will be injured, trapped and caught.
Listen then to the word of the Lord, you arrogant men
who rule this people in Jerusalem.
You say, "We have made a treaty with Death
and signed a pact with Sheol:
so that, when the raging flood sweeps by, it shall not touch us;
for we have taken refuge in lies
and sheltered behind falsehood. (Is. 28:9–15 NEB)

We are ready to make agreements if they seem to serve our appetite for security and power even if we have no intentions of keeping them. Our fear of commitment makes us unwilling to see an agreement, a friendship, a marriage, a religious community through the hard times.

Barbara Tuchman's contempt for Christianity is not unusual, though while dismissing it as a superstitious and meaningless mythology, perhaps in an attempt to dismiss all religion, she has at the same time created one of her own.

Yet there is some justification for her dismissal: somehow in the history of Christianity the religion of infinite possibility has taken on the characteristics, not of a dynamic, symbolic, and open description of life that helps explain truth about the interrelationship of the human person with the Divine, but assumed properties of the very closed mythology of death against which it has always stood in essence.

At times it has become a confusion of realities: the use of human or "worldly" power in the name of a gospel whose purpose is to show the folly of that power.

The idea of death often has been narrowed to mean mortality.

The idea of salvation often has been narrowed to a "heaven" of questionable desirability, and its alternative, nearly always presented as a threat, held up as far more likely.

The God of infinite mercy, of infinite possibility, often has been represented as an implacable judge to be appeased in a closed system of justice from which there is no exit.

References to "the world" often have been reduced to hatred of creation in order to assure us eternal life with the Creator, instead of the rejection of the very qualities of evil routinely used in the name of religion by many of those who have dominated and dominate its political power structures. These qualities of evil are: control of perspective, removal of another's sense of reality, scapegoating, deceit, violation of trust, expediency. They combine as psycho-spiritual rape and destruction of the creation.

Political evils seem virtually inescapable. To quote a saying I made up, when two or three are gathered together there is politics. To remain unentangled from politics, to be truly solitary, truly *monos* in the best sense; to cultivate the kind of solitude that is necessary to make community of any sort, is one of the most profound ascetical tasks any of us has to face.

Each of us has the urge to be *monos*, no matter what our way of exterior life. What do I mean by this? It refers to the Only-Begotten, the Single Only One, the Holy One of God, that is, Jesus the Christ whose life is meant to indwell in us. It means unity in the sense of healing of fragmentation, and unity amongst one's fellow humans. It means single-heartedness, that is, chastity, sometimes expressed in celibacy, with which it is frequently confused.

But above all it means the kenotic, self-emptying life that makes a person one with God, or rather allows God to enter in so that in a very real way one becomes and pours out the power of God.

It is precisely of the lust for control that we must be emptied so that God's love can be poured through us.

One of the early followers of this tradition was St Anthony of Egypt. He has long been a model for Christians, not only monks. Today we know that his famous "life" has little or no consonance with historical fact. But we do know that it is very likely that his letters are authentic. They give us the impression of a spirituality which perhaps can best be summed up in the word *kenosis*. The scriptural texts he refers to are those of self-emptying: Is. 53:5; Rom. 8:15–18, 32; Phil. 2:6–11.[61]

The idea of "living the gospel"—or the obstacles to doing so— seemed to be understood precisely in these "political" terms—that we are perpetually tempted in our encounters with others to have what we see as advantageous to us, with complete disregard for the others' freedom or possibility outside our own perspective.

For some of the ancient desert-dwellers, the only way to be weaned from this addiction to entanglement seemed to be physical, exterior solitude in order that they might battle alone in their weakness. Others saw that their particular makeup demanded confronting their weakness in community.

Ironically the lives of the desert saints have inspired not only holiness but also ambition, competition, envy, criteria for judging others, and desire to rule others. They were not meant to be thus used, and we always have to remember the difference between the ideal and the way Christian life has often worked out in fact. The ideal does not become invalid, but attempts at living it out have constantly to be reexamined.

In early Syrian Christianity, which was contemporaneous with the better-known developments in Egypt, there were few distinctions between monk and not-monk. There was one ideal for all: the single-hearted pursuit of God, whether this was expressed in a celibate life or an ideal held in the heart in married life.

Ephrem's biography also has no relation to fact. He was not a monk: he was an itinerant choirmaster. It is possible he had made some kind of religious consecration, but the demarcation lines then were not drawn as sharply as they are now. Single-heartedness lived out in Syrian Christianity is called "proto-monasticism".[62] And Ephrem's writing has an intensity about it that demonstrates his single-heartedness. Monk or no, he was *monos*.

There is debate about whether the cenobites or the hermits came first, or if the two ways evolved together. For our purposes it is not necessary to resolve these matters. But in either way of life— as for every Christian—the ideal is to become *monos*, to seek God alone in the heart and in the faces and lives of the people with whom one lives. It is a process of inner conversion and inner concentration.

André Louf describes the outcome:

> Among his brothers he is a tender and gentle friend, not irritated by faults, understanding weakness. He is infinitely mistrustful of himself, but foolishly trusting in God, entirely carried by his mercy and omnipotence. Only one desire remains in him, that it will one day please God to test him again, so that one time more, and always anew, and always more, he can throw himself toward him, and embrace humble patience still better and with more love. It is this which makes him like Jesus, and which enables God to continue his marvels in him, his man of affliction and his workman: *operarius suus.*[63]

Why—how—has this ideal been achieved?

> From this asceticism of the poor—*patientia pauperum*—he is each day reborn a new man. Henceforth he is entirely at peace, having been undone and remade from top to bottom by pure grace. He no longer recognizes himself. He has touched the depth of his sin, but at the same moment he has brushed the abyss of mercy. He has learned to surrender to God, to lay down his mask and his arms. Finally he finds himself weaponless before God, no longer having any defense against his love, he is despoiled and naked. He puts aside his virtues, his plans for sanctity. He painfully retains his wretchedness only to display it before mercy. God has become truly God for him, and only God, that is the Saviour from his sin. He ends by being reconciled even with his sin, with being happy in his weakness. Henceforth he is indifferent to his perfection: it is only soiled linen in God's Eyes (see Isaiah 64:6). His virtues he possesses only in God: they are wounds, but dressed and healed by mercy . . .[64]

But Louf is also aware that the ideal is not always what is happening in fact:

> This [i.e., repentance as a "system of justice"] was the monasticism that Luther tried to live to his cost, and from which, alas, he unduly generalised as an image at the moment when he was forced to end the experience through a report of failure. "Monasticism," wrote Dietrich Bonhoeffer, "had transformed

the humble work of discipleship into the meritorious activity of the saints, and the self-renunciation of discipleship into the flagrant spiritual self-assertion of the 'religious.' The world had crept into the very heart of the monastic life, and was once more making havoc. The monk's attempt to flee from the world turned out to be a subtle form of love for the world. The bottom having thus been knocked out of the religious life, Luther laid hold upon grace. Just as the whole world of monasticism was crashing about him in ruins, he saw God in Christ stretching forth his hand to save. He grasped that hand in faith, believing that 'after all, nothing we can do is of any avail, however good a life we live' " (*The Cost of Discipleship*, New York, 1963, pp. 50f).

The lucid words of Bonhoeffer denounce a monasticism which would become a "work of man" parading itself before God. The spectre of such a monasticism is not a mere caricature. It is an always present danger. It is perhaps today's most subtle temptation. Is any other result possible for a monasticism which would secularize itself in depth? *Only the experience of repentance can redeem monasticism from this sham and save it.*[65]

Whatever the ideal, the fact is that during the rise of the West monastic institutions became involved in the very worldly ambitions that are so foreign to the Christian ideal of the indwelling Christ, the meeting of the loving kenotic God and the kenotically responding human. While this may have been to advantage from the point of view of enriching culture, the inheritance of Christianity as "the work of man" is the main problem with which we are struggling today.

To put this bluntly, why has the religion of the mind of Christ, the kenotic One, become a religion of power politics? And don't we need to do something about it? Why has priesthood particularly taken on this attitude, especially in the debate on the ordination of women, which among other egregious oversights, ignores their particular, inherent predisposition toward a kenotic life?

Knowing they are powerless allows women to feel and perceive suffering in others. They can identify with the suffering in others and can empathize with other human beings. What priests women would make, knowing that they do not have power unto themselves, but have power in the Lord. Fewer power struggles would occur because power would not be the major center for operating one's business of living.

Achieving, even when in pain, brings about a self-confidence in the Lord. "He accomplishes all things," even through and in suffering. Women know this firsthand because they live with pain most of their vital, energetic years.[66]

Ms Fauvell may be too sanguine in her view about women and power struggles, but the rest of her point is well taken.

It is even more ironic that much of the theological debate has been argued against the ordination of women from the point of view of hierarchy, that is, *power*, ignoring the primacy of baptism, the priesthood of baptism, the kenotic life, the charism (see Chapter VII) given at baptism, and from which sacrament all others proceed. There is not one baptism for men and another for women. One of the ancient desert fathers said, "If you still see men and women you have not the mind of Christ."

It is Mary who, in her mysterious relationship with God first put on the mind of her Son, emptied herself, said, "*Fiat*", and it was from her emptied hands that we first received him. If we have thus received him in the flesh from a woman, how is it that there is difficulty about receiving him from a woman in the Body and Blood of the eucharist?

And where, in this vicious power struggle, this attempt to control—to denigrate and spiritually rape—where is the repentance, the tears, Louf speaks of? The question of the ordination of women is not a question of equality of a democratic process, but an equality of recognition that God can and does give vocations to the priesthood to all creatures, and to some of them, be they woman or man, the vocation to the ministerial priesthood.*

For what are we to have compunction? Not our wounds and liabilities, certainly. Our sin is turning from our indwelling vision of God as God and in each other. And when we pursue our ambitions, the "proud imaginings of the heart" in this unkenotic hierarchical struggle, the mind we have put on is that of the Father of Lies.

For some people in every age, Christian vocation unfortunately has meant trading one set of power structures and securities for an-

---

*I hope to treat this subject at length in the near future.

other. Thus in addition to the struggle to become willing so that God can empty us of self-image, many people, in order to receive the blessing of the Church on their vocation, have had to take on an additional self-image of a group or organization. For some this may lead to greater holiness. For others it may be a liability. Today new options are being opened up, albeit with great difficulty and much persecution from a few of the established (and threatened) religious structures.

The idea of "vocation" has itself become part of the power structure, and because the significance of every individual Christian vocation (not to mention vocation as a creature of God) has been so devalued, there are some people who feel that one is only "fully" Christian if one is in the ministerial priesthood, that there is some standard of preferment or special access to God of which ministerial priesthood is the pinnacle.

Each of us is called to union with God. We are already united to God, or we would not exist. God has poured out God's life for this. To set up a particular set of methods or mores and say they are the way to salvation is a complete travesty of what the Christian message is all about.

The monastic way is one among many. Fortunately there are enough authentic monasteries and monastics to keep the ideal going, just as there are enough good marriages to keep that ideal going. But Louf is right in counselling vigilance, because as soon as the ideal becomes twisted in its living out, enormous damage is done not only to the inhabitants of the monastery or other community who struggle not to be similarly infected, but also in a ripple effect to those who surround them. The same is true for every Christian in every walk of life. As someone who has embraced the monastic and solitary life, and who depends very much on my sisters and brothers living in community, I am hardly anti-monastic. But Louf's fears are solidly grounded, and, in addition, monasteries are easier to talk about because they are better documented.

Further, in the last twenty years the realization that monastic life is in drastic need of reform has led to much experimentation, some of which has borne fruit and a great deal of which has not because it has been primarily concerned with the living of externals, not with fundamental change in attitude of heart both of those living the life, but more especially of those in power who dictate how that life is to be lived.

The politicisation of monastic life virtually obviates being able to grow into the vision of God as God and in neighbor undistracted by political "dues". Monasteries no longer wield powers of the state, but without vigilance they can harbor as much political infighting if they were states in their own right.

There is no question that the cenobitic way of life has been a way to holiness for many men and women, but because of some of the problems of history it has often been a source of confusion to call it "monastic"—*monos*—in character, because the wealth and power of the cenobites has so often been a scandal to the evangelical ideals of evolved simplicity. Until very recently, as Thomas Merton pointed out in so many of his writings, it was virtually impossible to live *monos* in a cenobium in the way the life was recovered after the various European revolutions, and as the victorian revival was passed on to the Americas. The irony was that *monos*—a very subversive word when you stop to think about it—was often held up as an ideal while at one and the same time it was made impossible to follow.

Further, it is increasingly evident that the way monasteries have been structured by men for women is entirely inappropriate, and left to themselves, free from censure and fear—two sources of much competitive envy in women's communities—would doubtless evolve their own forms of monasticism. Women's monasteries are particularly subject to political distractions, and it is quite possible that if they were not required to authenticate themselves in the opposite sex, while still requiring the complementarity of contact, many of these women's problems would disappear.

Nor is the solitary spared from these "political" involvements. They are the demons to be fought alone in the heart just as the cenobite battles them in the matrix of community. Yet one cannot help but wonder if the impulse for more solitude did not often come in order to simply get on with the task of becoming willing, and detached from distracting political involvement. While the desert way is dangerous, for some it is more fruitful.

It depends on vocation, not on merit. It is not a matter of registering a certain mark on a scale of holiness. It is a way, just as marriage is a way. One is not better than another. God's relationship with human beings is no more dependent on their exterior state or measuring up on some human holiness scale than it is on their mental or other health.

But what I have said here about monasteries is no different when applied to any other form of Christian life. Our choices for power, status, dominance, and control, most particularly in the name of Christ, have a gathering resonance we can generally term "evil".

Mere awareness will not solve the problem. In spite of the fact that we live in a supposedly enlightened, post-conciliar, ecumenical age, the old wars amongst Christians are still being fought. Fundamentalism is no longer the exclusive property of an extreme Protestant wing, and tyranny within religious hierarchies still quashes those who would question the appropriateness of the existence of such power, as well as the divisions caused by quarrels more political than theological.

The discernment of "tradition" vs "change" has similar criteria. It is not true that those who are wary of change are *always* trying to control others' lives: change can also be a power-base. The questions that have to be asked are: Do our customs help us to pray? To love God and God in each other more? To make us more alive in the freedom of possibility? To make us less afraid? To help us drop our defenses and become exposed?

Or does our tradition—or the proposed change—mean we maintain and even reinforce our defenses, become less human, more frightened?

What will make us rejoice in each other rather than compete with each other? What will help us fix our gaze on God rather than on religion as a work of man?

In sum, in every part of our lives we still insist on arrogating to ourselves the power that lies within the provenance of God. We are intent on confining the mercy of God to certain doctrinal formulae. We demand that a kenotic God become a controlling God, and we resort to ritual formulae that, for all our insistence to the contrary, still leave a subliminal message of magic that will control the Controller.

Mystery and Mystique

A God who is mystery, who is unpredictable, who disturbs the *status quo*, who conceals in the process of revealing, who demands not only that we choose whether or not to be in relationship but also to take responsibility for that relationship; a God who offers salvation as infinite, unpredetermined possibility—such a God is not a comfortable God. Such a God offers security in the form of risk and faith, and self-fulfillment in self-forgetfulness.

Such a God is a radical God for a human race still desperately and necessarily concerned for minimal survival, dependent on security and caution. But mere survival of the species has never been written into the created order. Growth and change have, even if that evolution takes place so slowly as to be as imperceptible to us as it was to the early tribes who encountered this astonishing diety.

Then there was no doubt about the relative inability of the human race to control events. Today we are in much the same situation but with the added factor that we have the illusion of control in so many parts of our lives while coming ever closer to extinction. The fact that we ignore that the enabling technology is itself out of control and progressively narrowing our freedom even as it seems to enhance our lives evidences the depth of our illusion.

With the advent of our ability to destroy our selves and everything around us, the universe has become an even more perilous place than it was for the groups of nomads who first encountered YHWH, and like them we are continually tempted to abandon our responsibility and retreat into magic and mystique.

Mystique can be defined as the creation of a deliberate illusion. Its purpose can be to educate, to entertain, to convey power, to deceive and control. Mystique can be used for good or for ill. The mystique of English Royalty can help unify the nation; the mystique of the Bhagavan Rajneesh, absurd as he may seem to some, can enslave and exploit.

Early biographers wrote lives of saints with an idea of communicating an ideal rather than factual descriptions, thus creating a mystique that would surround their lives. At the time there was no intent to deceive, since everyone knew that the intent of the stories was to inspire. But through the centuries, these stories have been passed on as literal truth, sometimes in ignorance; often with the purpose of insisting on the ineluctable inferiority of believers in order to enhance the power of those holding authority.

Such use of mystique tends to encourage those on the receiving end to abandon responsibility; yet the romantic in us in a certain sense *wants* mystique, because at its best it can inspire as it reveals itself as a kind of benign illusion, even as it points toward mystery. But mystique too often is used to intimidate, to discourage the wish for transfiguration, to make transformation seem impossible unless the authority holding the mystique is obeyed, and prescribed ritual and subservient behavior followed completely.

Mystique, like certain kinds of mythology, offers a closed system that, while removing the freedom and insecurity of possibility, also offers the security of fear and known cause-and-effect.

This kind of mystique that fails to point beyond itself results in the esoteric and the occult, in magic and ever-narrowing perspective. It thrives on tyranny and subjection; on abandonment of reason and mass psychology. It feeds and feeds on the desire for control and the desire to be controlled, so that the painfulness of growth, of becoming, of moving into unpredictable newness, which requires continual adjustment, cannot disturb this tomb of existence.

Words ending in "ism" are often words that denote mystique. Fundamentalism can be a kind of mystique; so can the word "mysticism" (which ought to be dropped from our vocabulary) when it denotes a dualistic elitist knowledge of a selective god. Jerry Falwell, Jim Jones, Archbishop Lefebvre and certain extreme forms of Anglo-Catholicism are all examples here: might as right is sold as representative of the gospel; liturgy becomes ritual control of the Controller. Every mystique pushed far enough has the distinct possibility of ending in mass suicide greater than any Jim Jones could have imagined.

Mystique of this sort says that there is an accessible power but only on condition that one lay down one's freedom of choice, and subscribe one's mental faculties to living with inherent contradiction—as opposed to paradox, which is only apparent and *does* express reality.

Mystique demands an obedience which is opposite to the obedience of the gospel. Mystique demands an unthinking, unchoosing responsibility that shuts out all but a narrow band of attention. True obedience to God demands thought, feeling, using every capacity given to human beings in an ever-increasing awareness. Mystique inspires fear that can result in emotional highs; dread of God can end in love which is beyond emotion and unaffected by emotional highs or lows.

A person interested in acquiring mystique as opposed to engaging with others in mystery is interested in isolation, in creating the illusion of importance and specialness and power by increasing the gulf between him or her self and others. Such a person is interested in making decisions and requiring others to accept responsibility for these decisions; is interested in having followers who aspire to supposed hidden knowledge which the perpetrator has no intention of giving, but yet promises as long as the follower will yield him or her self unquestioningly.

Those who have embarked on a path of mystique are interested in themselves—in acquiring power for themselves or knowledge for themselves. It is an involuted and involuting mentality. Fear eliminates possibility and creates a prison. The spiral winds ever tighter. In true growth, the spiral winds ever larger.

Optimism, the creation of more illusions and fantasies, is sold as hope. Salvation is presented as an article to be possessed, and as the trap closes, the seeker finds her or him self possessed instead.

Mystique is not confined to fundamentalism (of whatever religious stripe), drug cults, and weird collections of loonies. Mystique is omnipresent. It can be as harmless as that created by Tom Sawyer painting his fence. But most is less innocent.

There is the mystique of the family which causes untold misery every year during holidays; there is mystique that results in mental illness, incest, and lifelong enslavement in the name of "love" at its worst. There is the mystique of prolonging "life" which is really the prolongation of dying. When the machines no longer sustain a thread that long ago snapped, the relatives of the deceased feel cheated and terrified: cheated because death was not averted; terrified because they realize the ultimate freedom of being released into greater life can now be postponed against their will.

There are as many kinds of mystique as there are human beings, human ideas, and human organizations. Self-image is a kind of mystique. It has to go. It is a distortion of mystery of the person created by God, and in whom God is met by one's self and by others.

Illusion and Reality

While all mystique is illusion, not all illusion is mystique. When we go to the theatre we are willingly entering into an illusion in order to be enabled to perceive reality on a deeper plane. We see our illusions exposed by illusion in comedy and tragedy; we are moved through emotions we had the illusion of having safely controlled or repressed or that we have simply forgotten about. We are confronted with a kind of truth that is outside of and widens our limited perspective.

The *katharsis* of theatre is analogous to the emptying of self-image that takes place in the way of tears: we are confronted with extremes of reality brought into shocking unity; we are devastated and uplifted in the same moment.

When we participate in good theatre we enter a kind of mystery: the play points beyond itself; the whole—the play, the actors, the audience interacting—becomes more than the sum of its parts. We are shaken, disturbed to our roots by good theatre. It is no wonder that theatre has long been associated with the divine.

The "magic" of theatre is not magic at all, because, as any good actor will tell you, there is only so much technique involved and in the end there is, in the occasional ineffable moment, a kind of possession that occurs which submits to and yet transcends the skill of the actors, the words and movements, the listening hearts of the audience. It is no wonder that ancient actors considered theirs a divine vocation, and were humbled before its mystery.

The "magic" that attracts, however, is usually not this magic but mystique. For some, the vocation that attracts by its mystique of power, riches, and sycophants becomes a true vocation, bringing greater life to themselves and their audiences. For others, the mystique becomes an end in itself; the illusion is no longer willingly entered but snaps shut on the greedy, would-be controller of a personal, private and closed universe. The horror of the end of this life, in this life, for those who have made this choice is beyond all the hells ever imagined by the human mind.

I have painted this choice in either/or colours to make a point, but the fact of the matter is that the balance between illusion willingly entered to reveal reality, and the willfulness to deceive are usually not that clear-cut, and there is always the danger that those who engage in theatre will begin to be unable to distinguish the illusion from what really is: *for we tend to become what we pretend we are.*

There has been much writing through the ages about "perfection" and "imperfection", of "false self" and "true self" as if each of us has two clearly defined faces, as if it is but a matter of flipping from one side to the other as one would flip the actors' mask from the comic face to the tragic. We have seen our selves in the same generation knowingly create illusion and then believe in its spurious truth, from the incident of the golden calf at Sinai to the incident of the Vietnam war in Southeast Asia.

We, our selves, are not so easily sorted out. We are never "perfect" and it is presumptuous to say that we know what is the perfection that lives in the mind of God. It might be objected that we know Jesus the Christ, but we do not understand who and what Jesus the Christ is, either, as he was and is on earth, and in the will of the Father.

Even if we did, the fact is that we do nothing without unmixed motives: we can have a preponderance of good over less good, but that is our limit. That is one reason pain is always a groundnote to joy.

Thus we have to be watchful when we find our selves wanting to "help" someone, to insure we are in fact not trying to control; we have to listen to our talk of "righteous" anger and "just" wars and even "self-defense" with the knowledge that we are listening to the first stage of a developing lie.

We may have no choice in our anger; at that moment it may be the only psychological glue we have available; we may be forced to enter war by circumstance, or to kill in self-defense as the lesser of other evils. But there is no point trying to whitewash these situations for which tears are the only adjective, verb and predicate, and which tears are probably the closest to purity and guilelessness we will ever come.

Solidarity in Sin

When we lie to our selves and to others we are trying to cover up the fact, opt out of the reality, that we all sin: not just the laundry list of petty, boring faults many of us were taught to confess, but the fundamental, nameless horror—nameless because evil in itself has no name, no substance, and no power until we allow its coiled potential in each of us to strike.

Sins may be the "dreariness of evil . . . the endless string of silly lies"[67] but there is underneath a flaw, a slippage, a tension that runs through the human community and binds it as surely as does resurrection in one Body.

And this brings us to the most extraordinary fact of all: that the divine nature is so kenotic that Mercy is willing to enter and pour through us, not only when we are at our best, but most of all when we are at our worst. The only conditional factor is our willingness. Even as the serpent strikes our cry is heard, and the possibility of life frees us from the prison we would create for our selves—if only we are willing. Christ is the Serpent raised up to heal, and all we need do is look upon him.

We try to cover up, and in covering up we deny our membership in the human race. We try to be better than others, and we isolate our selves from the common guilt as well as the common redemption. We put fig leaves over the canker of control, and say it is the farthest thing from our minds.

The still, small voice of God persists, and we deny that we have heard. We feel we have to make our selves "right" for God, when only God can do the righting. We lived for centuries having forgotten that our relationship with God *begins* with union, not union as a goal after a lifetime of abuse of the very creation God loves.

We have confused our selves with one word: forgiveness. We have taken it to mean both God's forgiving and our enabled forgiving of others. We have forgotten that forgiv*en*ness is just that: a given, and that any understanding or ability to forgive grows out of this given.

> 'Look at him,' John his forerunner and baptizer cries, 'he is the Lamb of God who is taking away the sin of the world' (St John 1:29). As the use of the present participle in the verbal form makes plain, this continual taking away of the sin of the world is his never ending priestly function.[68]

We speak of "forgiving" others as if it were yet another piece of religious technology, not realizing that in the long agony between the recognition of the need to forgive and the goal of actually forgiving is the salvation, for both myself and the one with whom I mourn for what has passed between us. This healing can take place even if the other is unaware either of having done hurt or of the forgiveness at work.

We are always in need of repentance, of this willingness to acknowledge our state of forgiveness; we are always being forgiven,
transfigured, and forgiving, and thus being part of God's transfiguration of creation.

Sin both matters terribly and matters not at all: matters terribly
as a vehicle for evil, and matters not at all because it can be transformed in the love of God. Sin, which we cannot avoid, and the
acknowledgment of sin, can be a balancing factor, not a morbid
preoccupation. It is rather a knowledge that adds reality to the assessment of decisions we are about to make, and brings us to a kind
of self-knowledge that surpasses gladness because of the fire in the
dark, and the fire in our tears.

And because we are one organism our tears cannot stop with
our selves; our responsibility cannot stop with a narcissistic perception of where our sin leaves off and another's begins. The more we
participate in transfiguration, the less we fear, the less we feel we
have to control. Thus the boundaries between our selves and others
become less defined and finally disappear altogether, not because we
are finding our selves by testing our selves against the actions and
reactions of others, but precisely because we are being found in God
and thus need less self-reflection.

We come to a knowledge of our selves and, at the same time,
who we are no longer matters. Thus our acknowledgment of our
responsibility is not the devouring, passionate, neurotic assumption
of responsibility that is false guilt, but rather a recognition of the
dynamic process of being privileged to acknowledge membership in
the human race, and thus be a bearer of responsibility, a sharer in
the royal priesthood, enabling the kenotic God to bear it within us.

The House of Cards

As children, most of us played at building things. Some of us
learned the art of building fragile houses with playing cards. It was
a delicate, often frustrating business to learn to balance one edge
against another to form an arch, do it again with another pair of
cards, and then gently balance a fifth on top as a platform for yet
another storey.

It is a good exercise for children. It teaches lightness of touch
and manual dexterity. It teaches patience. No sooner do we learn

the trick of balancing yet another layer than a breath of wind, a passing pet, or mischievous sibling comes along and jiggles just one card. Down comes the tower to the accompaniment of our impotent rage.

This is the point where we need to stop. Maybe the story goes on: maybe we return to try again; maybe we learn the trick of building really enormous and artistic houses of cards until our new-found skills find other outlets; maybe we perfect them until we make the *Guinness Book of Records.*

We need to stop the story at the fall of the house of cards because we need to look at the rage that appears when we realize we have no control, whether it was control that we in fact had and lost; whether it was illusory control; or whether some unforeseen force took control.

This is not a difficult parable. We handle our rages in different ways. A small child might vent frustration by bursting into angry tears and sweeping the remains of the card-structure away. An older child might explode briefly and go back to work. Children learn not-so-acceptable and acceptable ways of behavior.

By the time adolescence comes, life is a little like a fancy dress party as one personality and then another is tried on and paraded in all seriousness before equally serious peers and secretly amused or not-so-amused adults.

Somewhere along the line a personality is put together, a self, or not. Until that self is more or less there the person is always reaching out to complete it, acquiring bits and discarding them; bouncing off others' selves. Some of this self is "real" and some of it was built with similar skills as those that built the child's house of cards: a balancing act of flimsy materials, and poker face set against the fear of death, mortality or—infinitely more terrifying—the collapse of the tottering edifice erected against the world.

If we are lucky, someone wiser than we gently points to a different way that allows the cards to be blown away and another sort of activity begun.

If we are not so lucky we start to cheat: we take our first set of illusions and harden them into lies, which, glued together into a false front become the foundation for another layer. Pretty soon, in spite of all the inventions we can make, more and more energy goes into maintaining the illusion of reality of our unreal structure. Our terror grows along with the lies, and we believe them firmly in order to make our selves feel secure.

If unchecked, these mental structures become firmly established. More and more energy and resources go into maintaining this ego-empire; more people are exploited, more money spent, more natural balances upset to feed the enclave the builder makes to reassure him or her self that Everything Is All Right, and that the closed system will be in steady state forever.

Even death cannot shake this bastion of unreality—as long as it is the death of someone else. A person who has visited one of these enclaves will know what I mean: here are people who have spent all their lives managing problems so they do not have to go through the pain of solving them.

This creating of lifestyles that will mask terror and allow the minimum of intrusion into a well-ordered routine is not confined to the wealthy: it cuts across every class and race and economic division. The enclaves of the wealthy are the most familiar because they are not only the source of media hype but also the examples in Jesus' parables. But none of us is entirely free from this kind of building: all of us have to be willing to again and again be stripped of the fantasies that our desire to control our fate creates.

How we react to that stripping, whether it occurs by chance or is sought, is crucial. The almost universal reaction when it comes is rage, expressed or repressed. When we lose power we are frustrated, and when we are thwarted we become angry. *My* sense of power is being challenged. *My* sense of security, of control, of manipulating the familiar is taken away. Worst of all, *I* am left exposed in all my nakedness and poverty.

At this point there is a choice: we can start rebuilding the house of cards as fast as possible and as strongly as possible, or we can stop and take a long hard look and ask some difficult questions about the way we have lived and the way we intend to live. The first is willfulness. The second is willingness.

Everything in this book so far has led up to this moment: greater (chosen) and lesser deaths; open or closed systems; faith versus mythology; control versus willing powerlessness.

If we choose willfulness we proceed on our suicidal way of narrowing tunnel vision. If we choose to be willing, we choose the death that leads to greater life. If we choose to be willful, we go through a known suffering that is far greater than the cleansing and illuminating pain of willingness. If we choose to be willing, we enter a strait way, a chasm that echoes with the life-flood of tears that leads into unknowable and limitless joy.

IV

I called upon the Lord in my distress and cried out to my God for help. (Psalm 18:6 BCP)

I cried to you, O Lord; I pleaded with the Lord, saying,
"What profit is there in my blood, if I go down to the Pit? will the dust praise you or declare your faithfulness?" (Psalm 30:9–10 BCP)

And now, what is my hope? O Lord, my hope is in you. (Psalm 39:8 BCP)

Sorrow that is because of God is compunction which turns one to salvation/life. . . .

And when someone has been delivered from servitude to death, he serves the Lord in joy, and not in sorrow. . . .

It is the same with people who sin and so are distanced from our Lord and his righteousness: they weep with sorrow, just as someone weeps when he is far from his friend and feels sorrow concerning him. . . .

If they then turn away from their sins and are justified, they can draw close to our Lord and their tears turn to ones of joy. And when they become sinless [without any sins] and are delivered from sin, they weep with joy as they encounter our Lord, just like the person who sees his dear friend he had not expected to see, and he falls on his neck, weeping over him with sobs and tears of joy.[69]

For he who does not lay open his old ways by confession cannot bring forth the works of a new life. He who cannot lament for what weighs him down, is unable to produce that which raises him up. For the very power of compunction opens up the pores of the heart and pours forth the plumage of virtues.[70]

All the saints yearn for this means of entry; and by weeping the door is opened in front of them through which to enter that place of consolations in which the footsteps of God's love are impressed by means of revelations.[71]

Give me, O great God, in this world (I will not hide it), against the pains of the torments, fierce floods of tears.

Let a vessel unsullied reach me as it flows, so that, though all alone, I may surmount every treacherous danger.

Alas, holy Christ, that thou bringest no stream to my cheek as thou didst bring a flood to the weak wretched woman.

Alas that no stream reaching every part flows over my breast to be a cleansing tonight for my heart and my body.

For the sake of every venerable elder who has abandoned his inheritance, for thy glorious kingdom's sake, for the sake of thy going upon the cross,

For the sake of everyone who has wept for his wrong-doing in this world, may I, O living God, bewail my wickedness.

Especially for the sake of thy goodness and for thy griefless kingdom's sake, speedily, opportunely, grant me a well of tears.

O my love, my God, may thy blood flow in my heart. Who but thee, O God, will give me tears?[72]

Clean the stains of my soul and give me tears of penance, loving tears out of love, tears of salvation, tears that clean the darkness of my mind, making me light so that I may see You, Light of the world, Enlightenment to my repentant eyes.[73]

Love bade me welcome yet my soul drew back,
    Guilty of dust and sin.
    But quick-ey'd Love, observing me grow slack
    From my first entrance in,
    Drew nearer to me, sweetly questioning,
    If I lacked anything.

A guest, I answer'd, Worthy to be here:
    Love said, You shall be he.
    I, the unkind, ungrateful? Ah my dear,
    I cannot look on thee.
    Love took my hand, and smiling did reply,
    Who made the eyes but I?

Truth Lord, but I have marred them; let my shame
    Go where it doth deserve.
And know you not, says Love, Who bore the blame?
    My dear then I will serve.
You must sit down, says Love, and taste my meat:
    So I did sit and eat.[74]

There may not be two kinds of time in the world, but there seem to be two kinds of sympathy: one that weeps and disappears, and one that never leaves the watch. Sympathy, unlike pity, must have some application to the future. If we do not feel deeply the deaths we are powerless to prevent, how would we be alert to the deaths we might put an end to?[75]

    Low at his feet lay thy burden of carefulness,
    High on his heart he will bear it for thee,
    Comfort thy sorrows, and answer thy prayerfulness,
    Guiding thy steps as may best for thee be.[76]

Clearing the Watercourse

When the house of cards falls we are confronted with at least two ideas: the shining option (if often deceptive in regard to our power) that might have been, and the awful fact of the ruin that lies before us. The reaction that follows is a momentary flash of disbelief, usually followed by rage. Before we can talk about another possible reaction, we have to understand this one.

The rage is often the reaction to loss: of our beautiful creation that was an expression not only of an idea but also of our power, control, and expertise; of the face we wanted to present to the world that we are *somebody* who should be deferred to, paid attention to, respected. The house of cards is an easy image to cope with because it is relatively simple. Real life can get a little more complicated.

Perhaps our accomplishment, now destroyed, was more than a fantasized ego-trip (and ego-fantasies comprise an amazing number of reasons for rages). Perhaps we had accomplished something real and good with a relatively pure motive. Perhaps it was of great benefit to others. Now it is gone.

Perhaps, worse, someone deliberately destroyed it, gratuitously, out of jealousy, competitiveness, or some other base motive. Perhaps in the process trust was betrayed. Perhaps—worst of all in the eyes of some of us—our character has been besmirched in the process.

This scenario can be applied to a limitless number of situations in daily life, from home and school to corporate giants and big power diplomacy. Perhaps what has come tumbling down was real and good, or perhaps it was all a sham or even a bluff—in which case the reaction tends to be all the more violent because we have to shore up the lie. Choose an example in your own life before you read on.

A Brief Look at Anger

There is an appropriateness to anger, and we do our selves harm by repressing it, pretending we don't feel it. It is part of both grief work and the way of tears, and sometimes it acts as a kind of glue that seems to hold us together when everything else has been shattered or destroyed.

To repress anger is to invite trouble on biological, as well as psycho-spiritual levels. At the same time, there is a new awareness in the world of psychology that "rehearsing" anger repeatedly can be extremely destructive, and tends to fix the anger within a person. Within grief work there has to be found a middle way in the expression and forgetting of anger. There is a difference between being grieved and being aggrieved.

We need to acknowledge our feelings, however much we would rather not own them. Our feelings can tell us a lot about our selves, if we will only look, and we need to find out *why* we are angry, and follow it through all its healthy and sinful roots so that it can be healed. Anger—and pain—can be useful tools for self-discernment.

In the way of tears and fire, however, anger is seen as being related to the struggle for power. Hebrew scriptures talk often of anger, but a careful reading shows them to be suspicious of it, even when it is "just" or "righteous". There seems to be a kind of running commentary that as long as anger is present, the one who bears anger of any kind will never attain unto wisdom. To God alone belongs judgment, although this does not preclude the need for human discernment.

The New Testament carries this view of anger much farther. There is no qualification in the Sermon on the Mount when it comes to anger. The person who is angry is subject to judgment, whatever crime, real or imagined, has been committed. If a person tries to cope with anger by becoming contemptuous, he or she is subject to the fires of hell. It is important that this view be seen in the entire context of what Jesus is talking about, and not taken in and of itself. Jesus is talking about the coming of the Kingdom, and pointing out that sacred time and the eschaton can be brought into ordinary time by the fulfillment of the law of love.

Healing Anger With Tears

One of the ways of the kingdom is giving up the desire for, securing of, and manipulation of what is at the root of anger, that is, the thwarting of the illusion of human control and power.

The desert fathers are uncompromising in their stance against anger. While many early sayings have come down to us, it is perhaps Dorotheos of Gaza (6th c) who has the most comprehensive discussion of anger. "Humility [does] . . . not grow angry, and does not anger anyone . . ." and Dorotheos rightly sees this anger as connected with pride of place, or status.[77] Dorotheos' natural history of anger[78] is unique, and he speaks of this way, though without mentioning tears *per se*, when he says:

> If, from the beginning, you take the blame when you are reproached without trying to justify yourself or make counter charges and so repaying evil for evil, you will be delivered from all these ills.[79]

Dorotheos knows that anger is something endemic to humankind. If something makes you angry, it is because the anger is already there within you.

However, he does not hold up an impossible standard without suggesting means, extraordinary as they may seem, to us who are used to justification and rationalization of all our failings:

> How then can this be put right? By prayer right from the heart for the one who had annoyed him, such as, 'O God, help my brother and me through his prayers.' In this he is interceding for his brother, which is a sure sign of sympathy and love, and he is humiliating himself by asking help through his brother's prayers. Where there is sympathy and love and humility, how can wrath and other passions develop?[80]

Note that Dorotheos' "humility" is not a false self-abasement, and is not self-destructive, but rather comes from a profound understanding of the roots of anger and the need to move from involution to evolution, from looking within to looking at God in one's brother or sister. Although he does not say this explicitly, it is implied. He sees the situation in the light of divine pity (and tears, we would add). The response he recommends not only restores a proper scale of priorities but also is appropriate for one who would fulfill his or her vocation in becoming the kenotic image of the kenotic God engaged with creation and human history.

Nor can we plead that Dorotheos' way is inappropriate to our more complex, stressed, and biologically evolved human personality. We have only to experiment to see the wisdom of what Dorotheos recommends to see how astonishingly we become willing, thus enabling God to empty and transform.

If at the first signs of anger and hurt we ask, "Why do I hurt?" and realize, almost invariably, that it is because we feel injury to our self-image in terms of loss of status, control of others' perceptions, and acknowledge the cause inwardly, then the process of change has begun. A silent cry of the heart brings help, and within a short time it becomes evident that profound changes are taking place as long as we wish God to make them, and may even be surprised when anger eventually is completely bypassed.

A woman was badly hurt when a close friend said something completely unnecessary about her past to an authority figure. The friend was a person who needed to show his fund of inside information, but the woman, although she understood this, was nonetheless upset. The remark brought to light one of the more traumatic incidents in the woman's life, which had by this time taken a wholly different course. She didn't stop to think what the hurt was saying about her and the amount of healing still to be done in her past.

She writhed for a while; and finally went to the friend and took him aside to tell him a thing or two. With the angry words on her tongue, and her mouth open to say them, she was suddenly seized with the tragedy of the whole situation: his weakness; her weakness at being so worried about her reputation; and instead of reaming him out, she shocked them both by bursting into tears.

When she had recovered she was able to explain why she was weeping, and in the end they both wept at the mercy of God.

If we persist, we can go directly to tears and skip the anger, and all anger's unfortunate consequences. This is not repression but a completion of the process of which anger is a part. Understanding the process can telescope it.

There are situations that so devastate us, however, that anger acts as psychic glue: rape, for instance, which can be psycho-spiritual, as well as and not necessarily connected to physical rape. But even in situations as serious as rape—concentration camp living, for example—the time for choice comes: to be eaten alive by hate (when the anger is no longer needed as glue) or to forgive. Viktor Frankl's work on concentration camp victims has been very illuminating in this area.

But while we have to allow for situations of extreme damage, most of the time our anger is due to unwillingness to face the hurt we feel and the real reasons behind it. To learn to weep in order to be free of anger and know "rest" does not obviate self-respect and is not related to putting oneself down.

On the contrary, if we are struggling to seek God single-heart-edly, to learn to weep the anger out of our selves is a matter of self-respect.

The idea of tears washing anger from us is alien to the mores of power-oriented Western society. We are conditioned to justify our anger, to find the right place to put blame, and to always feel good about our selves. Most of us associate anger and tears with tears that spring from anger, not tears that cleanse us from anger. But as we have seen, these tears of anger are themselves an admission of powerlessness and a sign of choice, of potential change.

But sadly, most of us—even those consciously embarked on the way of tears—usually find anger too satisfying. We try to patch things up as well as possible under the circumstances. We might try to rebuild the house, card by card; certainly we will be on the look-out for those who destroyed it, and wait for an opportunity to get our own back. Most of all we try to gather the threads of our—rightly or wrongly—ravelled reputations around us with all the dignity we can muster, and voice outrage at the untruth of the matter to all who will listen. And most assuredly we will lick our wounds hoping—or do we?—that they will heal.

We want sympathy and we want attention and we want the world to recompense us for the indignity we have suffered. We want, sometimes, to hang on to our hurt to squeeze as much mileage out of it as possible. Then one day, if we're lucky, we come to the realization that this can't go on: either we find some way to break the grinding pain of obsessive thinking about having been hurt (with, of course, no examination of how we might have been guilty in bringing about our own downfall), or else we will spend the rest of our lives being dominated by resentment which daily grooves deeper into our selves.

To change the image slightly, Frederick Buechner points out that anger is a most satisfying meal, one we savour and smack our lips over. But sooner or later we discover that we are feeding on our selves; we are the skeleton at the feast.[81]

Some of us try to fulfill a different self-image. We pretend to our selves that we have heroically and courageously and magnanimously dealt with the disaster, and as a result repress our true feelings. Or perhaps we cannot allow our selves to shatter this noble image we have of our selves. Or perhaps it simply is not safe to express to our selves or to others what we feel.

This is particularly true of people in tightly-knit, highly-structured community situations, such as family, and in those where other people's opinion is not only a matter of self-image but also survival in that particular group.

Government is an extreme example of people who need to define themselves by power over others, often to the point of obsession, and people in government do often seem "in thrall to some person with magic powers". They are indeed in thrall, but the magic is magic's primary component: control. Their house of cards has grown to such grandiose proportion that much of their energy is spent shoring up its far-flung parameters, not realizing that by its very expansion it has begun the process of disintegration.

Some of the rage we are coping with is at our selves: how could we have been outwitted? How could we have been so vulnerable, gullible, naive?

Some of us do not feel it is safe or appropriate to acknowledge our feelings so we turn them on our selves. Some of us misunderstand Christianity and the Judeo-Christian heritage and feel it is against moral precept to have feelings, that it violates an ideal of perfection (which is definitely not Judeo-Christian) that requires a kind of imperviousness to life around us.

Whether we take the path of self-examination, or the path of coverup, these feelings will out one way or another. If they are not acknowledged at least inwardly, they will find some other outlet, physical or psychological.

The Biochemical Background

These days we hear a lot about stress, and much stress is due not only to overloaded timetables (which are an expression of our need to see our selves as important, as powerful, super-people), but also to the constant thwarting of our grandiose fantasies and sense of omnipotence, the constant challenge of circumstance to our wishful thinking about our selves.

As part of the study of stress, medical researchers have begun to study tears. I would like to give a brief summary of this research because we are a single organism, and what affects or effects one aspect of our life will affect the whole. The research is very suggestive, but it is still very new and it would be premature to jump to conclusions.

Additionally, the kind of tears that are the major concern of this book not only have *not* been singled out as a particular kind of tears but also would be virtually impossible to study. At the same time they are real tears and thus subject to physiological laws. While they are related to other kinds of tears and probably often mixed with other kinds of tears they cannot be controlled in the same sense that someone can cry tears of anger or grief for a lab experiment. Even if someone were able to capture some of these kinds of tears, divine grace is not something that can be measured by electrophoresis.

There have been a lot of magazine articles on tears recently, and just before this manuscript was to be mailed to the publisher I received the first book to gather the biochemical research together: *Crying, The Mystery of Tears*, by William H Frey, II, PhD.[82]

The research can be summarized briefly: there is a tantalizing correlation between heart attack and stroke rates in men and women (women have fewer). Women weep more than men, and there is a cultural taboo against men weeping, although this seems to be changing. While body levels of certain hormones seem to affect ease of weeping, at the same time the composition of tears of men and women are the same and do not contain hormones. Additionally, conditioning can be reversed.

Tears are possibly the only way certain amounts of toxic proteins are excreted from the body. One article suggests that different kinds of tears have different chemical composition: the components of tears of grief will be different from tears of anger. Another points to the differences in concentration of salts in tears of men and women.

Most recently, in a particularly poignant and ironic development, the AIDS virus has shown up in tears.

Dr Frey is particularly interested in tears as a natural way of maintaining the body's chemical balance, which is upset by stress, whether the constant pressure of adaptation, or the possibility that we live in a more artificially stressful age. His research suggests that many people think they are more stressed than they may actually be.

But it also may be true that the loss of manual labor has increased stress. Manual work, especially manual work that contributes materially to one's survival, is a kind of tears, a way of grieving out mortality. It is possible that by the simple fact that we have lost manual work, we have also lost a stress neutralizing factor.

Jogging and other sports are not the same as heavy manual labor. It would be interesting to know if there is a biochemical relationship between sweat and tears.

Dr Frey distinguishes between two kinds of tears: irritant tears, such as those caused by onions, and "emotional" tears. Under this latter category he lumps all tears that are not irritant. One fact he has come up with supports putting holy tears in a separate category: his research showed that tears of joy lasted about two minutes at the most. The tears that are a gift can last for days, even weeks and months. We might speculate that the "tears of joy" Dr Frey describes are self-reflective; holy tears are other-oriented.

The relationship of certain kinds of stress and certain kinds of transformation is also tantalizing. For example, the process of becoming willing can be quite stressful. It is often described as the "warfare of the soul". However, when the point of quiet, or *hesychia* has been reached, tears change, and the gift of discernment is given. Willing powerlessness has healed anger, and clarity of vision intensifies.

This clarity, too, will bring tears, but they are different from tears of "rapture", which are always tinged with illusion. These tears come from the intensity of the light as we gaze on God, the light which continues to transform us, and to which we have consented. Anger faces always toward our selves.

In the book of Jonah, God asks Jonah if his anger is appropriate (4:9):

> that is: Does anger open up your understanding of what is happening? It is clearly a didactic kind of question raised by God in the expectation of a negative answer.[83]

To see with this kind of discernment is possible only from a neutral posture. Dr Frey points to high manganese concentrations in tears, a chemical which may be linked to aggressive behavior. For the one who has *hesychia*, aggression is not a question, nor is defense. Thus it might be that the discernment comes because of the adaptation to constant prayer, often constant-prayer-as-tears, the tears being related to the ongoing commitment to willing powerlessness. Novices are known to go through a period of "monsoons" related to their adaptation to monastic life. Possibly these tears are a sign of the struggle to let go defenses and become willing to receive from the community.

Here are some quotes from Frey's subjects about weeping and its aftermath:

> One subject described her post-crying feelings as "clearer, easier to see reality."
>
> [Another felt] "refreshed, cleansed, relaxed after a good cry."
>
> [Stopping tears:] Others stop their tears by becoming angry.
>
> [A folk saying:] Tears wash the cobwebs from your attic.
>
> [Polarity—see Chapter VI:] "I'm torn by crying. It's a weakness and yet it's a strength to be able to cry."
>
> Washington Irving goes so far as to say, "There is a sacredness in tears. They are not the mark of weakness but of power. They speak more eloquently than ten thousand tongues. They are the messengers of overwhelming grief, of deep contrition, and of unspeakable love."[84]

This is not the usual dry study one might expect from a biochemist.

Although he is skeptical about animals weeping, the histories he reports are all concerned with animals losing power, i.e., being in a captive situation or losing those (offspring or humans) to which they are attached.

There are areas where I disagree with some of Dr Frey's conclusions, but they are relatively minor. One example is the statement that women are not taught to suppress their tears. Nearly all the women I grew up with *were* taught that tears were not acceptable.

While the research background is important, we need to avoid the kind of stampede to the lab occasioned some years ago by the discovery that people who meditate produce alpha waves, and that we can be conditioned to produce them at will, as well as have control over the autonomic nervous system. People seeking instant enlightenment were disappointed. Changing brain waves did not produce personal transformation. It did not make them holy. It did not give them ecstatic experiences. Holiness cannot be taught in a lab, and in any event will never by its nature be subject to spiritual greed.

The same is true of any other gift of God. There are some people who can cry on cue, and perhaps we could learn to cry tears of a particular chemical composition on command, in order to release a particular kind of stress. But these tears would not be the ones with which we are concerned.

Isaac struggled with the taboo on tears in his time, and asks his readers not to laugh at what he is about to write on tears. He points to the distinction between tears artificially induced, and the gift of God:

> I am going to tell you something at which you must not laugh; for I am telling you the truth. Do not doubt my word, for those from whom I have received it, are trustworthy.
>
> Though you should suspend yourself by your eyelids before God, do not imagine that you have attained anything in your rule of life until you encounter tears; for until then your hidden self is still in the service of the world. That is to say, you are leading the same way of life as faithful lay people. For you toil with your outward self in the service of God, but the inner

self is still without fruits: his fruits begin at the point which I have indicated.[85]

The sort of tears which are part of *kenosis* cannot be grasped and turned into a technique any more than kenotic life by its nature can be grasped, organized, technologized, automated or controlled.

It is interesting that while statistically more women weep than men, most of the writing on tears has been done by men. Perhaps it is to encourage one another, or perhaps the cultural taboos have been so strong that when they re-learned tears they were able to describe them with a certain detachment. It is also true, however, that few words from women have survived from the days of early Christianity.

Tears and kenosis are the opposite and the antidote to the need to control.

So if anyone promises instant holiness, ecstasy, or nirvana, or winning, or even self-improvement by teaching you the gift of tears or the way of tears, pay no attention. We can only be willing, and the rest is up to God.

Want, Willingness, Will and Willfulness

The word willingness has a broad spectrum of meanings, and has often been misunderstood. Willingness is not the terrible ogre of "will-power", which has been pushed for centuries in the Church as a kind of pelagian raid on heaven. Willingness is not a technique. It cannot be acquired by technique, although there are techniques that can show us who we really are if we will let them.

But right here is a contradiction: if we let them. If we are willing. We are right back where we started. In the end, a technique is a technique. It is good to know a technique for calming yourself down if you get upset. It is a good idea to know a technique to make your self quiet. But what issues from that calm, and what issues from that quiet depends on the attitude of your heart.

The changing of the heart is a long, slow business.

It can also happen mysteriously, seemingly instantly.

There are a lot of counterfeit changes of heart around, but the sort that is permanent has been longed for, wept over, and coming for a long time. Just wanting, not even willing, is a lot of it.

There is a famous story told of a confessor of the old school who went to see an ancient mariner on his deathbed. The old sailor wanted to be reconciled to the Church before he died, and so he began to make his last confession. As he seemed to reach the end of what he wanted to say, the priest asked, "Is that all, my son?"

The old man thought for a moment. "Well . . ." he paused, "there is one thing. I really can't be sorry about those dancing girls in China." At this he coughed and his breathing changed.

Knowing time was short, the priest had to think fast. "Are you sure you can't be sorry?"

Unable to talk, the old man smiled and shook his head.

The priest became desperate. "Can you *want* to be sorry?"

Silence. Then an imperceptible negative movement.

Realizing the end was coming, the priest said softly, "Can you want to want?"

The ancient suddenly sat up in bed with glory shining in his face and said clearly, "Yes, I can want to want."

And died.

To want to want: if we are honest, sometimes this is all we can manage: to want to want to be rid of our rage. To want to want to be able to forgive. It sounds cheap and mean, but it is realistic. If we want to want it allows a chink in the wall. It is the first step of the way of tears, the way toward being receptive to the gift of tears.

To want to want.

And then, suddenly perhaps, we want.

And finally find we are willing.

Willing for what? Willing to give up control and illusions of control; willingness to give up the need for power over others; willingness, first and most of all, to be shown that hidden under other motives is our desire to control the universe and have it our way, have it fair, have it more than fair: have it loaded in our favor. Have it the way our tiny minds and minuscule perspective want it so we can feel secure and immortal; so we can shut out fear of what is bigger than we are; fear of change; fear of having vast spaces of health, of possibility, of salvation thrown open before us; fear of the responsibility of co-creating with God, of being poured-out-through.

Fear of seeing our selves as being as small as we really are—not running our selves down, but seeing that, for all the glory that we are as creations of God, as human beings, we are just one glory in a universe of glories. Just one density, just one expression of the love of God within us and more intimate than the energy that holds the atoms of our hearts together and keeps them beating.

It is this perspective that makes holy men and women say, "I am nothing!" It is not a cry of self-denigration; it is not a cry that says the creation is to be abhorred in favor of a future world to come; it is rather seeing that even the full glory of redeemed humanity in a universe struggling through transfiguration is infinitesimal when one's eyes have been opened to the glory of the transcendent, kenotic, and indwelling God; that, even more, such a vision is so captivating that to tear one's eyes away and return to navel-gazing, narcissism, self-reflection, and even dispassionate self-observation, is absurd.

More, and this is closely related to tears *per se,* a person who has been given wider vision in this way sees the full magnitude of human potential for evil as well as good, the powerlessness to defeat evil by one's own efforts, the despair of this discovery, and the willing powerlessness that enables divine kenotic power to enter in and enable us to come to salvation and possibility.

Such a person realizes that wanting to want, much less willingness, is not a one-time struggle but a task for all of earthly and eternal life. As we are gradually or suddenly broken open into everlarger worlds of perspective, wonder and astonishment leave us transfixed. We see that we have hardly begun; we see the possibility God holds out to us and the immense abyss that lies between that and what we are; we know that only the compassion of a kenotic God can bridge the abyss, this God who sustains us as we fall short or even turn away. We are always neophytes.

Our astonishment shows us that what we thought was willingness is, in the light of salvation, only the very beginning of wanting to want. And yet in this humble beginning, God's power is allowed to enter, and it is accomplished in the wanting.

For some of us, the awareness of union, of the divine Mercy reaching across the abyss even when we turn and deny it is something that comes upon us with shattering clarity, changing the direction of our lives in a dramatic moment of conversion.

For others, it is a growing awareness that emerges into consciousness and gently opens our eyes to make us want.

For each of us the conscious part of the process begins in a slightly different way. But we begin with the knowledge of our union in the love of this kenotic God seeking to enter and transform our prisons and our sufferings, and it is the knowledge of this union that makes us begin to want to want the vision of glory, the potential density of our being in that glory, even if all we experience is a blind groping toward we-know-not-what.

The eighth chapter of the Letter to the Romans is unsurpassed in its expression of this mystery:

> In the same way the Spirit comes to the aid of our weakness.
> We do not even know how we ought to pray . . .

How far is this phrase from the security systems we have set up for our selves, rigid formulae to "assure" us that, by God, we have prayed and God cannot—as if God would—deny us what we want, even if we may have to put our request into words opposite to what we mean, that is, our narrow idea of salvation against God's limitless one. It would be a greater hell than any of us could imagine if God responded to our words rather than our secret, frightened hope.

> But through our inarticulate groans the Spirit himself is pleading for us, and God who searches our inmost being knows what the Spirit means, because he pleads for God's people in God's own way . . .

. . . which way is kenotic: willing powerlessness, neither taking power to our selves to force our idea of God's own way *nor* being a doormat for "fate" or the steamrolling of others' self-interest.

And why?

Not to subject us, not to trap us into a closed system, not to manacle us into a "heavenly" slavery of fear that is set in opposition to the diabolical slavery of fear, but to woo us, to elicit our yearning by the divine kenotic yearning, to show us the beauty of freedom that willingly gives up self-seeking power and comes to maturity, is free from fear of either the process of *kenosis* or of mortality. In this silence of mutual listening and expansion from mingled divine and human *kenosis* the will of God is found.

The longing of God to bridge the abyss

. . . enables us to cry 'Abba! Father!' In that cry the Spirit of God joins with our spirit in testifying that we are God's children. But if we are children, we are heirs as well: heirs of God, heirs with Christ, if only we suffer with him. . . .

—not by imposing artificial, pointless, masochistic punishment on our selves, but by being willing to undergo the greater death of learning willing *kenosis*, abandoning our pretentious shams, "so that we can share his glory".*

This glory, this splendor is not in the apocalyptic future but is the "new world" that becomes available to us through this cry of the heart. This is mystery, not mystique. This is the very God, not seeking, like the false teacher, to keep us in subjection, to maintain the abyss between us and the promise of secret knowledge by asking us to give up our freedom, our minds and our souls.

This is the very God seeking like the true teacher to bridge the abyss, to enable us to take our place in the fullness of possibility as images, icons, windows of this divine *kenosis*.

But . . . I am leaping ahead. The language of the Letter to the Romans has become so familiar to us that it might be a good idea to hear another expression of coming to want, to willingness. Here is Luther:

> . . . a man feels himself to be lost in the very moment when he is on the point of being saved. When God is about to justify a man, he damns him. Whom he would make alive he must first kill. God's favor is so communicated in this form of wrath that it seems farthest when it is at hand. Man must first cry out that there is no health in him. He must be consumed with horror. This is the pain of purgatory. I do not know where it is located, but I do know that it can be experienced in this life. I know a man who has gone through such pains that had they lasted for one tenth of an hour he would have been reduced to ashes. In this disturbance salvation begins. When a man believes himself to be utterly lost, light breaks. Peace comes in the word of Christ through faith.[86]

The language of the 16th century can seem extreme to us. Underneath it there are several points to keep in mind for this discus-

---

*I have blended several translations here.

sion. One is Luther's affirmation that death is the same as becoming open to salvation, being ready to be powerless. Another is that God's wrath is God's love relentlessly pursuing us even when, especially when, we are at our worst, what Karl Barth calls "God's 'no' to man's 'no' ".

It is in the light of this love that we look on our selves in horror, and in the light of this love that we decide whether to further set our will against God's (note the danger of the popular idea we have of "will power" today), or be released from that slavery into the silence and emptiness where the vastness of possibility no longer seems terrifying because we know it is possibility borne on love.

André Louf has resources that were unavailable to Luther's community, locked as they were in a system of "salvation" from which there was no exit. It is interesting to speculate what Luther's path—and the history of Christianity—might have been if Luther's confessor had such insight. Here is part of Louf's very tightly presented article, "Humility and Obedience in Monastic Tradition". It should be read in full, but it is worth the risk to quote a portion. It was written for monks, but his wise insight into the paradox of weakness and strength applies to anyone, man or woman, monastic or not.

> Let us take a concrete case: A young man applies to us thinking himself called to our life. Such a vocation, when there is one—and I am not calling it in doubt—because of the culture patterns by which we live today, is naturally deeply interwoven with a certain human striving for perfection. This young man is captivated by a conscious monastic ideal. He sees in it all that is beautiful, noble, lofty. The contemplative life will be represented to him as that which the Gospel calls the "better part". All this appeals to his generosity and he is ready to answer whole-heartedly. He has made a decision; he will undertake huge sacrifices; he is determined to reach this ideal; he wants— and what novice doesn't—to be a good monk. He will be the ideal monk (this word is very ambiguous). He will be a perfect monk, perhaps even a holy monk. With all his enthusiasm and energy he sets himself to the task.
>
> I won't call in doubt his vocation at all, but his call is entwined with this *pagan* striving for perfection. To the young man, however, this is by no means evident. He isn't aware that

his calling doesn't correspond to the Gospel, *that his striving in fact goes quite contrary to evangelical holiness. . . .*

And there is something else he doesn't know: that he has an unconscious striving for perfection. It is rooted deep in his subconscious and will impose on him what the psychologists call the super-ego. He bears an ego-ideal within himself with which he must come to terms. As you know this is a condensation of all that the young man has experienced from authority figures. These then make demands on him and unconsciously he has to be at peace with them, and even to love them. What binds him to these authorities is the unconscious need for love, *for safety and for affection and security. And naturally all authority, power and certainty are involved in this unconscious need of his. . . .*

Without knowing it he is a slave of this unconscious predetermination. *In a very real way he is held by terror and is not free. . . .*

The answer lies in learning to live out of our deepest longings, our needs, our troubles. These must all surface and be given their rightful place. For in them we find our real human life in all its depths. And when one begins with these unacceptable feelings and desires, which have to be submitted to examination, we must learn to look closely at, and learn to live with, this amazing degree of weakness of ours. On the face of it this may seem dangerous, but gradually one realizes that it isn't really dangerous, that it's just here that our deepest strength lies hidden as the source of our growth and all our possibility of growth. This is already true at the purely human level, but it is also true in an even deeper way from the Gospel point of view: *when I am weak, then I am strong! For to live out of our weakness is to live by grace. Grace inserts itself only in our weakness. . . .*

Every form of true ascesis must somehow bring [a monk] to this zeropoint, the point where his strength fails, where he is confronted with his extreme weakness and at which he can do nothing further. His heart is crushed and broken to become in this way a *"cor contritum"*. Along with his heart go all his human plans for perfection. The power of God is now able to step forth and renew the whole man. Then ascesis becomes a miracle, a continuous miracle, in this battered and crushed heart where one's own weakness is joined to the power of the Lord. I'm convinced that the only ascesis possible for any follower of the Gospel consists in this *realization of our poverty and weakness to the point where we turn to grace as our only hope:* oth-erwise *ascesis is pagan.*[87]

Louf's article touches the heart of the way of tears. That he writes for monks and nuns is not the point. We have already seen that the "monastic" impulse, that is, the desire for a single-hearted seeking of God lives within each of us. What Louf has written ap-plies to every Christian life, every seeker of transfiguration in what-ever tradition without exception.

It should be clear now why the distinction between wanting to want and willingness on the one hand, and will and willfulness on the other, is so important.

Tears and Power

It might be useful to examine Louf's discussion in the light of control and the gift of tears. I hope he will forgive me if I explore his elegant discussion in somewhat cruder terms.

In the first place, each of us should read the predicament of the "novice" as our own predicament. It is one from which we will never fully escape. The novice wants to make great sacrifices and become an heroic monk not only because of the compelling inner forces that drive him or her, but also to satisfy the urge to control and to con-quer. These urges are all of a piece and a result of the forces within. The novice wishes to feel good; she or he is constantly comparing him or her self with others; there is a perhaps not-so-secret fantasy to have their adulation and astonishment, and perhaps even a place in the legends of great ascetics.

It is important that Louf has named all this effort "pagan" be-cause it is synonymous with what I have labeled the "house of cards" and what Isaac calls "the world". Pagan effort is a cover-up, how-ever sincere, for the monsters that haunt our depths, which we lie about to our selves and to others, which we struggle to encapsulate.

We want to "look good" for our selves, those around us, and God. Some of us sandbag our shaky structures so quickly and thor-oughly that despair never gets a toehold. We pile our defenses and self-righteousness faster and faster as our terror increases, and never reach the point where the flood of tears and love sweeps them away, and we come to understand that our monsters are the blessed means of hope, and our fault a *felix culpa.*

The longer we persist in our own efforts to insure that we have the security of what we know, as opposed to the insecurity of the "miracle" of the power of God entering at the points of our greatest vulnerability, the more radical the despair to which we will be brought. None of us is proof from this, nor is despair encountered but once.

Despair is a frightening word and much of the pelagian and stoic influences on Christianity linger in the many prohibitions against yielding to despair. Of all the sins to admit to, this seems the worst in the eyes of those who would keep up appearances. It is the despair that we are forbidden to despair that is the mistaken religion that drives people to the brink and often over the edge of suicide as their last act of integrity.

Not everyone would want to say that one must fall through despair into the hand of God (see Chapter VI). Surely despair for each of us represents something slightly different. But for many it is not a matter of walking up to despair and finding God: it is going through despair *with* God.

In the first part of this century, Staretz Silouan of Mt Athos received the Light of Tabor very early in his monastic life. He was terrified of becoming spiritually proud, and so God gave him another gift, a Word to help him keep things in perspective: "Keep your heart in hell and despair not."

While this Word was given Silouan in a particular context, like many such Words it has taken on wider meaning for those of us who live daily under the threat of extinction of our planet. To keep one's heart in hell is to live in despair with God, but not to despair means to know by faith and hope beyond faith and hope, and beyond any experience of consolation that as long as we resist returning to our tried and true methods that lead only to dead ends, God can fill our weakness with the power of possibility. There are political implications that proceed from this idea, which will be discussed in Chapter IX.

And the gift of tears?

The gift of tears often comes at the moment of despair and entering in of grace; the moment when we look at who we are and say, "Yes, it is all true. I can do nothing of my self or for my self, and it is only the immense and ineffable love of God that I see now sustains me even in my sin, and heals me even as I am wounded."

The gift of tears is often given as a sign that we want to want, that we are ready to want to want, and in that wanting are already moving light years from the point of our first awareness of our selves as we really are. The gift of tears is often a sign of the presence of God when we feel most abandoned, forgotten, and alone.

Over the ages there has been a lot of misunderstanding about self-knowledge and the role of self-knowledge. People who are terrified of looking within themselves often scoff at those who do. Sometimes they are right: the seekers have turned aside and become absorbed in themselves, and lost sight of the One they seek.

However, a certain self-conscious awkwardness and narcissism is inevitable with any new task of learning we undertake, whether it is as ordinary as a sport, or as complex as acquiring that "knowledge of oneself as called in to creative, redemptive collaboration with God".[88]

In time, if we are not seduced away from the path—which happens frequently due to poor teaching and direction (see Chapter VIII)—we grow out of narcissism. Indeed, the less self-knowledge one has, the more narcissistic one tends to be; the more true self-knowledge one has, the more self-emptying one tends to be.

It is vital not to confuse self-knowledge with "self-improvement", or with "health". True self-knowledge is always a gift and eventuates in self-forgetfulness. It is a gift we must always desire greatly. It is true that such a desire can lead us to look for a magic formula, and without the willingness truly to see our selves, we will fall only into more illusion.

Anthony Bloom has noted that each generation tries to water down, make easy, the hard facts of the journey into God. We think that by "understanding" a gift we can bend it to our own sloth.

In a personal letter, Dom Armand Veilleux, Pachomean scholar and abbot of Holy Spirit Abbey, Conyers, Georgia, put this more directly:

> I sincerely believe that much of the superficial use of Eastern spiritual techniques, and much of our use of methods of meditation and prayer, are part of that silly, irrespectful, irresponsible tampering with spiritual forces. It is a new version of the Promethean myth. Instead of becoming one with the spiritual world, in all harmony we try to use it, manipulate it.

It cannot be emphasized enough that the gift of tears is a *gift*. Like any other gift, it can be accepted or rejected. While it cannot be forced or manipulated it can, like unceasing prayer of which it is a part, be nurtured. It is an "ambient" grace. It is not the special possession of a spiritual elite but always available, waiting to find us receptive. It is an ineffable gift, and one of its distinguishing marks is that it always points us away from our selves even as it illuminates our selves.

Tears and contemplation (the two are synonymous) are gifts, and both gifts of a deep encounter with Fire that tears ignite and salt through our whole being.

The gift of tears frees and is a sign of being freed both from control and from the fear from which control springs, and the *desire* for the safety our fears offer us and the *desire* to try to control in order to feel secure. It is to the love of God and an initially terrifying freedom that this gift opens us, the freedom to become part of the all-holy I AM, to be poured-out-through.

At this point we can perhaps see the relationship between the tears of grief-work that is primarily associated with mortality, and the way and gift of tears. As we have noted, the former have a beginning, middle, and end, and the latter are a commitment and a sign of that commitment.

Both are concerned with separation. Karen Horney has given us the term "separation anxiety", and her essay is a useful one. Grief work done in the process of mortality is certainly separation anxiety—separation from a whole complex of securities and givens. But it is perhaps something more as well.

A friend of mine has a particularly difficult time with tears of any sort. She is one of those people who, as a child, was beaten when she wept. Over the years she has gradually begun to lose her fear of weeping, which has also freed her to be ministered to as well as finding her vocation in ministering to others. For a long time she had felt that her only worth as a human being was determined by how much she ministered to others no matter how inappropriate for her own condition.

When her husband died, she said, "We think of tears as a sometimes thing. It hurts to cry. It hurts worse if you don't. It hurts more in the short term if you do weep, but even more in the long term if you don't. What hurts too is not only admitting that E___ is gone and all of what that implies, and the loss of control over his death, which of course I never had, but also the loss of control over his life, and the control he had over me, and worst of all, that either of us ever had that control in the first place."

This is the intersection of grief work and grieving. The loss she speaks of is more than her husband: it is all of the illusory self built up as a house of cards in the relationship: the self that was in control; the combined self "separate" or individuated as a couple; the selves in "possession" of each other in an image projected on the people and the world around them.

What I have termed grief work is related to dealing with emotions and loss related to a particular event, but there is no question that in these tears there are often mixed those that are holy, and it would be folly to try to separate them out or differentiate them.

For in holy tears is the grief of the whole human tragedy, and at the bottom of these tears are the silence and space to receive a new life from God in ordinary time, if one is the survivor, and in and out of time if it is one's own death one is mourning.

It is reported that the Fathers argued over whether it was appropriate to grieve over a friend's death. This argument recurred in the Middle Ages. But in reading these texts we have to understand that often they are embroidered so that their rigor makes their sanctity seem extraordinary, and additionally we need to remember that the combatants were involved in wars of ideas which could often lead to physical death if one were on the wrong side. We have to remember that much of the desert tradition was contaminated by a sort of stoicism that was anti-Christian, and manicheanism, interpreting "the world" to mean creation, instead of power politics. And it was this skewed attitude that was handed down which is only now being corrected.

In the next chapter we will look at different kinds of tears, but for the moment it is worth mentioning that all tears, even sinful tears used as a weapon, have this element of transformation potential in them: for once tears begin to flow there is the possibility of their being turned in midstream to tears of compunction.

In tears the invitation is always there to accept the grace of unflinching self-examination, radical honesty no matter what the cost, not in terms of self alone but self as interrelated to and interdependent upon other human selves and the biosphere as well. We cannot be half-hearted in asking for God's gifts any more than we can, at the opposite end of the spectrum, attempt to manipulate our selves or God into giving us a gift to satisfy spiritual greed.

We cannot ask without being ready to have God create in us the new person, which is the context in which the gift can be given.

Post-scholastic spiritualities emphasized guilt on a casuistic, personal basis that denied this interdependence to the point that a nun might write, as did de Sales' sister to him, that she had difficulty in finding something to confess every week.

In the reality shown us by the gift of tears, such a statement is inconceivable. This does not mean that we become overly scrupulous, or obsessive, or compulsive, or preoccupied with sin and gloom and horror. But it does emphasize that Christ died for *all*, and that we bear with each, as part of each, individually and corporately, sin as well as resurrection. This is one of the hard consequences of accepting the role of *alter Christus* to which each Christian is called.

No life is lived in isolation; no sin is exclusively either mine or someone else's. The more a life becomes transparent, holy, "sinless", the more it gathers to itself the sins of others, acknowledges, confesses, weeps, redeems, and precisely because it knows joy.

More than this, there comes a time when any kind of sorting-out process seems irrelevant. It is not that there is no distinction between good and evil, but that the tragedies of life, both natural and made by humans, are too tangled, too deep, too impenetrable to lay blame one place or another. Many tragedies are beyond any classification, and over these such a person weeps not *de haut en bas* but as an intimate, as a participant. From this it can be seen why such a person must be able to distinguish this kind of guilt from neurotic guilt.

Lacrimae rerum: the tears *in* things; the creation that bursts with the potency of transfiguration bleeds also with the tears of its redemptive Creator. Deep calls to deep; not some sentimental "might have been" but a divine call to a reality whose density of holiness can be seen only through the veil of tears.

Moses had to put a veil over his face to protect the people from the glory of God that shone from him. They needed protection because they were not sure they wanted God's gifts; their desire was conditional; their hearts were hard and complaining. Perhaps if they had been converted, if their desire and willingness had been one, their own tears would have been veil enough and they would not have demanded that Moses wear one.

In the Hebrew scriptures we are repeatedly told that no one can see God and live; yet there were exceptions. In the New Testament there are further references to seeing God, but with a difference. Although St Paul speaks of seeing through a glass darkly, he already seems to have a glimmering that all has changed, that because of Christ's passion and our baptism and resurrection, we *already* see God face to Face in some mysterious way. Jesus becomes the veil and is utterly transparent, and we come to know a little that it is God who sees us Face to face, Heart to heart, becoming one in the exchange of love and tears.

Père Jacques Bernard, to whom I am indebted for much of the rabbinical tradition that appears in this book, was one day looking at an icon of the Mother of God of the Burning Bush. He spoke of the mystery of the Incarnation, that somehow Christ, through whom all is made, was incarnate also in that fire.

Tears unite in us what is most human and most divine.

Interlude

Tidepools and Transfiguration

One year at the Feast of the Transfiguration I found myself on the beach at a very low tide. Its ebb had left huge rocks exposed, whose spray-washed surfaces glittered with even greater intensity than the blaring sun.

Between the rocks were havens of water, tidepools, which harbor unique creatures.

Life in the intertidal zone is marked by fragility on the one hand, and an amazing adaptation to extreme environmental conditions on the other. Here delicate coraline algae grow, algae that imitate the fronds of fan polyps. Here anemones ranging in color from shocking pink to lime green wave their flower-like tentacles, and close up to become ugly lumps as the water withdraws. White barnacles and purple urchins cling to the rocks with their companions, the many-rayed, bejewelled starfish whose colors glow topaz, amethyst, ruby.

Crabs and small fish lurk in and among these denizens.

Each creature seems to have its own way of adapting to the quickly-rising temperature of the pools as the sun heats them before their water is renewed by the incoming tide; each to temporary dryness when water withdraws completely.

These animals and plants live at risk: if they implant themselves too high along the littoral they will die of exposure. Most are slow movers, and should they miscalculate during an extreme tide, they would perish at its ebb before they could reach the nearest water.

They must choose carefully where they fix their feet, and when they open and expose their inmost selves. They need to discern between incoming tide and the occasional large "sleeper" wave.

So also does the observer.

Along the Pacific coast currents are swift and treacherous, and sleeper waves can wash over the unwary, rapidly carrying them to an unexpected and ineluctable death.

There is an analogy here to life in the love of God. Our consciousness is a little like the intertidal zone, and we must beware where we fix our lives and choices.

Too often we think of the Transfiguration as a feast of light only, one that dazzles like the sun reflected off the mothering sea. Too often we seek to fix our feet in light alone, unrealistically or pridefully thinking that our transformation has reached a point where we will not be burned by uncreated light.

To understand more fully our life in this littoral of sin and redemption, we have to see the Transfiguration in its context, especially in the Gospel of Matthew: it extends far beyond the mountain top.

The story of the Transfiguration is surrounded by darkness: it is no mere ecstatic vision. It is surrounded by losing one's life to gain it, by denial of prophets, by being tossed between fire and water by the fits of our sins writhing under the light of God, and in the end by the glory of crucifixion.

Mere ecstatic vision is vain and ephemeral, and if like Peter we wish to fix our feet in that light, we will perish.

We need to understand that our life, like the Transfiguration, is a consummation of polarities. We need to understand that our besetting sins, as Dame Julian glimpsed, are necessary to our transfiguration.

Sometimes, after severe psychological, spiritual or physical trauma, we are left with residual emotional reactions that seem anything but holy. Anger, for instance: it can grind in our souls like sand against the soft parts of a mollusk, and wash over us unexpectedly like a sleeper wave. If our feet are not firmly fixed, or sometimes even if they are, we can be swept before we know it into a sea of rage.

I used to think there was never any excuse for anger because, being pride's cowl, it is never justified. I used to think this, that is, until I underwent an experience so painful that my anger was the only vehicle through which my sanity was kept intact. I lived with this anger, struggled with it, fought it, nearly drowned from my thrashing, and finally simply allowed it to run its course.

It was, perhaps, the most painful year of my life as I waited, exposed to the light of God, for the gift of tears to extinguish this terrible wrath that was yet somehow necessary for life.

Finally I began to understand more clearly what was happening to me. I began to face more honestly how vulnerable I was to the particular kind of betrayal and rape I had experienced in the name of God's obedience.

I began to see that, like the occasional bizarre reversal of ocean currents, the life-saving anger at least this once had served a healthful function in me, had kept me afloat. And I also saw that the time had come to let it go, that it must have no root in me.

Like the creatures in the intertidal zone who wait in simple trust for the laving of incoming waves, I finally came to stillness.

I began to understand that under such extreme circumstances to use spiritual techniques to bring oneself to some kind of artificial peace or repression is a travesty.

I began to see that the tides of darkness and light are indeed both alike and, as the tears for which I had prayed for a year finally broke over my lacerated self, I saw also that in that year I had been crucified between rage on the one hand, and the longing to have the obedience of the love of God fulfilled in me on the other, and that this even deeper wounding, deeper than what I had originally suffered, was necessary to heal the hurt that had gone before.

Tears, like the incoming tide, brought unfolding, new openness, awareness of a deeper peace that had never left me. Once again my life took on its ordinary patterns.

On to this littoral of conscious and unconscious, seen and unseen, earth's wedding to heaven, the deepest rhythms of God's sustaining love once more made their upwelling, dispersing the hot currents of El Niño, that dark child whose disruptive reversal somehow, too, has its role in the journey toward adaptation to endless and uncreated light.

The healing process is never complete, nor is the pearl of great price completely formed in our wounds until we are brought into greater life. We go on, day by day, hour by hour, seeing our failures as they come, bidden and unbidden, with more acceptance of our forgiveness, yes, and by grace, with more tears. "My soul and body crieth out/yea, for the living God!"

Our tears, bearing the salt of God's love, ignite God's fire on the earth, opening the floodgates of joy which no one can take from us.

V

He heard my voice from his heavenly dwelling, my cry of anguish came to his ears. (Psalm 18:7 BCP)

Weeping may spend the night, but joy comes in the morning. (Psalm 30:6 BCP)

My tears have been my food day and night, while all day long they say to me, 'Where now is your God?' (Psalm 42:3 BCP)

Fear not to enter his courts in the slenderness
Of the poor wealth thou wouldst reckon as thine!
Truth in its beauty, and love in its tenderness,
These are the offerings to lay on his shrine.[89]

By the beginning of 1985 I could no longer cope. I was overwhelmed by the constant stress and the effort I was making to suppress something. I went out with a friend for a couple of drinks. It was enough to crack my whole defense system. I sobbed and heaved forth agonizing cries for hours. This was a turning point, and a dark night of despair.

During the next few weeks I made a more or less conscious effort to let my real feelings surface. I tried not to resist, channel, or change them. . . . I finally recognized in the watching, in the unresolved grief and mourning, my anger against society and those institutions who were uncaring or damning. I recognized my resentment against the church which was offering little in the way of pastoral care and seemed more concerned with airing an antiquated moral theology which was contributing to the atmosphere of homophobia. I saw this was preventing society from responding to AIDS. All of these feelings and angers surfaced like old dinosaur bones from the tar pits. I recognized that mine were the same angers and fears as the AIDS patients I had met.

But most of all, as I listened, and waited, I discovered my own fear of death and dying, my own fear of AIDS, my own fear of being labeled and tarred with the same brush, my own homophobia. I had been suppressing fear for over three years.

Suddenly, when I was able to speak the monster's name, it began to melt away. The process is still unfinished, but I am aware of my feelings and fears at a more conscious level . . .

After I celebrated the sacrament of reconciliation, the sacrament of the sick, and the Eucharist with Louis, he began to weep. He said to me, 'I am so happy—no, it is more than that, it is like pure joy.' I cried for joy with him.[90]

If you had eyes to see it and ears to hear it, Pastor Pete Rose presided over the biggest theological lesson of the century during his successful run at Ty Cobb's 57-year-old record. . . . his dirt-stained uniform hardly the icon of a religious man. And he openly professed that baseball was everything, the only thing, his ultimate concern. But in the end, this earthly brawler was a heavenly convert and a powerful preacher by deed. Standing at first base after breaking the record, he recalled looking to the sky and seeing a vision of his father, who died in 1970, and Cobb "looking down at me." He wept openly, and his tears did more to explain the precarious balance between faith and works than did the recently publicized agreements of Anglican and Catholic theological heavy-hitters. This blue-collar hustler, this self-made player, this bragging factbook of every hit made and every record set—this quintessential example of tireless merit—stood in powerless abandonment before a capacity crowd and graciously accepted their freely offered favor with tears of gratuitous joy.[91]

And when Sam heard that he laughed aloud for sheer delight, and he stood up and cried: 'O great glory and splendour! And all my wishes have come true!' And then he wept.

And all the host laughed and wept, and in the midst of their merriment and tears the clear voice of the minstrel rose like silver and gold, and all men were hushed. And he sang to them, now in the Elven-tongue, now in the speech of the West, until their hearts, wounded with sweet words, overflowed, and their joy was like swords, and they passed in thought out to regions where pain and delight flow together, and tears are the very wine of blessedness.[92]

The Mirror in the Pool

Our tears are precious to God.

> You have noted my lamentation; put my tears into your bottle; are they not recorded in your book? (Psalm 56:8 BCP)

The reference to the bottle for tears refers to an ancient practice of collecting one's tears and preserving them. Just as certain organs in the body were thought to be related to specific emotions, so tears were regarded as the organ of grief, laughter, and joy. Tear bottles were made of glass. They came in many shapes, but the most common was one with a bulbous bottom and long neck with a flared top to facilitate collecting the tears.

The chapel on the Mount of Olives known as *Dominus Flevit** is dedicated to Jesus weeping over Jerusalem, and the altar looks out over a spectacular view of the Old City. Its architecture reflects the use of these bottles.

It is possible that the woman who bathed Jesus' feet with her tears (Luke 7:38) was pouring out her bottle of tears. The Greek verb could be translated in this way. Having found her Lord, she no longer needed to hold to herself all her joys and sorrows, but could pour them out and be free. Her tears became undammed to flow with the waters of life into the river of life. Her heart had been broken open so that she had become a vessel for the oil of anointing, part of the fire that Jesus came to bring to earth.

Similarly the precious ointment of Mark 14:3 and John 12:3 is

---

*I am indebted to Jim Fleming for having taken me to this and other sites in Palestine.

a sign both of this fire and of the death, the *kenosis*, through which he must pass in order that the conflagration of the Spirit may begin.

We need to learn to recover our tears, whether for the sake of our bodies only, or the welfare of our entire being. Dr Frey speaks of his own experience of becoming willing to have his childhood conditioning taken away, and tears given again:

> So I consciously made an effort to get back in touch with my feelings, to allow myself to get upset when events warranted it, to give myself permission to feel sadness and pain, and to *cry*. It took a long time to accomplish that, but the result was worth the effort. I do cry occasionally with flowing tears when I'm very upset, and my eyes fill with tears on many occasions when I am touched by something.[93]

Note that although he has put this in the language of achievement, he did not force tears, or practice a technique to produce them. He simply gave himself permission to lose control not only of the barrier to his own weeping, but also of the self-image he wanted to project to others. Responding to reality was more important than the values of "the world" in terms of ambition, status, or "what people think" on seeing him weep. Further, he realized that "feeling good" was misleading: that he would not in reality feel fully human until he embraced humanity's pain.

He does not tell us if he first wept privately or publicly, and his surveys show that people recover their tears in both ways. He reports several techniques to help people whose tears are blocked, from onions to films, to concentrating on sad thoughts. The point here is not that the tears are being forced, or that a technique is being used to produce tears artificially for show, but that *the tears are already in the heart* and seek expression. Frey and his subjects recognize that one form of tears may turn into another: one woman said, "Peel and mince onions to start the tears and don't stop until you feel better."[94]

This is not out of line with what the ancients said about praying for tears:

> Who does good works and has been deemed worthy to have received some gifts from God, but has not yet received tears, he must pray for this in order to weep, either thinking about the

last judgment or longing for the heavenly kingdom or repenting over evil past deeds, or kneeling before the Cross of Christ, seeing Him suffering for us, our Crucified Savior.[95]

Jacob of Serugh considers those without tears to be in a desperate state. He recommends:

> You have no tears? Buy tears from the poor. You have no sadness? Call the poor to moan with you.[96]

He is commenting implicitly on who is poor and who is not, since those who are most in need of tears are usually those who have spent the most energy acquiring wealth to prove to themselves that they are above the pain of being human.

The ancient monks are all for weeping in solitude:

> If we arrive at stillness, we shall be able to be constant in weeping. For this reason we should beseech our Lord with an unrelenting mind to give us this. If we receive this gift—a gift which surpasses all others—then through weeping we shall enter into purity; and when we have entered there, it will not be taken away from us again, right up to the day of our departure from the world. Blessed, therefore, are the pure in heart who at all times enjoy this delight of tears and through it see our Lord continually.[97]

For us, this does not necessarily refer to an exterior solitude, and for all of their rigor, these desert dwellers knew the place for compassion. There is a touching story of one of the Old Men with a novice who fell asleep with his head in his lap. One wonders if the abba were helping him to weep.

In our day tears, especially tears related to loss, are often a signal that we need support from others. While all kinds of tears often come in solitude, we should not be ashamed to weep in public either as a signal of our own need, or as a witness to the loving presence of God. At St Macarius monastery in Egypt the monks can be seen today standing in prayer with tears pouring unashamedly down their faces. We need to be free from constraint to weep holy tears; and we need to learn discernment of tears so as to know when these are solitary tears wept in public, and when they are signals for help.

Ephrem speaks of the experience of group repentance in his commentary on the book of Jonah:

> 'The touching tears of these children caused all around them to weep. The little ones' voices penetrated hearts and moved them. Old men covered themselves with ashes, while old women tore out their hair and cast it away. Venerable whitened heads wrapped themselves in pain and shame. Young people, on seeing their elders, redoubled their groans. Old men provoked the young, those staffs of their old age, to tears.'
>
> [Hausherr continues] And so on, for many long folio pages. Yet the longer and harder the mourning, the more exuberant will the sinners' joy appear later when Jonah will announce to them, although somewhat reluctantly, God's pardon. The Syrian poet enjoys describing the struggle between the goodness of the Holy Spirit and the harshness of his prophet. A man with no heart, or simply with a bad temper, can resist tears, but never a father; his severity comes from his love. . . . No-one is so much a father as God. . . .[98]

Whether one begins to recover his or her tears alone or with another, tears have the character of solitude. The way of tears is not solipsistic. But in order to have and maintain kenotic community, one must have first kenotic solitude that is not dependent on exterior circumstances. Each heart must be pierced; each must weep his or her own baptism.

Criteria of Discernment

As we have seen there are many kinds of tears. Additionally, some tears may be transformed into another sort, and different kinds of tears may be mixed together. Most of the time it is not necessary to sort out what kind of tears are being experienced: we cannot know for sure, and we run the danger of becoming fascinated with our selves and processes.

At the same time we do need to assess, from time to time, what direction our lives are taking, and tears sometimes can provide us with insight. Are we weeping from irritation or illness? Are we weeping because we are feeling sorry for our selves? Or are we weeping for other-directed reasons, for the incomprehensible pain in the world? Are we weeping for ineffable joy?

Dr Frey's book was the first place I found corroboration that tears of laughter and tears of sorrow are virtually indistinguishable. Both spring from incongruity, or as we shall explore in more depth in Chapter VI, from holding polarities in the heart. This was comforting because I had already written what follows on establishing criteria for "holy" tears, criteria established not from tears of compunction but from tears of laughter. The desert dwellers might be astonished—but then again, they were so shrewd that even though one or the other now and again rails against laughter, this method might not be a surprise to them at all.

I think tears of laughter must be considered holy tears for a number of reasons, and in looking at these reasons we will perhaps see suggestions for these criteria. Although tears of laughter seem to occur more frequently in groups, the criteria are not less valid for tears that come in solitude.

1. *Tears of laughter cannot be forced.* They simply appear. You are laughing and suddenly you are aware that the tears are flowing down your cheeks. Additionally, you cannot artificially create a situation in which the elements will guarantee that people will laugh until they weep. There is the same element here as in good theatre: a moment when there is an infusion of grace that lifts the combination of factors beyond the sum of their parts.

2. *Tears of laughter are not violent.* While they may stem from a belly-laugh, they are not accompanied by violent physical activity, such as contortion of the body, running about, throwing things, or banging one's head against the wall, all expressions of frustrated power. Isaac talks of the passing of the "violence" of weeping, but he is speaking of weeping relative to the silent weeping of *hesychia*. It would not be surprising if a person who is learning again to weep, or who is recovering from serious psycho-spiritual damage, wept with deep sobbing.

3. *Tears are the antidote to power.* Even the language surrounding the tears of laughter demonstrates this: "I was helpless with laughter". Helpless. Powerless. A person laughing in this way has let a vision of reality penetrate so deeply that he or she has been freed by this new vision into a willing powerlessness. What this vision is, in fact, may not be immediately evident on a conscious level. Often in

retrospect one will become aware of the new perception, even if it is not directly related to the situation that ostensibly caused the laughter in the first place.

4. *Tears of laughter are transforming and a sign of transformation.* Of all tears, the tears of laughter result in an awareness of change in a particularly powerful way. One may not know exactly what has changed (this is not important) but the change can be obviously physically, psychologically, and spiritually sensed and felt. Tears of laughter are powerful evidence of the interrelatedness of all our parts, of the necessity to consider the journey into God as an holistic one, and one which seeks to unify and heal fragmentation.[99]

5. *Tears of laughter are other-oriented.* Even if the source of laughter is one's self, the laughter is a result of a kind of detached perspective, and of one's relatedness to the world and other creatures. Tears of laughter almost invariably occur in a communal situation. They are "contagious", and while this contagion is extremely complex, one element is a communication of the depths of insight. Further, these tears take one "out of one's self". Whatever may have been the initial cause of laughter is often forgotten in the common sharing of the Spirit of divine play. (See Chapter IX)

Additionally, these tears leave one with a sense of sharp clarity, new knowledge of the other people who have shared the experience, and a more compassionate and benevolent outlook on the world. There may be mixed in thanksgiving, praise, and adoration.

6. *Tears of laughter lead to longing.* There is always a vague or not-so-vague sense of "something missing" when the laughter has died down, the tears have been wiped, and everyone has dispersed in the mysterious silence that follows on these tears. As one walks back into the daily round there is a longing for—for what? Often one cannot say . . . but there is a sense of having had, like Celia in Eliot's *Cocktail Party*, "a vision of something" which is wholly gratuitous and ungraspable, but which causes the heart to yearn and may even lead to further holy tears.

These tears are related to the holy tears most often spoken of by the ancients as "longing for heaven". This longing, so often misinterpreted as "life-denying" or hatred of creation, is in fact quite the opposite. This longing has grown out of one of the most profound of human, earthy experiences, and is an ineffable glimpse, conscious or not, of what the created order might be when fully reflecting the image of the Creator.

> The burning of the heart on behalf of the entire creation, human beings, birds, animals—even all that exists; so that by the recollection and at the sight of them the eyes well up with tears as a result of the vehemence of the compassion which constrains the heart in abundant pity. Then the heart becomes weak [lit. small] and it is not able to bear to hear or to observe the injury or any insignificant suffering of anything in creation. For this reason, even on behalf of the irrational beings and enemies of truth, yes even on behalf of those who do harm to it, he offers prayer with tears at all times that they may be protected and spared; he even extends this to the various reptiles, on account of his great compassion infused without measure in his heart, after the likeness of God.[100]

> The humble person approaches beasts of prey, and as soon as their gaze alights upon him, their wildness is tamed and they approach him and attach themselves to him as their master, wagging their tails and licking his hands and feet. For they smell from him the scent which wafted from Adam before his transgression, when the beasts gathered to him and he gave the names in Paradise—the scent which was taken from us and given back to us anew by Christ through His advent, for it is He who has made the smell of the human race sweet.[101]

This passage immediately reminds us of another great saint who wept, St Francis, who is surely better understood in the context of Eastern Christianity than Western. The affinity of animals for those who have made room in their hearts is one of the most frequent stories told of holy women and men.

7. *Tears of laughter are guileless tears.* There is no ulterior motive behind them. They are not wept for any purpose, or to achieve any goal. Holy tears are probably the closest we ever come to complete purity of motive, emotion, and feeling. They are the gift of the Ghostly Reconciler.

A Word of Caution

There are some further marks of discernment it might be useful to note.

Many people have extreme difficulty weeping, and the sayings about them are particularly poignant.

> Regarding our tears, as in everything else about us, the good and the just Judge will certainly make allowances for our natural attributes. I have seen small teardrops shed like drops of blood, and I have seen floods of tears poured out with no trouble at all. So I judge toilers by their struggles, rather than their tears, and I suspect that God does so, too.[102]

Frey speaks of overcoming childhood conditioning, and giving oneself permission to weep. But there is perhaps more to it than that for some of us (and I am one of them) who find weeping difficult or impossible, as much as we might want to weep.

For some, the inability to weep is evidence of a power struggle. Often people who have this difficulty will experience a great desire to weep during the days just before making a sacramental confession, but the tears will not come. Sometimes in the confession itself the tears will come. This can be a sign of a skilled confessor, in that he or she will, by being the mirror of the God who both confronts us and weeps with us, enable the surrender necessary for the tears finally to flow. It doesn't matter whether the power yielded is the person's rebellion, or some force from "outside", which is part of the larger struggle in which every Christian is engaged.

This raises the question, too, about the relationship between tears and interior struggles, not only with frank rebellion, sin, and the constant warfare between good and evil, but also how much of the struggle is related to unresolved and much-needed grief work over our past life, parts of which perhaps we cannot bring to consciousness, but that block our tears. Perhaps each time a tear comes some further blockage is broken through, some further fragment is bonded, some small part of a wound healed.

One way some of us weep who cannot otherwise is in our sleep.

There was a woman who, on leaving her religious community, was unable to weep. In fact, she was so numb that she didn't realize it was an option. Her eyes began to swell shut, and when antihistamines did not help, it became evident that this was a reaction to unshed tears. A doctor friend suggested that for the next few months she sleep as much as possible. Perhaps he was thinking of Aeschylus:

> He who learns must suffer. And even in our sleep pain that cannot forget falls drop by drop upon the heart, and in our own despair, against our will, comes wisdom to us by the awful grace of God.[103]

Isaac also has something to say on this matter:

> If you do not have the strength to take hold of yourself and to fall on your face in prayer, wrap your head in your cloak and sleep until the hour of darkness passes from you. Do not, however, leave your cell. This form of trial especially befalls those who wish to conduct themselves in mental discipline, and who throughout their journey yearn for the consolation which comes from faith. For this reason this dark hour, when the mind is in doubt, upsets them more than does anything else. . . . All these things we have frequently experienced, and we have put this into writing for the comfort of many.[104]

Not all the fathers agree with Isaac's message, but for some of us his advice may be comforting. There are, in fact, many people who weep primarily in their sleep.

But Isaac experiences the beatific end of tears in sleep as well:

> Now, I know someone who in his very sleep was seized by wonder at God through the contemplation of something he had read in the evening. While his soul was amazed at this contemplative meditation, he perceived, as it were, that he had meditated a long time on the thoughts of his sleep and was examining that vision in wonder. It was in the depth of the night, and suddenly he awoke from his sleep as his tears ran down like water on to his chest; his mouth was full of glorification and his heart was meditating in contemplation for a long time, with a delight which knew no satiety. And through the many tears which were shed without measure by his eyes, and through the stupefaction of his soul by which all the members of his body became relaxed, and of his heart in which a certain delight was stirring, he was not even able to accomplish his usual night office, apart from a

psalm—with difficulty—at break of dawn, so overwhelmed was
he by the multitude of tears which burst forth involuntarily from
the fountain of his eyes, and by other things.[105]

On the other end of the spectrum there are those who weep
copiously and easily. I have met people who weep like this who are
quite obviously other-oriented, weeping from compassion. It seems
to be their vocation to weep for the world, and to shed the tears some
of us find so difficult. At the same time I have met people who
seemed to be dramatizing themselves and were deceived by their
tears; others who were simply very emotional people.

As with the discernment of any other gift of God the biggest
danger is ending up wanting gifts to have gifts for the sake of gifts,
and not for the sake of the Kingdom. There is no question that interior weeping occurs without actual tears—although material tears
are always a blessing when they accompany this interior weeping.
There is also no question that one who prays or is prayed without
ceasing weeps continually, whether these tears are inward or actually emerge from the eyes.

Whether the joy of the knowledge of God or of faith, tears evidence the continual breaking into time of eternity, of transfiguration, and the vision of God, even when nothing, and more than
nothing, seems to be one's lot.

This may seem paradoxical at first, but we have only to look at
Thérèse of Lisieux's dying words of love uttered from what she
called le néant, the abyss of annihilation, nothingness, emptiness,
and even futility. (See Chapter VIII)

The Universality of Tears

It is important to underline the universality of the experience
of holy tears. They are neither confined to Christianity, nor to those
who consciously profess religion.

> I had been allowed to sit on my daughter's bed and hold my
> granddaughter in my arms. No mask, no gown, no rubber
> gloves, no thick window to peer through. Just I and my grand-
> daughter, to hold and to touch—the way it must have been in
> the beginning. I came very close to weeping with . . . What?
> Love, pride, joy, relief, I suppose, and something more. . . .

The family provides more than love and belonging and security. It provides a sense of continuity, a sense of infinite purpose. I have never been able to believe that we evolved on this tiny planet circling a third-rate sun on the fringes of a mediocre galaxy sailing through a boundless universe only to die on this planet. . . . I thought of all the millions of years we had come; I thought of my own impending end some day; but above all, I thought of her fresh beginning, of the millions of years to come to get where we are going.[106]

There seems to be a fairly consistent understanding of tears in other cultures and religions, from Native American to Zen Buddhist. Maloney reports:

A friend of mine has been working for the past year with a Zen Buddhist Roshi. Reporting to him the success he had been having with the repetition of the *koan* given him by his master, he was told: "Until I see you on the floor, your face bathed completely in tears, I will not believe that you have broken into the inner meaning of that koan."[107]

The traditions also have migrated. Someone told me that there was a text I must have for this book that was at the heart of Zen enlightenment. Some weeks later I received the quotation in the post. It was not a quote from a roshi. It was from Isaac the Syrian.

The gentle wing of divine Tears brushes the faces of men and women in every culture and age, and often is expressed in less self-conscious and structured ways than by the inheritors of the Western Christian tradition.

The Shock of Recognition

In 1944, Irénée Hausherr published *Penthos* in French. It was the first attempt to gather together texts on tears and make some kind of systematic sense out of them. In 1982, *Penthos* was translated into English. It concentrates for the most part on later patristic writers. But Hausherr's interpretation, while still very valuable, is couched in the language of a spirituality as comprehensible to many people today as Ge'ez. His presentation is also slightly chaotic, but he communicates the fundamentals, and makes many texts available to a wider audience for the first time.

Hausherr begins with a distinction between *penthos* and the sort of sadness or melancholy which the ancients occasionally regarded as sin (they are not consistent on this) and *accedia*, or ennui. Today we have a more detailed vocabulary—in spite of Evagrius' 77 varieties—with which to describe sadness or depression, and know that some types stem from biochemical imbalance, as well as destructive patterning and catastrophic events.

However, at the same time our psychological knowledge tends to dismiss ideas of sadness that are *sinful*. This is as wrong as insisting on the reverse. But, at least in the United States, there is a tendency toward sloth in every area of life, sloth which on its positive side is a motivating factor for much American ingenuity. (Sloth, not necessity, is often the mother of invention.) On its negative side, however, sloth is explained away by every conceivable sort of rationalization, not least in the context of the current revival of interest in the interior life. The effort to change—or lack of it—stems not only from emotional paralysis but also from sheer unwillingness: willfulness.

Hausherr next makes a distinction between *katanyxis* and *penthos*. It is, he writes, "a sudden shock, an emotion which plants deep in the soul a feeling, an attitude, or a resolution", or "a shock which comes from without; the latter [*penthos*] is the psychological reaction".[108]

However, he then lumps the two words together, calling them "through metonymy, virtual equivalents."

Here he and I part company. While it is true he is talking about the abbas and ammas, it is unlikely that human reactions have changed fundamentally in 1800 or so years. One who has a shock that makes him or her aware of the reality of a situation may not necessarily proceed immediately to *penthos*.

A person may dodge and defend him or her self in many ways. It may take a long time before a person is ready to own up to the reality and perspective which has been glimpsed. Soloveitchik agrees:

> A great gap often intercedes between the idea and the act, for crystallized thinking is the end-product of intuitive, undefined thoughts. They take hold of one in the darkness of the night, they emerge from the innermost recesses of the secret self,

and man tries to fend off some of them and hide them from himself, not to mention from others. The road that leads from these
first stirrings to the actual contemplation of repentance is long
indeed, and even then, after the rational idea is clearly formed
in thought, it must be reborn and translated into action.[109]

A specific example of this gap can be seen in the person coming
to terms with psychological damage from childhood. (I am not now
talking about situations of child abuse or other kinds of assault from
which there is no escape.) Sooner or later we all have to realize that
while we have suffered at the hands of another's inherited psychological problems, or brutality, at the same time we ourselves have
allowed the situation to continue as easier than walking out on it, thus
breaking the destructive cycle, even when we know this is what we
must do.

This is classic behavior in the families of alcoholics, which is
why the family members need treatment as much as the drinker.
There is often an enormous gap between the shock of realizing one
has been a "co-alcoholic", enabling the other's drinking and one's
own self-destruction, and doing something about it. These are lethal
behavior patterns which imitate the best of altruism, and are often
a subtle distortion of religion in the popular mind.

A person going through this recovery process faces a long and
complicated process of sorting out and assuming *appropriate* responsibility. For the "co" as well as the drinker, to make the break, and
later to nerve him or her self to ask forgiveness and make amends,
can be a shattering, but also transforming, process.

As long as I have used this example it might be useful to note that
Alcoholics Anonymous and Al-Anon, the two organizations for alcoholics and their families and friends, teach a version of practical
Christianity that is often more accurate and profound than what is
taught in most churches and religious establishments. More than one
seeker after God has been sent to meetings to learn. It is not necessary
technically to qualify as an alcoholic (although more of us are qualified
than we know; one does not have to be a falling-down drunk.)

Ours is an addictive culture, and as a society we exhibit all the
emotional and psychological mechanisms typical of acute alcoholism. Addiction takes many forms, and Alcoholics Anonymous has
spawned many similar organizations, which help people with prob-

lems such as gambling, child abuse, overeating, and recovery from mental illness.

I am not alone in this thinking: Esther de Waal, author of *Seeking God*, is currently at work on a book in which she compares the 12 Steps of AA to the Rule of St Benedict.

The stigma that still attaches to alcoholism—"the chemical problem with the spiritual solution"—is itself evidence of the capacity for denial most of us have when faced with a mirror.

Olivier Clément sees *katanyxis* not only as a piercing of the heart that is a sign of relatedness to God and other humans, but also as a shock that turns us outward:

> Those who receive the gift of *sympatheia* become by the grace of God able to heal the most secret suffering of their neighbour. Crucified with Christ they attain to his infinite tenderness—*katanyxis*. They would wish to be like the apostle. . . . 'to be anathema, separated from Christ . . . for their brethren' (Rom. 9.3). They pray for universal salvation.[110]

Hausherr describes the main source for *penthos* or compunction as awareness of sin, and goes on to discuss what disposes a person to be able to receive this grace when it is offered. The first is mourning for lost salvation. He quickly relates this to thanksgiving. "*Penthos* without thanksgiving would be despair, sorrow that was not godly, while thanksgiving without repentance would be a presumptuous illusion."[111]

Already we begin to see that tears and fire, the inward-outward movements are inseparable. One cannot remember sin without having a knowledge of the goodness and the glory of God.

Soloveitchik speaks of the energy with which the sinner returns:

> Sooner or later the cloud of mourning will inevitably descend, and then will come fear and loneliness, estrangement, alienation, remoteness and separation; sadness will grow and emptiness will spread in the soul, and a man will begin to yearn for the Almighty, and when he apparently sights God's Image from afar, he will begin to run toward it rapidly with all his strength . . . .

In Christian tradition we immediately think of the Prodigal Son, and the Father, prodigal with love. Soloveitchik continues:

> The power of unleashed nostalgia in man's bosom, after such protracted incarceration, propels him onward; he will run more quickly now than was his wont before growing apart from God. Through this nostalgic drive the penitent surpasses the completely righteous, who has never sinned, who does not know sin or recognize it.[112]

In later passages he develops this theme:

> By sinning, he discovered new spiritual forces within his soul, a reservoir of energy, of stubbornness and possessiveness whose existence he had not been aware of before he sinned. Now he has the capacity to sanctify these forces and to direct them upward. The aggression which he has discovered in himself will not allow him to be satisfied with the standards by which he used to measure his good deeds before he sinned; it will rather push him nearer and closer to the Throne of Glory.[113]

Hausherr goes on to describe the same sense of loss as that of a "heavenly kingdom" so that, as Gregory of Nyssa writes, mourning is found even in the prayer of praise. Here again is the linking of polarities.

Another primitive urge to *penthos* is fear. The ancients had several interpretations of fear. One is the scriptural fear of the Lord. "Awe" and "dread" might be better words to use for this kind of fear. Although at this writing the word awe, as commonly used in the United States, has become a travesty of itself in common speech, perhaps it is a sign of hope and longing for something beyond our selves, of knowing that we do not have to seek to control everything in the universe, and wonder and mystery at knowledge of a power that lies beyond us.

Fear can mean not only the utter transcendent mystery of God, but also the unknowability caused by separation. This fear sadly can become the fear of a god who is implacable judge and destroyer, and a fear of hell. While this may be a misunderstanding of God's "wrath" (cf. Fretheim), it is still part of the history of spirituality. We see here an idea of a pagan god who has an attitude of inexorable *quid pro quo*, an idea which has unfortunately persisted to the present day.

But the vision of God's wrath as the relentless pursuit of sorrowing love is much harder to bear than the punishment I deserve and can therefore justify. To find myself standing in that Light is much more dreadful. It is not a legal understanding of justice that brings together my fractured, faulted self, but rather the anointing of tears-that-are-fire that flow from the eyes of God, and drop on the stone of my heart.

Perhaps the impression of "wrath" comes from the inescapable quality of this Love, the knowledge that I live always under that Eye, and from which loving gaze there is no escape and no hiding. Yet this fear is not fruitless, for from its tears love is born:

> Groans and sadness cry out to the Lord, trembling tears intercede for us, and the tears shed out of all-holy love show that our prayer has been accepted.[114]

Tears over our death produce fear, but when fear begets fearlessness, then what a joy comes dawning! When joy is without interruption, holy love comes blossoming forth.[115]

Yet another cause for *penthos*, says Hausherr, is compassion for one's brother. He speaks of this compassion primarily as it mirrors the judgment of God, that is, weeping for one's brother or sister because one has judged that person to be in sin and therefore "dead". The problem with this attitude is that it implies that "I" am capable of assuming the position of God, and it can lead to an insidious self-righteousness and pride.

But this is a one-sided presentation of the desert dwellers, and stories of Abba Moses were told as an antidote to the temptation to judge:

> A brother at Scetis committed a fault. A council was called to which Abba Moses was invited, but he refused to go to it. Then the priest sent someone to say to him, 'Come, for everyone is waiting for you.' So he got up and went. He took a leaking jug, filled it with water, and carried it with him. The others came out to meet him and said to him, 'What is this, Father?' The old man said to them, 'My sins run out behind me, and I do not see them, and today I am coming to judge the errors of

another.' When they heard that they said no more to the brother but forgave him.[116]

Not only did they strive to refrain from judging each other, but also themselves. Judgment is entirely in the provenance of God. To judge oneself is to grasp power and perspective that is God's alone.

Hausherr also speaks of "pure love of God" as a cause for *penthos*, and distinguishes it quite clearly from the tears of repentance. He also remarks on its rarity. It is difficult to see these tears either as unmixed or as being so rare. If one truly has pure love of God, then it would be impossible to know it, as such love precludes self-reflection, even as tears of love include tears of repentance.

> And from the very first staging-post of that hidden mode of life these tears will commence, and they will convey him to perfect love of God.[117]

Isaac speaks of tears that make one drunk with love, and the Syriac verb also means irrigation, a beautifully potent word, especially given the barren context of his environment. He also differentiates tears according to measure: intermittent, perpetual, and moderate. But Isaac goes beyond Hausherr's distinction: in Isaac's pure prayer (and he is not consistent in his terminology)

> . . . there is neither any prayer, nor emotions, nor tears, nor authority, nor freedom, nor supplications, nor desire, nor longing after anything of what is hoped for in this world or in the world to come.[118]

Hausherr goes on to describe cultivation of and obstacles to tears, but at this point we must leave him.

It might be useful to pause and look at some of the various movements of tears, which are really one movement constantly repeated as if in an expanding spiral.

Grief Work:	forgetting—remembering—forgetting
Way of Tears:	forgetfulness—remembering—self-forgetfulness
or	heart of stone—heart of flesh—heart of fire
or	fire—water—fire
or	fire of hell—water of baptism—fire of purity
or	silence of death—praise—silent praise.

The forgetfulness of the first phase is a kind of deadness, the personal hell of isolation described in Sartre's *No Exit*, the sullen fire of impurity and the silence of the damned. In the middle phase one is awakened to one's condition, given the gift of repentance, new life by baptism of the water of tears. One weeps for one's sin and separation, but equally and more in thanksgiving for forgiveness and resurrection that comes through remembering, and moves through thanksgiving into praise and adoration, pure love of God that is non-self-reflective.

The fulcrum on which the two extremes are poised is the basic Christian experience. At the end of this chapter I have listed some other groups of words that might be suggestive of this continuum balanced on an axis of this experience of the gift of tears.

The distinctions among various kinds of tears developed over the centuries; and since there are as many subtleties to tears as there are people to weep them, it might be useful to distinguish a few more.

Some Tears of the High Middle Ages

In 1983, Dr Brian McGuire, head of the Medieval Institute of the University of Copenhagen, presented a paper at Stanford University entitled "Monks and Tears: a Twelfth-Century Change". Dr McGuire begins by noting a most unusual situation in which a Cistercian monk asked for—and more astonishingly received—permission to learn about the way of tears from a holy woman in the town. Dr McGuire immediately injects a word echoing Climacus:

> Tears in themselves are not a sign of closeness to God. In the centuries to come, other writers make the same or similar point. Tears can be shed for the wrong reason as out of mawkish sentimentality. As the novice in one of Aelred of Rievaulx's dialogues concedes, he had had an easier time weeping over stories about Arthur than for his own sins.[119]

He first notes Aelred's forebear, Gregory the Great, the "doctor of tears", whose primary focus seems to be the kind of tears associated with the desire for heaven. Jean Leclercq has also noted that these particular tears have a literature to themselves in the medieval tradition.[120]

McGuire also reminds us of the dualistic tradition which we have already seen as part of the gnostic and manichean inheritance when he speaks of "the monastic refusal to allow a place for tears in connection with the death of friends" and, it might be added, family. To this day there are some monasteries that still give a questionably literal reading of scripture primacy over the greater law of compassion.

McGuire notes that about the year 1050 the monastic attitude began to change. But it is not until St Bernard of Clairvaux that we find a new sort of tears mentioned, tears that have "the taste of wine", that are tears of "brotherly compassion going forth with the fervour of charity" that produce "a certain sober drunkenness".

If we go by McGuire's description, there is a marked difference between Bernard's drunken tears, and Isaac's, or the tears of compassion mentioned in earlier literature. What does Bernard mean? I should like to suggest at least two possibilities. The first is that with the Cistercian recovery of parts of the desert ideal, a certain solitude-in-community, it is possible that the earlier experiences of desert compassion were recapitulated.

To know oneself is to know the agony of humanity on a universal level. This takes at least two forms: compassion for another's suffering, and rejoicing in the glory of God revealed in the other. As Isaac the Syrian says, "He surveys the flame of things."[121]

When this sort of self-knowledge is operative, to make any kind of discernment of one's neighbor is to take responsibility on one's self for what has been discerned. Thus to "judge"—not as God judges, and not *de haut en bas*—means that one implicitly accepts the judgment on one's self of what one has descried. Thus the opposite of "Judge not that ye be not judged" is operative: one willingly takes the judgment of another upon oneself.

Yet this is still not what Bernard seems to be saying. Another possibility is that if Bernard had the kind of self-knowledge implied by his writing, then he must have been fully aware of his failings, his brutality, his polemic, his power-brokering. It should not be assumed that he was proud of these faults, while at the same time we realize, whether or not he did, that his eloquence in writing and speaking was the flip side of his skill as a polemicist.

Still, his sense of compunction is evident, and in such a state what seems a hyperbole of self-deprecation is in fact very real, not because one is actively trying to be "more humble" than another: no comparisons are being made. Rather, one looks in the light of what one has somehow "seen" that God intended, and there is no way to express this glimpsed abyss in the light of one's gifts. It is precisely the gifts that show the depth of sin, pride, sloth.

For someone with this acutely realistic evaluation of gifts and failures, pastoral responsibility is especially painful because one realizes only too well how easy it is to do damage, and how much one's own sinfulness can get tangled up in the pastoral process. Thus to see someone evidence great growth and grace, and know that God has used one's self, warts and all, to effect this grace, is indeed a cause for a kind of holy drunkenness. We will never know exactly what Bernard meant, but this is certainly one interpretation.

Bernard's spectacular faults bring to mind another kind of tears, which might be called the tears of patient waiting. The waiting can be concerned with many things: to know the will of God; to see the coming of the Kingdom; to be given a new inspiration in solving a difficult problem; to be healed from illness or fault. While it is quite true that God can heal us of faults which we feel are hopeless, at the same time it is true that often we have faults which we intuitively know we are meant to have in order to have the energy for moving into willingness, as we have noted in Soloveitchik's sayings.

Thus these tears are tears of waiting-in-hope, crying with the prophet, "How long, O Lord?"

Tears of the Word

Dom André Louf adds another kind of tears to this investigation. He speaks of the Word as it appears in scriptural tradition as a two-edged sword, and goes on to define these two edges as doing battle with the powers of darkness in prayer on the one hand, and being pierced to the heart by the Word on the other. It is this latter that produces the tears we might call tears of the Word.[122]

However, these tears themselves may be of several types: there can be tears of illumination that finds no images or words; there can be tears of wonder and humility; there can be tears of piercing reality—the types, again, are as varied as humanity.

There is a passage from pseudo-Philo that speaks of a kind of tears we might call tears of covenant, which are very important when we think of tears igniting fire on the earth (see Chapter VII). We often speak of contracts signed in blood; the one between David and Jonathan was sealed in tears:

> And Jonathan answered and said: Come unto me, my brother David, and I will tell thee thy righteousness. My soul pineth away sore at thy sadness because now we are parted one from another. And this have our sins compelled, that we should be parted from one another. But let us remember one another day and night while we live. And even if death part us, yet I know that our souls will know one another. For thine is the kingdom in this world, and of thee shall be the beginning of the kingdom, and it cometh in its time. And now, like a child that is weaned from its mother, even so shall be our separation. Let the heaven be witness and let the earth be witness of those things which we have spoken together. And let us weep each with the other and lay up our tears in one vessel and commit the vessel to the earth, and it shall be a testimony unto us. And they bewailed each one the other sore, and kissed one another.[123]

The Jesus Prayer as Tears

While any prayer has the potential for being tears—and any kind of tears, prayer—the Jesus Prayer of all verbal prayers is the essence of the way of tears. There are many good books on this prayer, so I will do little more than note the fact.

The Jesus Prayer is sometimes translated, "Lord Jesus Christ, Son of [the living] God, have mercy on me [a sinner]." The words in brackets are sometimes used and sometimes not. "Living" is felt by some to be implicit in the word "God" and "a sinner" in "mercy". There is no hard and fast rule.

Some authors feel the bracketed phrases are vital to the prayer; others do not. And the prayer can change itself to be inclusive of other petition, praise, thanksgiving. It can shorten itself to be one word or total silence.

In some monasteries it is said in common. To observe simple men and women saying the prayer in turn is to see them pouring tears on their hearts, which are broken open to anoint the earth. To participate in such prayer is to feel one's self gathered and thrust through the darkness. The Jesus Prayer itself becomes tears in such a case. But it is better to leave writing of it to those who are adepts.

The Tears of Jesus

We know of Jesus both that he was the sinless One and also that he wept.

But this knowledge alone has not been enough to sweep away the onus attached to tears in some cultures. There is room here only to scratch the surface of scriptural accounts of Jesus' weeping, and no room at all to explore his sayings *about* tears. This discussion is only by way of suggesting an approach to scripture. The subject of tears in the New Testament is fruitful ground for an interested scholar to explore. To write of Jesus' view of tears and his own experience of tears requires every bit of biblical criticism that can be mustered, as well as the writer's own knowledge of tears.

The first passages I would like to consider are Mark 3:5 and John 11:33–35. The first is the story of the man with the withered arm who is healed on the sabbath, and Jesus' response of "anger and sorrow" (NEB) to the pharisees, who are trying to trap him. The second occurs during the raising of Lazarus, when Jesus sighs heavily within himself, and finally is overcome with weeping.

In the first place, it is significant that anger and sorrow occur in the same instance. Each of the passages about Jesus' tears seems to show a complex of motivations. In this one there is compassion for the sick man; compassion for the "obstinate stupidity" of the pharisees, along with anger both of frustration and resisting the temptation to force their belief other than by the bestowal of life and freedom.

There is a glimpse of reality of the political and human situation, and rejection of any illusions he might have had about himself and the impact of his ministry. He must remain kenotic to do his Father's will. The temptations of the wilderness never leave him.

The passage from John is even more complex. The Jerome Commentary puzzles over the word translated variously "inward groaning" to "sighed deeply within himself" and its connotations of anger without being able to find any reason for it.[124]

However, the commentary also relates this incident with the wedding of Cana, when his anger was more open and evident. Perhaps it is consistent, too, with his general exasperation at the unwillingness of his hearers to understand; their constant demand for signs and wonders. Perhaps he had a sense of being exploited.

Perhaps he was aware of the knife-edge he walked, the power he was continually letting go, not only in healing but also, and more, the power he chose not to exercise or grasp.

Yet he cannot resist the request of Martha and Mary any more than he could resist his Mother. His compassion for them and his friend, his compassion for those unable to comprehend, unable to break out of their stereotypes and fearboxes, his grief for his friend, which is also his larger mourning over the fact of death and perhaps—who knows—his mourning over his own—all in the end cause him to weep.

There is a terrible irony here. In what seems to be the most powerful act of all, the raising of the dead, Jesus is at one and the same time powerless to make his friends see the point of it all. His grief is as much for his own powerlessness as it is for other reasons.

The second pair of passages I would like briefly to consider are the two "mother hen" passages in Matt. 23:37 and Luke 13:34–35. These do not speak specifically of Jesus' tears, but they are definitely laments.

The Matthew passage is held by some to be more eschatological, and the Luke to refer to steadfastness in the face of persecution.[125]

Once again we see compassion, tenderness, perhaps even what the Russians would call *umilenye*, combined with a willing powerlessness. A mother hen does not force, *cannot* force—she has no way to do so—her chicks to take refuge under her wings. She can only call to them, plead with them, woo and croon to them. If they insist on ignoring her, they are taken by hawk or weasel. So with Jesus: Jerusalem will not hear his words and the inevitable awaits her. In both passages there is compassion for those who are fallen and those who will fall, either under judgment, or under persecution.

Again irony: what if indeed the message had been heard, and the power of willing powerlessness, the power of tears had been effected? Would the persecution have continued? Would the city still be under judgment? Or would the persecutors and conquerors be baffled? Must we always weep over our Jerusalems? (see Chapter IX)

Luke 19:45 is Jesus' speech over Jerusalem. The same commentary speaks of strong emotion at a time of departure, of regret, of "most tragic sorrow and sternest detachment". In the context, that of the last entry into Jerusalem, within the note of triumph is the rejection of the role of tyranny. The commentary says, "Yet this king remains one of the '*anawim*".[126]

The invocation of angelic hosts echos "Lord Sabaoth",[127] and recalls the tremendous might of this God who is now flesh, and who has become a kenotic King so that he may fulfill his vocation to be the power of God. (*See* 2 Kings 6:17)

Finally there are the accounts of Gethsemane. The Letter to the Hebrews speaks of Jesus' cries and tears (Heb. 5:7); but the gospel accounts show Jesus as the one who, though most in need, does the comforting. The tears and the chalice, the sweat and blood are figures of the deepest mystery of tears, but not the least is his role of servant to the very end.

WORD LISTS

*Continuum column **not matched** with Fulcrum/Axis column.*

Continuum	Fulcrum/Axis
inward-outward	contemplation
introversion-extroversion	experience of forgiveness
impressive-expressive	center
implosion-explosion	still place
grieving-freedom	singularity
I-as-subject toward object-I as predicate of subject	infusion
seeking-disseminating	meeting place
burying-raising	ground/Ground
sowing-scattering seeds from fruit of sowing	silence
(reproduction)	hub
emptiness-fulfillment	needle's eye
black hole-white hole	engagement-union-marriage
sorrow-joy	Trinity
mind in heart-mind of heart	tomb/womb
Word-apophatic fire	Person/Self
committed-uncommitted	Source
narrowing-widening	primordial moment
psychology-theology	dark-is-light
embraced-embracing	awakening
alone-with Alone—alone-with-Alone's creation	knowledge/Knowledge
passivities-activities and therefore Alone	Trinity-as-fire (bush kind)
focusing of life toward Source—Source pouring out	retort (laboratory)
through	I AM
cross-resurrection	wick
asceticism-spondicism (cf Bruteau)	Pointe Vierge
OT-NT	unified field
night-day	pilot light
self-consciousness in disposition-self-forgetfulness	core
in disposition	Presence
desert-city	Mystery
squalid (sterile) bush-squalid bush salted with fire	
stove indoors-desert outdoors and fertile (ashes)	
tears-laughter	
Fort Knox-Big Sky Country (not Marlboro)	
photograph-icon	
rooting-blossoming	
taper-menorah	
twilight-dawn	
constriction-expansion	
water-wine	

Add your own.

VI

He brought me out into an open place; he rescued me because he delighted in me. (Psalm 18:20 BCP)

You have turned my wailing into dancing; you have put off my sack-cloth and clothed me with joy. (Psalm 30:11 BCP)

If I go down to hell Thou art there also. . . . (Psalm 139, Coverdale translation)

Once you have reached the place of tears, then know that the mind has left the prison of this world and set its foot on the road towards the new world. Then it begins to breathe the wonderful air which is there; it begins to shed tears. For now the birth pangs of the spiritual infant grow strong, since grace, the common mother of all, makes haste to give birth mystically to the soul, the image of God, into the light of the world to come. And when the time of birth is come, then the mind will perceive something of what belongs to that world, like a faint perfume which an infant receives inside the body in which it has grown. Then, unable to endure what is unwanted, it (the spiritual infant) will set the body to weeping mingled with joy which surpasses the sweetness of honey. Together with the growing of this interior infant there will be an increase of tears. The stream of tears occurs when the mind has begun to become serene. I am talking about the flow of tears belonging to the stage which I have described, not that partial one which takes place from time to time. This consolation which takes place intermittently occurs for everyone who serves God in solitude; sometimes it happens when the mind is in contemplation, sometimes while reading the words of the scriptures; sometimes when the mind is occupied with supplication.

But I propose to speak of that total kind, which continues night and day without a break, and by the sincerity of his behaviour, when the eyes become fountains of water for a period of nearly two years. This happens during a transitional period; I mean mystical transition. At the end of the period of tears you will enter into peace of thought; and by this peace of thought you will enter into that divine rest of which Paul spoke, rest in part, according to [our] nature.

From this place of peace the intellect will begin to see hidden things. Then the Holy Spirit will begin to reveal before it heavenly things, while God dwells in you and promotes spiritual fruits in you. Then you will start to become aware of the transformation which the whole nature will receive in the renewal of all things, dimly and as though by hints.[128]

> These, though we bring them in trembling and
>   fearfulness,
> He will accept for the name that is dear;
> Mornings of joy give for evenings of tearfulness,
> Trust for our trembling and hope for our fear.[129]

Tapping the Fountain

In the above passage, St Isaac has shown the long-term effect of the gift of tears and the way of tears. As with so many aspects of creation, what is true in the larger view, the macrocosm, is also true in a more intimate perspective, the microcosm. His description is also accurate in describing the various phases of tears in general. As with all passages of the journey into God, there are no fixed times or necessary sequences. Some may skip the two years of copious tears; some may come to weeping very early only to find that the entire process is a spiral one, and is repeated again and again on different levels, almost as if one were reincarnated in one's own lifetime.

Additionally, women may experience the coming of tears differently from men, although the interior process, the triggers for tears, the matrix in which the gift is given, seems to be the same.

Before continuing it would be helpful if you stopped for a moment and recalled the last time you wept, for whatever reason.

The First Phases of Weeping

As Isaac observes there seem to be several stages, or phases of weeping.

1. *The Way to the Realm of Tears*

For many people this is the most difficult part of the journey, not only because it means facing themselves in all their nakedness in the light of God, but also because our society has so conditioned us against weeping. Weeping, according to this conditioning, is a

shame and a disgrace, a sign of weakness, mawkishness, and senti-
mentality, a sign that one is not able to keep a stiff upper lip.

While even Irénée Hausherr, author of *Penthos* feels that some
tears are "shameful" I would like to suggest that it is rather necessary
to draw a distinction between tears that are perhaps sinful and those
that are not. I wonder if any tears except those that are used as a
weapon are sinful *or* shameful, and even these are an admission of
lack of control, of loss of power in the situation.

Tears are often labeled "shameful" because they indicate "lack
of self-control". But I wonder if this kind of self-control is one that
we ought to seek, that is, a self-control that obviates all tears. Certainly self-control is necessary—we have to gain control in order to
be able to lose control in the appropriate way: in tears.

Certainly one can weep from rage and self-pity, but, if rightly
observed, these, too, are already an admission of lack of dominance,
that one's illusions of omnipotence have been shattered. Already
there is an opening because there is a certain grasp of reality; and
within this contact is the option for the tears to change.

> It is not to be wondered at if mourning begins with good
> tears and ends with bad, but it is admirable if ordinary and nat-
> ural tears can be turned round to become spiritual. This is some-
> thing that will be understood by those inclined to vainglory.[130]

Most of the early desert-dwellers were careful in the distinctions they made when seeking the way into the realm of tears. They
insisted that tears were not to be induced as a technique, but were
a gift that could be earnestly sought from God. This seeking was
not, however, to satisfy the desire to be regarded as one who had
gifts from God. Spiritual pride, they knew, was the surest way to
lose the gift.

Climacus can be devastating on this subject:

> He who has the gift of spiritual tears will be able to mourn
> anywhere. But if it is all outward show, there will be no end to
> his discussion of places and means.

> The man who mourns at one time and then goes in for high
> living and laughter on another occasion is like someone who pelts

the dog of sensuality with bread. It looks as if he is driving him off when in fact he is actually encouraging him to stay by him.

But he has comfort, to offer, too:

> Silly men [and women!] often take pride in their tears—hence the reason some are not granted the gift of mourning. And [men] of this kind, discovering that they cannot weep, think of themselves as wretched and give themselves over to sighs and lamentation, sorrow of soul, deep grief, and utter desolation, all of which can safely take the place of tears, though the [men] in question regard these as nothing and benefit accordingly.[131]

To be repentant to the point of tears was a primary goal of the beginner in the desert, and tears seem to signify whether the seeker had truly abandoned "the world", namely the basic desires of status, security, and control.

> Tears are to the mind the border, as it were, between the bodily and the spiritual state, between the state of being subject to the passions and that of purity. As long as one has not yet received this gift, the labour of his service is still in the outward man, and this is to such an extent that he does not even perceive anything of the hidden service of the spiritual person. Once he has begun to leave the bodiliness of this world and steps into that territory which lies beyond this visible nature, then he will immediately reach this grace of tears. And from the very first staging-post of that hidden mode of life these tears will commence, and they will convey him to perfect love of God. When he has progressed to this point, so rich in tears will he be that he will imbibe them with his food and his drink, so constant and abundant are they.[132]

It is important to remember what Isaac and other writers mean by the words "world" and "passions":

> 'The world' is a collective term, employed when we examine contemplation, to designate the various different passions: when we wish to refer to the passions collectively, we call them 'the world', but when we want to refer to them separately, we call them by their separate names.[133]

We have the problem of more than a thousand years of scholarship and controversy about the meaning of many key words. Complex and negative meanings have accumulated with time that obscure these sayings. For these and many other reasons, the distilled and evolved simplicity of tears has for centuries been lost to the West.

There is, as far as I can tell, no passage about tears that specifically refers to control and letting go control. But perhaps these are twentieth century concepts and categories. Nonetheless, I feel this is at least in part what the writers on tears were understanding by phrases such as "leaving the world", "being buried in the passions", "giving up the will" and "poverty".

As we saw in the quotation from John Climacus above, these writers recognized that one sort of tears might lead to another, and as long as the tears to begin with were natural, or authentic, and not induced as a vain show, it was only the end result that mattered.

Virtually all of them agree that what is most required to find the realm of tears are solitude and poverty. Though much has been made of external solitude and poverty, these writers are referring primarily to inward solitude and poverty. Climacus writes of both the distortion of what may seem the very qualities that should enable our *metanoia*—

> The forces against us are so abominable that they can even turn the mothers of virtue into the parents of vice, and they can turn into pride those very things that should produce humility in us.[134]

—and practically in the next breath points out that for those whose hearts are oriented properly, tears are always present:

> I have seen men moved to tears in cities and among crowds so that the thought has come that great assemblies of people may actually do us no harm.[135]

2. *Gaining Control to Lose Control*
Certainly self-control in the sense of self-discipline is greatly to be desired, and, paradoxically, in order to weep one must gain control in order to lose control. One must have learnt the self-control

of stillness, of silence, of dispassionate self-scrutiny. This kind of self-control is very different from some stoic ideas. Paramount is a tenderness vital to their idea of conversion, and a conviction that tears are a part of mortal life until its very end.

3. *Polarity*

While not losing sight of tears as a gift, we also have been talking about tears as a way. It is in one sense wrong to make a distinction between the two because the way, too, is a gift, and in the end not only are they one but also part of the oneness, the integration, the prayer without ceasing, the *monos* of single-hearted seeking of and living in God.

As the rain which waters the earth is created from polarized ions of oxygen and hydrogen, so tears spring from polarized feelings, emotions, and thoughts. Tears of frustration may come from the polarity of the thing desired set over and against its being out of reach. Tears of self-pity may ooze from vanity set in opposition to a real or imagined slight. Tears of rage may spurt from the illusion of power we think we have, defeated by a similar fantasy in another person. The polarities of tears are as prolix and varied as human personalities. These varied sorts of tears are usually related to concrete, external events, but so too can holy tears be triggered by external events.

One way the holy people of old came to tears was by *holding two opposing thoughts in the heart*. The difference in these tears will become immediately evident. They are a result of a vision of the fallen creation held over and against the mercy of the Creator; the vision of the horror of human interaction held against the knowledge of a good and loving God, a God who, most unbearably of all, continues to love us nonetheless.

It is a glimpse of the abyss that lies between earth and heaven, human and divine, the nothingness of humanity even at its best and most glorious, compared with that to which it can be and into which it will be transfigured. The key here is that whether the stimulus is internal or external there is an *innate willingness* to bear the tension of holding these opposite ends of a continuum in silent offering.

Love itself becomes the polarity in this exchange, and our tears are born of it.

Any self-deception or deliberate distraction diminishes polar-

ity, and as self-knowledge unfolds, so do our confrontation and exchange of love with God. Thus the gift of tears is itself a way that
unfolds and is not only transforming but also is itself transformed
from sorrow into joy.

Climacus says: "Mourning, after all, is the typical pain of a soul
on fire."[136]

> The man wearing blessed, God-given mourning like a wed-
> ding garment gets to know the spiritual laughter of the soul.[137]

> Tears over our death produce fear, but when fear begets
> fearlessness, then what a joy comes dawning! When joy is with-
> out interruption, holy love comes blossoming forth.[138]

Immediately it has to be said that, like joy, the gift of tears is
not dependent on emotions, nor ultimately do affective feelings play
a large role. Isaac says, ". . . for weeping lies beyond being subject
to the passions".[139] Thus everything that we desire that is not God,
all living that is not focussed toward God is held before the eyes of
the heart in the light of God.

Even more important, this weeping is of a different nature and
in a different category than weeping whose source is either irritant
or emotion. *It is the weeping of apatheia.* This distinction is particularly important as it mirrors the weeping of God; for being beyond
the passions, it is not ordinary weeping that evidences the idea of
mutability around which the controversies of Chalcedon raged, but
is something quite different. We will look at this in more detail later
in this chapter.

Weeping has much more to do with what God is doing in the
98% of our selves that is out of sight, that is fed through consciousness and irrupts into consciousness, a breathing in and out that perhaps could be compared to the transpiration of plants by which they
take in carbon dioxide and exhale oxygen.

Consciousness can inhale, and has the choice of what will be
given to the heart, will harden or soften it, will make it more willing
or less. Consciousness reflects our choices, both those consigned to
the heart and those coming forth; the deep choices of our hearts that
emerge in the stillness that pervades our lives as we come to know
God.

And God needs to work out of sight. Often we will be discouraged at the contents of our conscious minds, the petty, dreary thoughts. But often in a crisis God will surprise us with the choices our hearts have made that our thoughts may belie: that we are Christ's and Christ is God's. But if God were to allow us to see this, we might consider that our work was done.

In *The River of Light* Lawrence Kushner speaks of this activity of God in an analogy of dreaming:

> Without the dark womb of sleep there could be no sensation of light, emergence of consciousness, or place to which we might return. In the darkness there is no arrangement of past and future, no self-reflection, no ego, and no neurosis. The Talmud teaches that the days of our lives properly begin with darkness and move to daylight. And thus all genuine creating must originate in the darkness. All transformation must commence during the night. At the price of the "old ego" and its organization. You cannot predict what will happen in the darkness.[140]

The work of Light goes on in our darkness, out of our sight. This must be; otherwise we would become proud, like Lucifer the light-bearer, dazzled with the beauty Light had wrought, and, like him, we would come to believe that its power lies with us. Like him, we would come to believe that we are equal with it and can control it, and in opposition to Christ, try to grasp it even more violently than is our wont.

The Seeker in the Dark

Not only in the darkness of the self that is out of sight does God do the work of light, but also in the darkness of sin. Sin is necessary, says Lady Julian. Sin is behovely. Sin is part of the package, necessary because in the awareness of it we are brought to repentance, generate the energy that impels us toward repentance, and in repentance to tears, and in tears to the vast open place where, in the dark, all is new and ready to begin in the fires of Mercy.

The way of tears teaches us how little we know about either sorrow or joy, and how much we over-value our superficial reactions. If, for example, we use "feeling good with Jesus" to magnify or justify control over others or self-deception, we are in peril of our souls. If we use religion to bring our lives into *stasis*, into an illusory steady state where everything is familiar and we know exactly who we are and who God is; if we use the liturgy to hide from God, to avoid the uncertainty and dread of the still place where our new lives come to be, then we have opted for lies and for death.

We are afraid to weep because we are afraid of losing our imprisoning self-image.

In some ways this is a justified fear. As many writers, particularly Merton, have pointed out, ours is an age in which it is particularly difficult to find one's self in the first place. Often the task of the first years of Christian life is to help a person integrate his or her disparate parts in order to have a self, and thus a self-image *to* give away. God is working all the while, however, and is not confined to our ideas of health.

Many of us build our houses of cards in order to create some semblance of a self, or, having found our selves in part, to make the part seem the whole, to convince our selves that we know our selves thoroughly, our limitations and our potentials.

Often this process has involved great struggle, sacrifice and pain. To come to realize that the self we discover must continue to be transformed, that our images of self must be put to death one by one, can be a shattering insight. We want to say, "Enough already. I have been born enough. I want a respite. I have had enough of this unsettling pain and discomfort."

To be aware that we feel this way is one thing; to adopt it is to cut our selves off from the process of being transformed, and from our co-creativity with God as we are emptied of self-image, and God's *kenosis* mingles with ours.

As May has pointed out, it is quite possible that pain is an element in all creativity. He adds:

> Note here that suffering, the willful refusal to accept that which frustrates one's attachments, is not the same thing as pain. Pain, which is a simple stimulus, can certainly be felt during unitive experience. In the sense of realizing one's identity with all creation, pain may in fact be said to be a universal component of *all* unitive experience.[141]

Usually we think of this pain of being born as being related to specific crisis points or events in our lives. We go through a difficult transition and think that now we know how to cope with life; we go through therapy and discover a whole new world and think that now we know what our responses will predictably be, and how to meet the next fence, which is coming at us with startling rapidity even as the ground underfoot becomes less and less sure.

There is that experience in the process of transformation when we are brought to understand that we hang on to our unwanted behaviors because we are afraid. We have a dread of what is unknown, even—maybe especially—of health (and by "health" I mean here what God is leading us to become in unique relationship); we have a dread of what our new and unfamiliar responses might be and of the new responses these will ineluctably elicit from those around us. And indeed, the process of crossing over to that new land, the desert where we consciously recondition our responses to our selves, our life events, and other people is fraught with every danger any desert solitary ever faced. The reconstruction process is nothing if not painful—but worth it.

Having come through all that, we want to heave a sigh of relief and get on with life. We are happy to forget the preoccupation and self-consciousness that is the inevitable accompaniment of beginning any new task, but especially that of coming to know our selves, a process at first fascinating, then boring, and, in the end, annoying.

We wonder if self-preoccupation will ever go away so that we can live again with a measure of spontaneity. Or so it seems. The self-disgust with self-preoccupation is, of course, a sign of health, a sign that we do indeed have a self we can forget, and a self-image which must be given away.

And that kind of self-observation does, finally, go away. It may return sporadically; often it is transformed into another kind of self-observation that is less obtrusive, less negatively judgmental, less narcissistic; almost a new "instinct" that is not conscience as taskmaster, but a conscience that is neutral observer, that sees our selves and our lives in relationship. We start to understand that this birthing process never ends and that it is part of our relatedness to every other person and all of creation. But we also understand that we are not condemned eternally to the self-consciousness of first-stage conversion or therapy.

An Earnest of Joy to Come

But if this were all, it would hardly seem worth pursuing. It is not all. Self-forgetfulness *does* come and, put more positively, the vision of God becomes more and more our focus.

A constant flow of tears comes about in a man for three causes: [firstly,] from awestruck wonder arising from insights continually revealed to the intellect and replete with mysteries, tears spill forth involuntarily and painlessly. For with the vision of the intellect a man considers these insights, being held fast with wonder at the knowledge of things spiritually revealed to the intellect through the same insights and, [at the same time] tears flow effortlessly by themselves because of the strength of the sweetness that confines the intellect to gazing at the insights. The Fathers call such tears the type of the Manna that the sons of Israel ate, and the outpouring of water from the rock, "for that rock was Christ", that is to say, insights both mystic and spiritual. Or else, constant weeping arises from the fervent love of God that consumes the soul, and because of its sweetness and delightfulness a man cannot endure not to weep continually. Or [thirdly], constant weeping comes from great humility of heart.[142]

Who Writes? Who Weeps?

Love itself becomes the polarity in this exchange, and our tears are born of it.

Another way of looking at this process is through the analogy of craft. Carla Needleman has explored this metaphor as she experienced several manual crafts.[143] I experience it daily in writing.

I have always said that I "hate" to write. It is a much more complex feeling than hate, however. And hate is, in the event, entirely the wrong word. But I have often wondered why writing is so utterly painful for me.

Over the years I have discovered that writing—popularly known as a supremely egotistical process—is the most self-effacing, self-forgetful activity I engage in other than the adoration of God in still-prayer. In fact, writing for me *is* a form of adoration. It is also, each time I sit down to face the blank page—or screen—a chosen death.

Writing a letter, essay or book calls for me to lay everything aside that normally preoccupies my consciousness including what we ordinarily think of as thought, and simply allow the words to present themselves on paper. This is a very common experience amongst writers, who have always had a fascination—perhaps egotistical, perhaps its opposite—with the question, "Who is the writer?"

In an article entitled, "Does the Writer Exist?",[144] Joyce Carol Oates contrasts authors with their writing, and describes the astonishment and disappointment of people who have visited famous writers and found them to be utterly different from, and often totally indifferent to their writing.

In another article called "Strange Fish",[145] Lee Anne Schreiber explores the same question in a different way. She quotes John Gardner's *On Becoming a Novelist.*

> All writing requires at least some measure of a trancelike state. When one has experienced these moments, one finds, as mystics so often do, that after one has come out of them, one cannot say, or even clearly remember, what happened. . . . One knows one was away because of the words one finds on the page when one comes back, a scene or a few lines more vivid than anything one is capable of writing.

"The main thing about it," Barbara McClintock, the Nobel winner in cell biology reports, "is that you forget yourself." Schreiber also quotes Marguerite Duras: "I know of all kinds of people who don't write who are writers. By that I mean the world passes to us by way of them."

"Even," Schreiber adds, "if they can't explain how."

One explanation is attempted by Irvin Ehrenpreis' review of Ronald Bush's study of T.S. Eliot. Ehrenpreis first remarks of Gray's "Elegy" that it has something ". . . which seems to rise from the abyss of the human soul and speak to the universal condition of men".

> Eliot, [Ehrenpreis continues] . . . hoped to draw on depths of unconscious feelings or intuitions that normally resist the cre-

ative imagination. Like Freud, he was willing to experiment on himself. He tried to feel his way back to his most dangerous emotions and to secure from the energy that, concentrated in language subtly echoing earlier masters, would call up new, profound responses from the reader.

For an acutely self-conscious critic, at home in several national literatures and learned in philosophy, to grope his way below these difficult accomplishments and bring up essences that had hardly been recognized by psychologists, then to embody these in unforgettable speech, is a triumph enjoyed by not more than two or three poets in a century. . . .

I take seriously Eliot's distinction between the man who suffers and the mind that creates . . . I am willing to go a good deal of the way with Nietzschean esthetics, and to say that when Eliot explored his deepest sensations for the images and sounds of his most powerful verse, he was not examining the self apart—the ego that goes to the dentist or that gives instructions to a secretary. Rather I think he tried to reach for a self, or a level of self, *that shares the definitive experiences of mankind.* From this healthy, creative depth he tried to bring up figures, metaphors, that would seem to responsive readers to evoke their own inner life. Failure was a chronic danger. But success would be unforgettable. . . . it involved a contract with the reader such that the powerful images would not invite an inspection of the poet's domestic or social relations but of the reader's archetypal world.[146]

There are many echoes in writers on tears. Here is Isaac:

As soon as someone begins to be raised above the affections, this holy power will cleave to the soul, not departing from it either by night or by day, and it will show to the soul God's providence. And even the minutiae of all that is and happens, of yes and no, of what takes place for someone secretly and openly, and of matters relating to the creation of this world, are revealed to the soul by that power which cleaves to it, revealing to it the creative power of God and showing it the divine care which, without ceasing, follows and visits everything belonging to this whole creation. And it shows the soul how this providence follows a person at all times, and, even though he does not perceive it and is not aware of it, preserves him against adversities at all times, and directing him towards what serves for the salvation and the rest of his soul and body, and the discovering of his true life.

Now this same divine power, which effects all these things, shows itself to a person in secret, by revelation that can be understood by his spiritual nature, which is the intellect. When someone has been deemed worthy to receive this power within his soul, he has nothing left but wonder and silence, and tears all the time flowing like water; from that point on he ceases from all works.[147]

And while Eliot would never say, Isaac also describes what such explorations lead to:

Let this be for you a luminous sign of the serenity of your soul: when, as you examine yourself, you find yourself full of mercy for all humanity, and your heart is afflicted by pity for them, burning as though with fire, without making distinction of individuals,—when, by the continual presence of these things, the image of the Father in heaven becomes visible in you, then you can recognize the measure of your mode of life, not from your various labours, but from the transformations which your understanding receives. The body is then wont to swim in tears, as the intellect gazes at spiritual things, as these tears stream from the eyes as if from torrents, moistening the cheeks, involuntarily and without being forced.[148]

Like Isaac, I suspect there are many writers who feel that this level of common humanity is the level where all of us, writer or no, gaze on the Face of God, and where God seeks to become incarnate in each of us.

I suspect I "hate" to write in part because my subject matter pertains to the holy, and the encounter with my "most dangerous emotions" can be particularly painful. The energy secured from them is extremely dangerous. There is always that part of me that wants to write from my own illusory strength, and not from the knowledge that only through my brokenness and still-open wounds is God able to enter.

There is always part of me that secretly wants to say to God, "You may have redeemed the world, but in me you have met your match." Each time I write I am required to face this feeble rebellion, and surrender. Perhaps this ascesis of writing will one day lead to the knowledge which is neither affirmation nor refutation.

Another nonfiction writer in the August 25, 1985, "Talk of the Town" in the *New Yorker* touched on this theme from God's point of view.

> I can't *imagine* ever being able to write fiction . . . because for me the world is already filled to bursting with interconnections, interrelationships, consequences, and consequences of consequences . . . it all reminds me of an exquisite notion advanced long ago. . . . The Lurianic Cabalists were vexed by the question of how God could have created *anything* since he was already everywhere and hence there could have been no room anywhere for his creation. In order to approach this mystery, they conceived the notion of *tsimtsum*, which means a sort of holding in of breath. Luria suggested that at the moment of creation, God, in effect, breathed in—He absented Himself, or rather, he hid Himself—so as to make room for His creation . . . in a certain sense, the *tsimtsum* helps account for the distance we feel from God in this fallen world. Indeed, in one version, at the moment of creation, something went disastrously wrong, and the Fall was a fall for God as well as for man: God Himself is wounded; He can no longer put everything back together by Himself; He needs man. The process of salvation, of restitution—the *tikkun*, as Luria called it—is thus played out in the human sphere, becomes at last in part the work of men in this world. Hence, years and years later we get Kafka's remarkable and mysterious assertion that "the Messiah will come only when he is no longer needed; he will come only on the day after his arrival; he will come not on the last day but on the very last."[149]

The great Anglican theologian, Austin Farrer, recounts the same story:

> [A rabbi speaks:] Now I tell you that the question, why God permits this or that natural evil, is among the questions allowing of no way back, nor of any answer. And why? I will tell you this also. The Holy One (Blessed be He!) filled all immensity before the world was, and there was no place where He was not; and so neither was there any place where a world could be; for He was all, and in all. What did He do? He drew back the skirts of His glory, to make a little space where He was not; and there He created the world. And so, where the world is, there He is not. And that is why we look in vain for His hand

in the chances of nature. Nevertheless (Blessed be He!) He has visited us with His lovingkindness.

Farrer comments:

> Obviously it takes you nowhere, to speak of God's being present or absent, in any plain way, at one place or another. In one way, he is everywhere absent, for no place bodily contains Him. In another way, he is everywhere present; since whatever exists manifests His present will that it should exist; and as the Psalmist says, 'If I go down into hell, thou art there also.' For hell would not be, if God's will for its existence were withdrawn from it. . . .
>   . . . God gave the world room to be itself. He would not so inhabit it as to make it the passive reflection of His own ideas; or like the machine which does no more than embody the design of its constructor, and perform the wishes of its manipulator. God made the world, but He did not just make it; He made it make itself; for only so could it be itself. . . . Nevertheless (said the rabbi), the Holy One has visited us with His loving kindness . . .[150]

Farrer inserts this story in his essay on the Trinity, but the point is the same. God is willing to limit God, to "inhale"—whatever image seems appropriate. God is willing to become "empty", or rather, in this image, to make an "empty" place by dispersing a bit of the density of glory. God in this way as well as in the Incarnation becomes involved with creation.[151]

God's *kenosis* means that it is *God* who suffers. This is the parallel to "God Himself is wounded" of the Kabbalist. And God suffers in the Incarnation.

The statement "God suffers" may raise eyebrows. But as Fretheim has shown, the Hebrew Scriptures do not hesitate to know God as one who laughs and weeps, and to use all kinds of figures to convey this knowledge of their relatedness to God. Hosea even calls God "dry rot" to Israel (Hosea 5:12).

Ephrem, writing in a Syrian tradition still relatively untouched by Greek philosophical influence, understands this conveying of knowledge of God in metaphors with clarity (see Chapter VII).

However, by Isaac's time, the politics and problems surrounding the Council of Chalcedon, in which no one listens to anyone else (much less the mind of Christ), and in which saying the wrong thing can mean death or exile, dominate the entire Christian world.

The problem centers around the relationship of God and man in the Incarnation, that Jesus the Christ suffers, and yet that the Godhead is not subject to change. This controversy is still with us and is being discussed in theological debates over the problem of evil in the wake of the Holocaust and the bombing of Hiroshima and Nagasaki, and also in ecumenical dialogue.

I have no intention of trying to solve this somewhat recondite problem: I lean in the direction of being a spiritual semite.* While we need philosophy to help us discuss theology, at the same time there has been much heavy borrowing from stoicism, some forms of which are not compatible with Christianity and yet were introduced into it by Clement of Alexandria, to name one advocate.[152]

Just one of the problems associated with this kind of stoicism is the idea that rest in God, and God as God, is somehow static and unmoveable. Vann, in his otherwise very interesting discussion, falls into this language at the end of the chapter in which he tries to reconcile the idea of God weeping.[153]

However, I would like to suggest that the idea of *kenosis* has implicit in it the idea of "weeping". Human language is always inadequate to express knowledge of God, and this "weeping" is not weeping of irritation or emotion, which would indeed subject God to mutability. It is rather weeping that is mirrored in humans that is of a different kind, what we have called "weeping of apatheia" that is indeed part of *hesychia*, of that dynamic "resting" in God.

God's concern for the creation is unchangeable. God is love, of which the supreme form is compassion, and God has shown us the extent to which God will go to demonstrate this love to us.

Isaac has an extraordinary passage on this topic:

> Why did God the Word clothe himself in the body in order
> to bring back the world to his Father by means of gentleness and
> humble manners; and (why) was he stretched out on the Cross

---

*Toward the end of his life, Pope Paul VI stated, "We must all be spiritual semites."

for the sake of sinners, handing over (his) sacred body to suffering on behalf of the world?

I myself say that God did all this for no other reason, but only the love that he has, his aim being that, as a result of our greater love arising out of an awareness of this, we might be captured by his love [*or* captured into love of Him], when he provided the occasion of [this manifestation of] the kingdom of heaven's great potency—which consists in love—by means of the death of his Son.

Our Lord's death was not to deliver us from sins, or for any other reason, but solely in order that the world might perceive/become aware of the love God had for creation. Had all this astounding affair taken place solely for the purpose of the forgiveness of sins, it would have been sufficient to deliver/redeem (us) by some other means. For who would have made an objection if he had done what he did by means of an ordinary death? But he did not make his death at all ordinary—in order that you might realise the nature of this mystery. Rather, he tasted death in the cruel suffering of the cross. What was the need for outrage done to him and the spitting? That death would have been sufficient and in particular *his* death, without any of these other things which took place, would have sufficed for our salvation/redemption. What wisdom, filled with life, is God's![154]

In a time when the issues raised by Chalcedon were swirling about him, in the camp of those most adamantly insisting on God's impassibility, and in a culture where tears were considered a sign of weakness and mutability, it is astonishing that Isaac and other writers place such great stress on their importance. For me this confirms that they have perceived that there are tears separate from everyday tears of irritation or emotion.

From William James onward there has been an increasing insistence that emotions are physiologically based. This has taken some of the onus off emotions no one can do anything about. To repress them is self-destructive. However, it also confirms that there is a choice between attaching to or detaching from them, acknowledging them, but letting them go. Thus we can distinguish between tears that are emotional, and tears that somehow reflect the God into whose image we are being transformed, tears wept by the historical Jesus and the Christ who indwells.

But even more than this, I suspect that Isaac had a profound knowledge of God, a knowledge so deep as to risk this radical statement at a time when it was perilous to do so. Isaac saw that whatever the philosophical questions there is a truth that transcends them, and that the love of God as compassion is so immense that it would be more untrue and limiting of the revealed God to say that God does *not* weep.

Isaac is not alone. All through Christian history, writers have understood that in some mysterious way, because of God's willingness to limit God's power in *kenosis*, God needs the divinely created image, not only in the incarnation but also in Christ in us.

As tears are intimately related to, even synonymous with *kenosis*, *we find at the bottom of our tears that it is God who weeps and God who weeps with us.* Here is the exchange of love; here is the gathering of all our pain and all our joy.

These are the tears that wash Ezekiel the prophet; these are the tears of living water from the well of Jacob; these tears are the living water from the side of Christ, from the wound that incorporates all our wounds, and in which our lives are hidden and from which our new life comes.

It is God's tears we weep as God seeks humbly to become incarnate in us through the meeting and mingling of God's tears and ours.

And from this mingling of tears the will of God is born.

This may seem an astonishing statement, but if God is responsive to us, if God has limited God's own power in order that we should be free co-creators, then it cannot be otherwise. As Canon Vanstone has pointed out, God is as much at the bottom of the collapsed slag heap with the buried children as God was playing with them on it.[155]

It is God's tears we weep, and God's hidden, apophatic fire that is released on the earth when falling tears melt the stone of our hearts and ignite the oil of the Spirit, the oil of gladness, the fire lit upon the earth.

*Thus we cannot speak of the way of tears only, but rather the way of tears **and** fire.*

At this point of meeting in mutual *kenosis*, we *become God's power*, but *only insofar as we are willing to continue in willing powerlessness.*

We become God's power but only insofar as we are willing to resist the temptations of the wilderness, the temptation to grasp and dominate and rule. We become God's power but only insofar as we are willing to create unpredetermined possibility for others and for the creation, the infinite possibility of their becoming kenotic and thus free for this infinite possibility, part of the transfiguring process, and ultimately the *apokatastasis*, the final perfection of all things. In this meeting of mutual *kenosis*, in our becoming God's power is our vocation as co-creators.

These are only ideas, by the single handful. Lines, lines, and their infinite points! Hold hands and crack the whip, and yank the Absolute out of there and into the light, God pale and astounded, spraying a spiral of salts and earths, God footloose and flung. And cry down the line to his passing white ear, "Old Sir! Do you hold space from buckling by a finger in its hold? O Old! Where is your other hand?" His right hand is clenching, calm, round the exploding left hand of Holy the Firm.

How can people think that artists seek a name? A name, like a face, is something you have when you're not alone. There is no such thing as an artist: there is only the world, lit or unlit as the light allows. When the candle is burning, who looks at the wick? When the candle is out, who needs it? But the world without light is wasteland and chaos, and a life without sacrifice is abomination.

What can any artist set on fire but his world? What can any people bring to the altar but all it has ever owned in the thin towns or over the desolate plains? What can an artist use but materials, such as they are? What can he light but the short string of his gut and when that's burnt out, any muck ready to hand?

His face is flame like a seraph's, lighting the kingdom of God for the people to see; his life goes up in the works; his feet are waxen and salt. He is holy and he is firm, spanning all the long gap with the length of his love, in flawed imitation of Christ on the cross stretched both ways unbroken and thorned. So must the work be also, in touch with, in touch with, in touch with, spanning the gap from here to eternity, home.[156]

We become the power of God only as we are willing to remain powerless so that we may be poured-out-through, and as we are willing to absorb evil, to be handed over, to be crucified with God. Each solitude is a density of community as each of us is willing to become empty and willing for whatever emerges from the silence of meeting with God. It is not for us to determine how this is done. It is not for us to use the images of the past or to try to imitate the prayer or the gift of others—in part because we risk crowding out the gift God wishes to give and make of us.

Nonetheless, here is a contemporary account of one person's understanding of this exchange. It very nearly becomes a closed system, but it is almost impossible to express this most profound of mysteries:

> Imagine with me a solitary woman in a rundown New York apartment. She works enough to support herself, studies the world situation, watches the city from her window, and she prays—opening herself both to the love of God and to the pain of humanity. Such pain could be envisioned as horrendous, repressed anguish efficiently compressed by the wonders of technology into the explosive power of an H-Bomb. In being open to hold such pain, this woman's very soul becomes a battleground for the forces of good and evil, her heart becomes a crucible for the transformation of our unconscious collective agony. For she *is* conscious, willing to bear the burden of our fears and hates. Thus, her love purges and redeems the forces of evil. For one more day the bomb does not explode.[157]

It is easy to get romantic about such an image and picture our selves heroically absorbing and neutralizing all the sin of the world. It is easy to become pelagian. It is easy to forget that this is God's power we are talking about, and that it becomes available only as we are self-forgetful. It is easy to feel good about our selves and become smug about our calling to become God's power.

The reality is utterly different: the reality is a deep and imageless wounding and a blind trudging step by painful step through a sense of utter depression and despair, bearable only because one is haunted by something imperceptible which is, almost unbelievably, a foundation note of joy that is rarely perceived or felt.

Yet in this same moment Olivier Clément's words are also true:

> The man thus becomes prayer, offering the world on the altar of his heart. The condition of space-time which gives rise to the beating of the heart, is no longer an endless prison, but a temple walled with light. The man 'feels' (taking the apophatic

meaning of the 'feeling of God') the risen Christ, who is the face of the Father, in the light of the Spirit.[158]

To become part of God's offering there is no room for self-reflection, and even if reminded by someone else from time to time, there is little more than raising one's head in dumb wonder and thanksgiving before returning to the task.

There is a terrible danger here: as soon as we begin to realize what is happening, to be self-reflective, as soon as we begin to grasp at this power it is by our grasping turned to evil. As soon as we reflect that this power has come in to and is working through us, we already threaten to become luciferian, usurping mastery, a mastery that is by definition not kenotic, a mastery that dominates and twists and controls everything with which we come in contact in the name of all that is holy.

We begin to attempt to trap, maintain, possess, shore up the illusion of possessing the power of God; we become possessed by the terror of losing it. The power of God can be present only through the tears of acknowledged powerlessness and sin. As soon as we say we are righteous we are evil. This is not a doctrine of total depravity: we are created good, but when we use our free will to grasp power that belongs to God, that power becomes evil.

Many of us live under the illusion that if we are not for good or for evil we can exist in some moral limbo. The reality is that if we do not choose to be given for the purposes of God, then we are available to be used for the purposes of evil. To be unconscious is to leave oneself open to being manipulated; to be awake and weeping is to be in touch with reality and available to be poured-out-through by the love of God.

We come again and again to this precarious moment: the choice of willingness or wilfulness, of *kenosis* or self-aggrandizement; of service or dominance. The moment we waver this power ceases to be God's power and becomes our narrow enslaving fearful will turned on our selves. Listen to one who knows this wretchedness:

> "We exist for the glory of God," Charlene said in a flat, low monotone, as if she were sullenly repeating an alien catechism, learned by rote and extracted from her at gunpoint. "The purpose of our life is to glorify God."

"Well?" I asked.

There was a short silence. For a brief moment I thought she might cry—the one time in our work together. "I cannot do it. There's no room for *me* in that. That would be my death . . . I don't want to live for God. I will not. I want to live for me. My own sake!"[159]

Peck's solution, unfortunately, would pit one kind of willfulness against another. Here is a different point of view, not that we become God, but that we are lived by God.

> None of this by itself leads to God, and all of this, like any human endeavor, can be perverted into a mere ego trip. Yet it provides the necessary though elemental basis for what can follow: the arduous process of radical transformation or transfiguration in which we gradually uncover and surrender whatever prevents our being lived by God.[160]

The more we become the power of God the more we must know our need of God. To become part of God's infinite possibility is to live always within a question: what shall it be? Slavery or freedom? Prison or possibility? Death or life?

Becoming God's power in this mingling of *kenosis*, of tears becoming fire, is true priesthood. God's *kenosis* is a constant giving up of power, and God's *kenosis* is God's tears. This *kenosis* in us is a readiness always to engage but also always ready to disengage, so as not to limit possibility. This is how God's power must be expressed in our *kenosis*.

Although we are finite, God treats us as image and not as object, and thus infinite possibility becomes possible even in finite creation, although our *capacity* for the love of God remains finite. We are still creature. Our kenotic life is our life in the life of God and God's in us: this kenotic life is our life in the kenotic Trinity.

> The *kenosis* takes up again the movement of God who, in creating by withdrawing himself, leaves 'around him' a space of freedom, and then descends by the Cross into his own absence, so that everything may be filled with light, 'heaven, earth and even hell'. . . .
>
> For as Christ said to the Staretz Silouan: "Keep your mind

in hell and despair not." In the depths of hell the soul aspires to Mercy, and it is *there* that it finds itself to be loved. This is a permanent *metanoia:* the world ceases to be that of the 'me', which idolizes itself (and so at the same time hates itself) to become the world of God, the apparently upside-down world of the Beatitudes and of Communion. Then we understand that suffering, hell and death are spread abroad by means of the 'powers of darkness' in our hearts; but also that Christ is the Conqueror of hell and death, and that this risen life, light and freshness of Spirit, can increase in us from ever greater depths, according to the measure of our faith and our humility, to make of us beings of wonder, and sometimes of blessing.

And it is in watching, vigilance, *nepsis* (another definition of the monk is a 'neptic'). Man uncovers, beneath the social and moral expressions of evil, its satanic roots, and his own fundamental complicity. He discovers, deeper still, the incarnate and crucified Word, God descending by the folly of love into this absence of himself which I have become. Then in this encounter of Love with not-Love, the heart of stone splits, it begins to become a heart of flesh, and the grace of the Spirit flows in the man from the centre of this new heart.[161]

Who is the writer? God is the writer. We all have Eliot's task, even if what comes through us is written in our lives, not in words. We all have the task to write with our lives not to point to our selves, but to point with our selves beyond our selves in relationship: in becoming God's kenotic power, God's fiery tears; in relationship evoking God in each other to adore.

Love itself becomes the polarity in this exchange, and our tears are born of it.

The Second Phase of Weeping

The birth of the spiritual child of which Isaac speaks takes place in the dark. Tears come and finally merge into silence.

Grief and silence also belong together. Grief achieves a poise in the breadth of silence. The force of the passions is lost, and grief, purged of passion, appears all the more clearly as pure grief. The lamentation of grief is transformed into the lamen-

tation of silence. On the river of tears man travels back into silence.[162]

In weeping of whatever sort the second phase is a movement
into silence. There may be tears of laughter, violent sobbing, or
quiet drops slipping down the face, but at their end we all become
aware of a silence that is at once a desolation and an expectancy.

The silence of weeping is both rest and opportunity, attentive
stillness, true *hesychia*. In the silence of weeping God offers us possibility, the possibility of becoming fire.

But before we can become fire, we must learn of silence. Silence is the matrix of tears, and from silence tears issue. Isaac writes:

> What is the meditation of the solitary in his cell, if not
> weeping?[163]

> . . . which comes to him who has found truth in still-
> ness . . .[164]

> From works performed by compulsion in stillness there is
> born a fervour blazing beyond measure, which flames up in the
> heart as a result of glowing thoughts, which pop up in the mind.
> These labours and watchfulness refine the intellect by their fer-
> vour and give it sight. And this sight gives birth to the glowing
> thoughts just mentioned, by means of the depth of the soul's
> sight, which is called contemplation.

> Contemplation in turn gives birth to fervour; and from this
> fervour comes sight given by grace. Then the bursting out of
> tears is born, at first partial ones, that is to say, tears will burst
> out for someone many times in a single day. Then he will come
> to the state of tears without a break. As a result of the tears the
> soul receives peace of thought. From peace of thought the soul
> rises to serenity of the intellect; and with a serene intellect a per-
> son comes to the stage of seeing hidden things. For purity is
> stored up during the state of peace from warfare of passions.[165]

John the Solitary (5th c) describes five kinds of silence:

> Thus there is a silence of the tongue, there is a silence of the
> whole body, there is the silence of the soul, there is the silence
> of the mind, and there is the silence of the spirit. The silence of

the tongue is merely when it is not incited to evil speech; the silence of the entire body is when all its senses are unoccupied; the silence of the soul is when there are no ugly thoughts bursting forth within it; the silence of the mind is when it is not reflecting on any harmful knowledge or wisdom; the silence of the spirit is when the mind ceases even from stirrings caused by created spiritual beings and all its movements are stirred solely by Being, at the wondrous awe of the silence which surrounds Being.[166]

From a human point of view this is the moment, if we will but use it, to begin a new life. This is the moment when we are once more pure, empty sheets of vellum to be written on and illuminated with new words and new life. This is the moment when we can, if we are willing, receive the grace to begin to re-condition our old responses with the ones toward which we have been led and in which—no matter how much dread they may hold for us in their strangeness—we wish to grow.

It is perhaps the moment of most effort when we not only give thanks for our tears but also make a commitment to this emptying, this silence, this emerging into joy for life, this continual encounter and mingling of our tears with the tears and the joy of Being.

But there should be no illusion: there is effort, but it is effort not to effect these changes by our own power but by remaining in this silence so that the power of God can work in us. We engage with this moment of freedom but always with the attentive readiness to disengage and to wait.

We are at this point moving within the unknown, yet with an image of our selves-to-be that we have been given in some way, dimly held before us as we are slipping from the old skin into the new. But we must always be ready to let this image go, too, in another silence somewhere in the future, lest the new skin also become a trap.

Isaac gives us a summary:

> From stillness a man can gain possession of the three [causes of tears]: love of God, awestruck wonder at His mysteries, and humility of heart. Without these it is unthinkable that a man should be accounted worthy to taste of the wellspring of flaming compunction arising from the love of God. There is no passion

so fervent as the love of God. O Lord, deem me worthy to taste of this wellspring! Therefore, if a man does not have stillness, he will not be acquainted with even one of these, though he perform many virtuous deeds. He cannot know what the love of God is, nor spiritual knowledge, nor can he possess true humility of heart. He will not know these three virtues, or rather, these three glorious gifts. He will be astonished when he hears of certain men that they possess constant weeping, for he will suspect that they weep at will, or that they force themselves to this, and consequently he will think the thing incredible.[167]

Whatever is consciously occurring in the silence at the bottom of our tears, we need to understand that we travel through this passage not once but continually. Each moment we are beginning anew on the foundation of what has gone before. Because of this perpetual newness that penetrates more and more levels we cannot talk in terms of the geometry of progress, yet if an image is to be used perhaps a spiral is the best. But it is better if we can do without, lest we secretly feel we have begun to accomplish or achieve and thus grasp again the reins of control.

We need to understand that tears evidence a much greater dynamic. A few years ago I attempted a simple diagram of the movement through this passage that is repeated again and again throughout our lives, a spiraling toward potential of life greater than any double helix ever dreamed.

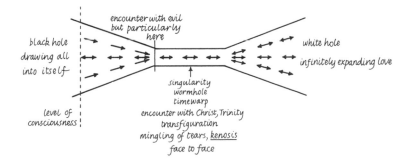

The analogy in this diagram is a shift in universes that takes place by moving down a black hole into ultimate density and emerging, or being thrust out of the singularity into a white hole. It is a distortion to try to show this in a two-dimensional diagram, but I am not attempting to talk about physics except by simple analogy. It is impossible to diagram the processes of *metanoia*.*

At the same time a diagram can be useful. In simplest terms we journey within, encounter God Face to face, and having encountered that Love are thrust outward by it.

On another level, we come to know our selves and struggle to give up the illusion of control and get past the anger of thwarted control and the fear of losing control. This is represented on the left side of the diagram. The single arrows are the movement inward; the double arrows are the movement of grace enabling us at every moment. There is a constant struggle with evil but most particularly immediately before wanting becomes willing and we enter the singularity. At least this is my experience much of the time. Others may come to this encounter in another place. We are all different.

There is still some correlation to the astronomical analogy. Although matter and antimatter are morally neutral, in a black hole matter is both created and destroyed with "unimaginable violence".[168] Before we come to the singularity where all laws break down, where we encounter absolute silence, there is in us tremendous warfare. The attraction of a black hole seems inexorable, yet some particles are emitted, and other gravitational forces tug at the stars being pulled toward it.

We are attracted to God, to the density of glory that radiates holiness. But other considerations tug at us, too, and as we travel through the repeating spiraled galaxy from one universe to another, we can encounter terrible conflict.

But tears help resolve them. At the end of all things, we are told in the Apocalypse, all tears shall cease (Rev. 7:17; 21:4). All tears pour into the river of the water of life that is the healing of the nations (Rev. 22:1). Tears cannot cease until the end of time because they are mingled with Christ's sacrifice that is offered until all is reconciled.

Tears are Eucharist.

In the singularity our weeping is transformed; we encounter our own *kenosis* and are filled with God's. We are freed from anger and fear and self-reflection and turned inside out so that the thrust

---

*Those familiar with *Blessed Simplicity* by Raimundo Panikkar may want to compare with the more complex "golden ass" diagram on p. 183.

of our lives is for the creation, and we become God's power, God's kenotic grace. We become "single":

> It is appropriate that it should be when the gaze of the human spirit is exclusively fixed upon God and when a single thought dominates the soul in prayer, that divine mercy should well forth from God. For we see that, when we offer the visible Sacrifice, it is when the mind is concentrated upon God in supplication and beseeching that the gift of the Spirit descends upon the bread and wine which we lay upon the altar.[169]

On yet another level we become by willingness dense with God's density; on the left side of the diagram we can choose the holy despair of letting go, sinking into the seemingly bottomless pit where the hand of God cradles us and we are changed. Or we can choose willfulness, the other kind of despair at the end of which is the ultimate act of control: suicide.

Olivier Clément puts it this way:

> What we must say to all those who are wounded by the 'terrorist' God is that basically what is asked of man is not virtue or merit, but a cry of trust and love from the depths of his hell; or who knows, a moment of anguish and startlement in the enclosed immanence of his happiness. *And never to fall into despair, but into God.*[170]

Perhaps another way to think of this is to fall through despair into the hand of God.

In the singularity where all laws break down we encounter transfiguration; we have fallen through despair into wonder and possibility; Christ comes to live in us and we in the blessed Trinity. We are carried through the singularity and poured out through the right-hand side of the diagram. There are many ways of looking at this image and many ways of understanding what this book can only intimate.

Quite simply it is another way of talking about death and resurrection.

As our tears are ignited we become willing for the gift to become a way.

Aeschylus' description in Chapter V is a way of describing willingness on the deepest level, where, in effect, we ask God to override our willfulness when we cannot; that by that "awful grace" and "against our will"—against our willfulness, our conscious and superficial will—we will be taught wisdom even "in our sleep", even in the sleep produced by tears; that is, the subordinating of what was written before, and the opportunity for something new to be written, which will supersede it. This necessarily happens out of our sight where our wounds become glorified, and our tears fiery joy.

But it is not, even in the singularity, a foregone conclusion that we will become willing. There is still the possibility that the silence will be too frightening, that possibility will seem too much like chaos, and that we will in our fear of losing control quickly try to fill up the silence with the noise of control, anger, and complaint; or, more subtly, new kinds of "methodology", or fascination with liturgy, or some other kind of devotionalism. We are always free to choose.

At the bottom of the silence of tears where all laws break down, God can work without our knowing even when we do try to evade the potency of the silence. This is the strait place we must pass before we come into the kingdom, into sacred time, into the things of the new world made available to us.

This is the control in order to lose control; this is the place where we are mysteriously made children of God and heirs with Christ.

What is happening? How can this be distinguished, described, this undescribable? Perhaps it can be likened to, perhaps it is, the indwelling with the Son in us; perhaps we not only dwell in the Trinity, but the Trinity in us. Perhaps this apophatic fire lit by tears is the Son and the Father gazing unveiled on one another, fire meeting fire, and thus we look on the Face of God and yet live.

Perhaps this is one of the meanings of resurrection: that Christ within us gazes on the Father; Christ our Wick, our fiery Core; this Gaze which is Spirit, and Spirit bursting into flame is this Gaze which is the incandescent wheel of the blessed Trinity.

> Held, held fast by love in the world like a moth in wax, your life a wick, your head on fire with prayer, held utterly, outside and in, you sleep alone, if you call that alone, you cry God.[171]

See God and die? We see God unveiled and live, and all creation ignites with us, and as daughters and sons we become in the density of our createdness redeemed a source of *theosis* radiating to and interpenetrating the whole.

We are moved into freedom and spaciousness; we are committed to moving with no boundaries, no security, no predictability, no strength but God's, no degree nor kind nor state nor experience into the ordinary now revealed salted with fiery tears, the pervasive distillation of divine life and unity, and presence of transcendence.[172]

We are released from geometry into circumincession; we are in exodus, the whole moving into possibility, leaving self-consciousness, leaving self-reflection, leaving all images, leaving all the garlics and onions and cucumbers that are involuting, and evoluting into desert, into promised land, which are somehow one in the burning of being-word-fire which we become.

The Way of Fire

The third phase of tears is the most subtle and the most difficult to describe. Isaac speaks of it as "rest", "revelation", "resurrection", "moderation of tears". It is obvious that this "rest" is a very active one.

Because it is Other-directed; because it is essentially non-self-reflective; because it is the imperceptible perception (explored in Chapter VIII), the third phase of tears is both kataphatic and apophatic at the same time and yet beyond both "ways": kataphatic in that the ordinary is the mode of relationship; and apophatic in that what is "seen" in the wondrousness is not "seen" in the sense of any categories either of "extraordinary" experience[173] or "altered states of consciousness".

This last term is very misleading as it uses static language, the language of "states" as if we proceeded from one level to another, instead of understanding consciousness as one, continuous, and many-faceted. This term has led to confusion with drug-induced experiences, which are indeed *altered* states of consciousness.

It is also apophatic because anything which smacks of "experience", while accurately perceived, has lost "significance". Even the gift of contemplation in its various forms is in some way a distraction.

We need to remind our selves again that people vary widely: for some, the way of tears will be much as Isaac describes; for others, totally unlike; for yet others, the way into tears will be more like a repetitive cycle, lifetimes within lifetimes. There is no one "right" description of this way, and the criteria for discernment, as we have already noted, are both subtle and flexible.

Furthermore, those who have entered this way deeply enough to realize there is no "way" except God's find it increasingly a waste of time to attempt to discern if tears are "holy" or not. In fact, these people when asked, "Who (or where) are you now?" will often reply, "I don't think that matters anymore."

This doesn't mean they are beyond self-examination, but such examination has become dispassionate, and functions more like the autonomic monitors in our bodies that determine how many beats our hearts make per minute.

It is important to distinguish between autonomic and automatic. An automatic response—I am not attempting to be medically accurate—is like a knee-jerk response: when you tap a certain place just below the knee, a healthy nervous system will cause the foot to jerk forward. There is little or nothing one can do consciously to effect this response, and it and other similar responses are constants by which a physician can determine health or disease without too much static from the mind.

An autonomic response, however, has to be a *response of readiness*. The autonomic nervous system governs not only heartbeat but such functions as breathing, the amount of adrenalin released into the bloodstream, and the amount of blood sent to each part of the body. These responses *can* be affected by the mind: one can easily learn to blanch one hand, or slow one's heartbeat, or cause certain kinds of brainwaves to be dominant.

Perhaps one characteristic of the third phase of tears is a similar readiness to respond. There is a readiness for possibility, a readiness both to engage and to disengage in order to prevent closing the system or taking control in a way that limits possibility. Perhaps this is one way of looking at that mysterious monastic word, *apatheia*.

Apatheia is one of the most commonly misunderstood words in our monastic inheritance. Many people see it and mentally record "apathy". The ancients saw a characteristic develop in sincere seekers that they felt was an important sign of growth into God, but they could not agree on its description. Some of this disagreement was possibly due to warring philosophical schools and political intrigues. But possibly, too, the ancients simply did not have the descriptive language which is available to us now, thanks to the expansion of human knowledge, particularly in human sciences.

Thus *apatheia* has been claimed to be this or that depending on what philosophical school predominated in the author's mind. Perhaps we are subject to similar fallacies, but perhaps it has taken this long to develop a descriptive conceptual language that can suggest a common vision which itself can be determined only from the distance afforded by the passage of time.

The Danish scholar Lars Thunberg has suggested that *apatheia*, *ekstasis*, and *kenosis* are in some way interconnected in Maximus the Confessor. But the idea of this relatedness is interesting on its own.[174]

We begin to understand each of these words by reflecting one off the other. For example, anyone who has lived under the vows of poverty, chastity and obedience for a time will say that they are in reality one vow. It is virtually impossible to say what characteristics are exclusive to one as opposed to another, or where one breaks off and another begins. Further, it is virtually impossible to talk about one without talking about the others.

There have been attempts to make analogies to life in the blessed Trinity, Father, Son, and Holy Spirit, and these attempts, while not to be taken literally (nor are the traditional name-images of the Trinity meant to be taken literally) can also be illuminative.

The temptation exists to do this with the triad that includes *apatheia*, but especially when approaching Son and Spirit, which is which? Surely the Son has the same *apatheia* as the Father and the Spirit, who is the Communicator. Or, which is more "like" *kenosis:* the Father who is willing to "absent" to make room for the creation; the Son who is handed over, or the Spirit who is self-effacing? One can reflect on these analogies for hours with great profit.

I would like to spend a moment looking at *apatheia* and *ekstasis* as I have begun to understand them, since I have already spent a good bit of time on *kenosis*.

I would like to characterize *apatheia* in Maximus' terms of ever-moving repose, which is another way of talking about readiness to respond willingly. If it is possible to associate *kenosis* with willingness for whatever, so perhaps *apatheia* can be associated with this word readiness.

Apatheia is a far cry from our modern word "apathy", and equally distant from the popular idea of passivity or "stoicism". It has often in the past been presented as "impassibility" in the sense of shutting out; I rather see it as a constant passage to greater immediacy and openness. (See Chapter VIII)

Ekstasis is also related to this readiness. It is not, in my understanding, the much-discussed "states", often catatonic, which have been written about out of all proportion to their importance, especially in the lives of saints and by those who would have their friends officially canonized. This is not the place to enter a discussion of the psychological problems with such concentration, but it should be clear from this book so far that to emphasize what seems extraordinary is to create illusions about power, and an atmosphere of unreality.

The sort of "state" summed up by Bernini's marble of Teresa in ecstasy is far from, if not entirely opposite to, what I suspect is meant by *ekstasis*. This may seem harsh, but it is difficult to counteract the popular conceptual distortion that has proceeded from this powerful visual symbol. It is possible that Bernini was, like so many artists, attempting to make a visual analogy to the ineffable—always a dangerous business.

Part of the problem is in the word itself. It really means to be taken out of one's self; yet it has come to mean a kind of self-absorbed grasping of a spiritual goodie. *Stasis* implies "static", which often to us has the nuance of inanimate, or fixed. The idea of a "sum of the qualities involved in a particular kind of existence or existence at a particular time and place" (Webster's New Collegiate) is not what many people think of when they think of someone in a "state" of contemplation, or in the "unitive state".

Indeed, many people seem to feel that a prayer "state" is somewhat synonymous with rigidity, or at least, that such a "state" is akin to immobility.

Kenosis is a word that implies unceasing outpouring or self-emptying and so is a good word off which to reflect *ekstasis*. Additionally, if we understand *apatheia* as related to readiness, we again introduce an idea of alert response. Thus we begin to see that perhaps *ekstasis*— which means to stand outside—is not a self-reflective state where one narcissistically enjoys "special favors" of God, but rather a dynamic readiness of outpouring response that is the opposite of narcissism.

The readiness of a self-emptying response is a far cry from "achieving a state", which often to us suggests both a win/lose situation, and that it is possible to acquire these states by our own efforts, which idea smacks suspiciously of technology or magic, but in any event, a closed system.

The way of fire is by its nature apophatic. It is a way of seeing; it is a way of living that is alert, unself-conscious, without illusion, all-embracing without being either defining or devouring. In practical terms it is a way of seeing without reflecting that one is seeing the hidden potential, hearing the hidden music, being fed by the hidden manna, all of which are both unseen and yet seen, both impossible in terms of being subject to empirical testing—subject to being made an object—and yet more "objective", more real than any empiricism.

The way of fire is a life in which discernment is implicit and continually operative, seeking the reality through the appearance and under the appearance, discerning one from the other; constantly alert for mistaking means for ends, and disordering of priorities. A person growing in this passage is aware of prayers that prevent prayer, such as insisting on more "rigor" in terms of set prayer in the Office, in order to escape from the silent encounter with the Face of God under which there is only nakedness.

A person in this phase will be quick to see when expediency is being masked as a good, and when a goal is uniformity instead of unity. Such a person will, without regard to his or her own risk, call attention to the fact that the emperor, far from sporting magnificent new clothes of magical and fantastic stuff, has no clothes on at all.

Apophatic fire breaks out everywhere, and in the white hole passage a person will not only perceive it but also become an agent for it, become part of it, and feed its flames. In possibility there is a fecundity, true fecundity that can grow only out of single-heartedness; fecundity whose seed, shell, is split by fire and becomes itself a flame, a sign of unseen conflagration. In the possibility that comes on the other side of tears we are made flame and become conflagration with the fire we see in each stone, each leaf, each person no matter who or where; we see the fire hidden in each, and each feeds ours.

It is the fire of sacramentality, but the fire in which we are both sacrifice and priest, giver and given, forgiver and forgiven. We are at once thrust into the fire and by the Fire thrust out.

> What is repentance? 'The desisting from former sins and suffering on account of them'. What sums up purity? 'A heart that feels compassion for every created being'. And what is perfection? 'Profound humility, which consists in the abandonment of everything visible and invisible'. Now the visible comprises everything to do with the senses, and the invisible means all thoughts on such subjects. On another occasion the same Old Man was asked, What is humility? 'The embracing of a voluntary mortification with respect to everything'. And what is a compassionate heart? 'The heart that is enflamed in this way embraces the entire creation—man, birds, animals, and even demons'. At the recollection of them, and at the sight of them, such a man's eyes fill with tears that arise from the great compassion which presses on his heart. The heart grows tender and cannot endure to hear or look upon any injury or even the smallest suffering inflicted upon anything in creation. For this reason such a man prays increasingly with tears even for irrational animals and for the enemies of truth and for all who harm it, that they may be guarded and be forgiven. The compassion, which pours out from his heart without measure, like God's, extends even to reptiles.[175]

In the way of tears we are in all three passages at once. We seek the realm of tears in order to be stripped of all that is not God, of all that keeps us in the shabby costumes we substitute for the clothing of the children of God. One must be removed before the other can be put on.

We live in the singularity, being at once stripped and focussed, bathed and burnt, and part of the fire streaming from its density into infinite expansion and possibility.

We live in a distilled and wide-awake ordinary, where bushes burn on every side, and a bag lady finds a pearl of great price in every dumpster.

Who then devised the torment? Love.
Love is the unfamiliar Name
Behind the hands that wove
The intolerable shirt of flame
Which human power cannot remove,
We only live, only suspire
Consumed by either fire or fire.[176]

We see the field of energy that is God's love, and God's fiery tears silently permeating all of creation; we know each moment the holiness and glory, the density bursting from every tree and every face; we see and do not see because we too are burning with these tears, tears that break open our hearts to release the oil of messianic anointing on the earth; tears that far from veiling us from the Father's gaze magnify it to salt everything with fire (Mk 8:49).

Tears and fire are one.

VII

Yours is the day, O God, yours also the night; you established the moon and the sun. You fixed all the boundaries of
the earth; you made both summer and winter. (Psalm 74:15–16
BCP)

When God decided to create the world, He first produced
a flame of a scintillating lamp. He blew spark against spark,
causing darkness and fire, and produced from the recesses of
the abyss a certain drop which He joined with the flame, and
from the two he created the world. . . ."[177]

In the system depending on mathematical concepts, which
is sometimes linked with images of light and rivers, the first *Sefirah* is nothingness, zero, and the second is the manifestation
of the primordial point, which at this stage has no size but con-
tains within it the possibility of measurement and expansion.
Since it is intermediate between nothingness and being it is
called . . . ('The beginning of being'). And since it is a central
point it expands into a circle in the third *Sefirah*, or it builds
around itself a 'palace' which is the third *Sefirah*. When this
point is represented as a source welling up from the depths of
nothingness, the third *Sefirah* becomes the river that flows out
from the source and divides into different streams . . . until all
its tributaries flow into "the great sea" of the last *Sefirah*. . . .
From the mystery of *Ein-Sof* a flame is kindled and inside the
flame a hidden well comes into being. . . . It is as if all the possible images were assembled together with this description.[178]

. . . and the fire and the rose are one.[179]

. . . The beautiful fire of spiritual tears. . . .[180]

. . . water is also viewed as the oven, and the Spirit appears in the guise of its fiery heat.[181]

Blessed, therefore, are the pure in heart for whom there is
no time when they do not revel in this delight of tears, and
through it constantly see our Lord.[182]

. . . and after a little chastisement they will receive great blessings, because God has tested them and found them worthy to be his. Like gold in a crucible he put them to the proof, and found them acceptable like an offering burnt whole upon the altar. In the moment of God's coming to them they will kindle into flame, like sparks that sweep through stubble . . . (Wisdom 3:5–7 NEB)

Was there pain before there was a world? Was the world brought forth in pain? Yes, I am sure of this, I am convinced that it is so. What knowledge can there be of this? As these words come on to the paper by way of what goes by the name of Pilgermann I note that theoretical science has worked its way back deductively to the very first moments of the universe and the bursting forth of everything from the time-space singularity which had contained it just before that moment. All of this is imprinted on the waves and particles of me, it is in the mystical black letters that rise above all flames. It is the Word that is at once the birth-scream and the death-cry of the cosmic animal that is God, the It that is both creator and created. How should there not be pain? One has only to listen to music run backwards to sense the reversing cycles of consummation and creation, the continual ordering and reordering of the disturbance of the manyness of its being.

It is not from the loss of Sophia, the loss of Christ and the loss of God as He that the pain comes, no. It is from the pain that God comes, that Christ with his lion-eyes comes, that Sophia in all her beauty, her splendour, and her passion comes. It is from the cosmic intolerable of the nothing-in-everything alternating with the everything-in-nothing that all things come. This great pain, this ur-pain, swims in its monstrous bulk in deeps far down, down, down below that agony of loss in which I grind my teeth remembering the golden bell of Sophia's nakedness and the sharpness of the knife of joy.

Knife of joy. At this thought almost do the waves and particles of me laugh. Perhaps this almost-laugh is seen somewhere as the shaking of a leaf in the evening wind, the shaking of a leaf seen in the light of a street lamp under a humpbacked moon in a modern place where the few trees speak to the dry stone. 'Knife of joy,' I said, and immediately there came to mind the knife of unjoy, the knife that drew the line for me. Now of course I know what I did not know then: I know that the pain waits in the joy as the dragonfly waits in the nymph. Almost I sense that joy, as the nymph to the dragonfly is a necessary stage in the development of the pain.[183]

The Fountain Is the Furnace

Tears are a mark of having touched reality, or having been touched by Reality, of integration and regeneration. They are a sign of the reunifying of the person, the healing of fragmentation. Tears are the body's participation in God's indwelling life in the person.

Tears are fire.

At the foundation of the world, so the rabbinical tradition tells us, God struck spark on spark, and took a certain drop from the abyss.

> In the beginning of creation, when God made the heaven and earth, the earth was without form and void, with darkness over the face of the abyss, and a mighty wind that swept over the surface of the waters. God said, 'Let there be light', and there was light; and God saw that the light was good. (Gen.1:1–4 NEB)

What is this "certain drop" from the abyss? I think it is God's first tear: I think it is the weeping of God's self-limiting, that self-absenting of God that not only made creation possible, but also necessitated the abyss. God weeps because of the abyss between God and creation, that the abyss must be a condition of creation. Only God, through continual self-outpouring—only God can cross it. And God does, in the *ekstasis* of God's love for the creation.

Perhaps this first tear is God's weeping over the ineluctable consequences of the perilous freedom God is giving to creation, and the knowledge that God will suffer within the ravaged weeping of time and mortality. Does God foresee the consequences God will suffer along with God's people—*all* God's people? There is a tradition that as the pillar-and-cloud led the people beyond the Red Sea that God wept, saying, "Do not rejoice that my people is set free, for my people are drowned in the sea."

Perhaps this first tear is the Child emerging into the agony of the world, and laid in a manger, the Child whose first gifts were the longing and suffering of the poor, and the longing and desolation of the rich. Only a Word, only a promise brought them there, and the tear of the abyss is God's first promise.

> . . . in His mercy [He] modified His might,
> descended and took up residence in Mary's womb
>
> Blessed is He who took up residence in the womb
> and built there a temple wherein to dwell
> a shrine in which to be,
> a garment in which He might shine out. [184]

In the primordial moment this tear and this spark were one, and the rabbis (as well as the physicists) know that the river of fire and tears pours into the creation and finally into the great and fundamental sea.

So is our God made human.

Ephrem saw it better than anyone:

> As the Daystar in the river
> the Bright One in the tomb,
> he shone forth on the mountain top
> and gave brightness too in the womb;
> he dazzled as he went up from the river,
> gave illumination at his ascension.
>
> The brightness which Moses put on
> was wrapped on him from without,
> whereas the river in which Christ was baptized
> put on Light from within,
> and so did Mary's body in which he resided,
> gleam from within.
>
> Just as Moses gleamed
> with the divine glory
> because he saw the splendour briefly,

how much more should the body wherein Christ resided gleam,
and the river where he was baptized?[185]

And Ephrem saw how this ecstatic outpouring has changed the
world and time, made it possible to look on this radiance, and to be
translucent with that same light:

> . . . and how a womb of flesh was able
> to carry flaming fire,
> and how a flame dwelt
> in a moist womb which did not get burnt up.
> Just as the bush on Horeb bore
> God in the flame,
> so did Mary bear
> Christ in her virginity. . . .
>
> Formerly there was none who dared
> to see God and still live,
> but today all who have seen Him
> are saved from second death. . . .[186]

Ephrem's unified vision sees the coinherence of the Creator and
created because of God's continual crossing of the abyss to enable
God's wondrous and ongoing gifts at whose appearing we tremble
with tears and joy:

> In your Bread is hidden a Spirit not to be eaten,
> in your Wine dwells a fire not to be drunk,
> Spirit in your Bread, Fire in your Wine,
> a wonder set apart, [yet] received by our lips!
>
> When the Lord came down to earth, to mortals,
> a new creation he created them, like to the Watchers.
> He mingled fire and spirit in them,
> to make them fire and spirit within.
>
> . . . New wonder! Our mighty Lord gives to bodily creatures
> Fire and Spirit as food and drink. . . .
>
> Fire came down on Elijah's sacrifice and ate it up;
> the Fire of love has become our living sacrifice.

Fire ate up the offering;
in your Offering, Lord, we have eaten Fire.

'Who has ever grasped the wind in his hands?'
Come and see, Solomon, what your father's Lord has done!
Fire and Spirit, against their nature,
he has mingled and poured into his disciples' hands.

See, Fire and Spirit in the womb that bore you!
See, Fire and Spirit in the river where you were baptized!
Fire and Spirit in our Baptism;
in the Bread and the Cup, Fire and Holy Spirit![187]

So too in the way of tears and fire are we invited to mirror our
God fully, to know that tears and fire are one. Caught by beauty
and knowledge-without-mediation, we are in equipoise, in ever-
moving repose: we are haunted by the knowledge and pain of sin
and the knowledge of the flawed beauty of creation, while at once
we see God in all God's terrible love and beauty, as we know and
are known. So are we stretched cruciform by and with our Lord on
the Tree of Life.

> If a man, who possesses within him the light of the Holy
> Spirit, is unable to bear its radiance, he falls prostrate on the
> ground and cries out in great fear and terror, as one who sees
> and experiences something beyond nature, above words or rea-
> son. He is then like a man whose entrails have been set on fire
> and, unable to bear the scorching flame, he is utterly devastated
> by it and deprived of all power to be in himself. But, through
> constant watering and cooling by tears, the flame of Divine de-
> sire in him burns all the brighter, producing yet more copious
> tears, and being washed by their flow he shines with ever-
> greater radiance. And, when the whole of him is aflame and he
> becomes as light, the words of John the Divine are fulfilled: 'God
> unites with gods and is known by them.'[188]

In this density of holiness we are raised out of time to that first
singularity, that first point of God's tear and God's spark, from
which primordial silence all expansion, all possibility are held in potent stillness as our tears mingle and ignite with that single, certain
drop from the abyss.

Christ's Body has newly been mingled with our bodies,
His Blood too has been poured out into our veins.
His voice is in our ears,
His brightness in our eyes.
In His compassion the whole of Him has been mingled with the
    whole of us.[189]

Tears are our bodies' participation in *theosis;* in these tears we
see the beginning of the transfiguration of all creation which will be
accomplished by Christ in and through us. Tears are the Refiner's
fire; tears are the sorrow caught in beauty and joy; tears are the mirroring of the Consuming Fire who weeps. Tears are fire, fire, tears;
and within this crucible we too know the *ekstasis* that knows only
God.

Body and soul together exalt You,
for they have been baptized in You
and have put You on.

O children of the baptismal font,
babes, who without spot, have put on Fire and Spirit,
preserve the glorious robe
that you have put on from the water.

Whosoever puts on the robe of glory
from the water and the Spirit,
will destroy with its burning
the thorny growth of his sins.[190]

Tears are the renewal of the baptismal covenant, the existential
knowledge of vows made, cleansing of the soiled robe, purifying of
sins.
    When we speak of tears and fire we are dealing with elementals:
our immersion in Christ who sets the river ablaze; the river that
pours into the vast sea of love; the river of fiery tears whose final
glory is the pillar of the Cross.

The Holy Spirit as 'fire' has two aspects: the fire is a sign
of acceptance of a sacrifice, and at the same time it also conse-
crates it.

[A story of early baptism:] The water itself is described as going up in flames; this goes back to an ancient tradition that the Jordan went up in flames at Christ's own baptism—in the case of Christ's own baptism it is of course Christ himself who effects this, not the Holy Spirit (though Jacob [of Serugh] speaks of 'The Spirit of Christ' going ahead and heating the water); in Christian baptism, however, it is the Holy Spirit who sets aflame the water. Thus in the long list of exorcisms common to the Maronite service and the Syrian Orthodox one attributed to Timothy we find: '. . . the Father rejoices, the Son exults, the Spirit hovers; the baptismal water is set aflame with fire and the Spirit. . . .'[191]

Compare these quotations with Isaac on the tears of prayer:

Perpetual tears during prayer are an indication of divine mercy of which the soul is worthy because of its repentance which has been accepted; and with tears it begins to enter the vale of serenity.[192]

When we engage the Word, when we read scripture, we are compelled by images and symbols that transpond something of the reality behind them to the well of tears within us where fire waits. We often read images too literally.

Here are some words:

Tears	Fire
water(s)	fire
fog	lightning
cloud	glory
garden	barren land
river	desert
drink	thirst
well	wilderness
tears	salt
spirit	Spirit
lake	wine
darkness	oil
night	day
dread	light

womb	blood
rain	waste places
wind	breath
sleep	awakening
death	resurrection
sigh	laugh
tomb	birth
waves	coals
sea	lamp
smoke	name
ashes	holocaust

I have not put these words in any particular opposition to each other. They are found mixed in different combinations in scripture but there nearly always seems to be an image of water with an image of fire.

In virtually every theophany we find these two elements, although they may be more obvious in one than another. But these polarities always seem to be held in tension for the irruption of fire-and-cloud that is glory.

Like all symbols, each can be and is used to reflect opposite aspects. Fire, for example, can mean punishment as well as bestowal of the Spirit. Yet even these fires must be seen as deliberate wrong meeting purity; the conflagration that arises when sin meets the ineluctable flame of Love, the judgment of Mercy. These fires always have smoke, which contain the moisture of tears.

The same word in different places can signify not only opposite effects, but also fire on one occasion and water on another.

Breath in one place can refer to the Spirit of God, and in another to a sigh that comes from tears. Often the use of these words reflects the desert or wilderness environment. Darkness brings dew and even fog from the Mediterranean, and to spend an evening in a silent garden after a sweltering day is one of the earth's most sublime delights. One can almost hear the plants coming awake after sheltering themselves from the heat, stretching, and exhaling oxygen and moisture.

Barren places conceal oases, and wells, fire.

The power of spring makes even the smallest plants in the valleys to bud, warming the earth as fire does a cauldron, so that it sends forth the treasures of the plants which God has laid in the earth's nature, to the joy of creation and to his glory. Likewise Grace makes manifest all the glory which God has hidden in the nature of the soul, showing the soul this glory and making it glad because of its own beauty.[193]

And always they meet, tears and fire. The glory of God is itself revealed as cloud and lightning. In baptism, there is the continual renewal of the primordial point and the primordial silence, in the pouring of fiery water and the outpouring of tears, which is release from the prison of our darkness, and birth into the dawn of endless possibility. Eucharist, growing out of baptism, and baptism's recapitulation, moves us through this singularity of forgiveness. Darkness and light, we are told, we know, are both alike because they are one.

He recast our image in baptism as in a furnace . . .

He made his own handiwork into a craftsman for his creation so that it should recast itself in the furnace of water and the heat of the Spirit. (Narsai)

He who is good saw his image made ugly by sin; he recast it in the furnace of the water . . . (Eastern Syrian Breviary)

(Christ speaks:) though I need nothing, I enter the furnace of the water. (Jacob of Serugh)[194]

The Luminous Eye

This way of approaching symbols and particularly symbols in scripture is *anagogical*. It does not exclude textual criticism against which it has often falsely been set, when in fact it is a complementary polarity. It has often been dismissed as a way of prayer-thought called "monastic" theology. This way of seeing, for the last hundred years or so, has lapsed into embarrassed silence, but now, thankfully, we have begun to realize that there is more to seeing than textual criticism reveals, and that the merely rational can distort as much as the merely intuitive.

The imagination of poets and philosophers is able to view an abstraction as concretely as a living being. The mythopoetic mind does not need to choose between a figure of speech and reality, especially when the object of its concern is the enigma of the cosmos and the ultimate meaning of life.[195]

The luminous eye is the eye of the heart, the eye of those who see with more than their eyes, and whose engagement with God, whose meeting with God in mutual self-emptying, mutual powerlessness, admits a light not present in those whose hearts sleep in stone.

The luminous eye sees through symbols and beyond them:

It is our metaphors that He put on—though He did not literally do so;
He then took them off—without actually doing so; when wearing them,
He was at the same time stripped of them.
He puts one on when it is beneficial, then strips it off in exchange for another;
the fact that He strips off and puts on all sorts of metaphors
tells us that the metaphor does not apply to His true Being:
because that Being is hidden, He has depicted it by means of what is visible.

. . . For this is the Good One, who could have forced us to please Him,
without any trouble to Himself; but instead He toiled by every means
so that we might act pleasingly to Him of our free will, that we might depict our beauty
with the colours that our own free will had gathered;
whereas, if He had adorned us, then we would have resembled
a portrait that someone else had painted, adorning it with His own colours.

. . . The Divine Being that in all things is exalted above all things in His love bent down from on high and acquired from us our own habits: He laboured by every means so as to turn all to Himself.[196]

In this poem Ephrem is making two basic points: since humanity cannot cross the ontological chasm and so approach God, God has to cross it in the opposite direction first; only thus can communication be established: God has to descend to humanity's lowly level, and address that humanity in its own terms and language. And secondly, the whole aim of this divine descent into human language is to draw humanity up to God.[197]

It is Wisdom at play who is the mediatrix of communication.

To attempt to write of these signs, this eye, this God who calls us forth with tears from our tombs into the Uncreated Light of Life is to wish for Isaiah's burning coal, to long to feel the fire of purification and the touch of the Word; to long to hear the words, "your guilt is taken away, your sin is forgiven."

In his paper "The Thrice-Holy Hymn in the Liturgy"[198] Dr Brock explores the sources of this universal eucharistic cry, and the symbol of the coal which is tears and fire made one, the primordial, burning, potent silence; the fiery coal of mercy, the holy manna, the medicine of life. Note that the angel cannot touch the coal: this is a privilege only human beings have:

> The seraph could not touch the coal of fire with his fingers,
> and the coal merely touched Isaiah's mouth:
> the seraph did not hold it, Isaiah did not consume it,
> but our Lord has allowed us to do both.[199]

Only in Ephrem's attitude of wondering humility can we approach the God who willingly comes to us in names and fire and flesh. We who are a little lower than the angels can be touched by God's fiery tears in a way impossible for them.

It is difficult to write of one theophany or another, and the impact of speaking of one at a time is different from that of allowing them to cluster, if one dares.

It is difficult to make statements; easier to begin by asking questions:

Are the waters of the flood God's tears? Is the fire and the cloud which reveal the glory—*is* the glory—God's tears igniting the mountain and the people? Do we like Gideon and Elijah pour tears on our offerings to ignite them, or is it God's weeping in us that ignites the pyres? Like Abram, do we offer our divided selves, naked impotence in the trembling dusk, sealed by the brazier and the torch that sear us with the dark fire of the divine Name? Do we lash the water, the fiery river of tears, with Elijah and Elisha? Do we know the chariot of flame that awaits us, and the mantle of our loss?

> When Moses signed and anointed
>   the sons of the Levite Aaron,
> fire consumed their bodies,
>   fire preserved their clothes.
> Blessed are you, my brothers,
>   for the fire of mercy has come down,
> utterly devouring your sins
>   purifying and sanctifying your bodies. [200]

> In fire is the symbol of the Spirit,
> it is a type of the Holy Spirit
> who is mixed in the baptismal water
> so that it may be for absolution,
> and in the bread
> that it may be an offering. [201]

Here are the fire of the Bush and the tears of Moses' dread; here are the tears that stream from our wounds into the river of fire and the river of life that gushes from the side of Christ, that flows from the holy city. Here is the undamming of tears locked within our clay and fear, made wine to be poured at the marriage of heaven and earth.

> But when the gift comes, it breaks on the soul suddenly like a flood leaping over all the dikes set up by sin. . . . [202]

> The silence of the earth seemed to merge into the silence of the heavens, the mystery of the earth came in contact with the mystery of the stars . . . Alyosha stood, gazed, and suddenly he threw himself down upon the earth.
> He did not know why he was embracing it. He could not have explained to himself why he longed so irresistibly to kiss it, to kiss it all, but he kissed it weeping, sobbing and drenching it with his tears, and vowed frenziedly to love it, to love it for ever and ever. 'Water the earth with the tears of your gladness and love those tears', it rang in his soul. What was he weeping over? Oh, he was weeping in his rapture even over those stars

which were shining for him from the abyss of space and 'he was not ashamed of that ecstasy'. It was as though the threads from all those innumerable worlds of God met all at once in his soul, and it was trembling all over as 'it came in contact with other worlds'. He wanted to forgive everyone and for everything, and to beg forgiveness—oh! not for himself, but for all men, for all and for everything, 'and others are begging for me', it echoed in his soul again. But with every moment he felt clearly and almost palpably that something firm and immovable, like the firmament itself, was entering his soul. A sort of idea was gaining an ascendancy over his mind—and that for the rest of his life, for ever and ever. He had fallen upon the earth a weak youth, but he rose from it a resolute fighter for the rest of his life, and he realized and felt it suddenly, at the very moment of his rapture. And never, never for the rest of his life could Alyosha forget that moment. 'Someone visited my soul at that hour!' he used to say afterwards with firm faith in his words. . . .

Three days later he left the monastery in accordance with the words of his late elder, who had bidden him 'sojourn in the world.'[203]

We arc to meet this fire that weeps, and the mercy of tears cools our burns and in cooling ignites them once again.[204]

Even as we think we see our life's blood leach from our wounds, our wounds become other Wounds, salted and healed, though recognizable still as wounds; preserved and hidden and burning.

I ran to all Your limbs, and from them I received every kind of gift. Through the side pierced with the sword I entered the garden fenced in by the sword. Let us enter in through that side which was pierced, since we were stripped naked by the counsel of the rib that was extracted. The fire that burnt in Adam, burnt him in that rib of his; for this reason the side of the Second Adam has been pierced, and from it comes forth a flow of water to quench the fire of the First Adam.[205]

The beginning of our prayer should be watchful and alert, and with suffering of heart we should let streams of tears pour down our cheeks. The whole of our service should be completed according to the will of God, so that it may be without spot and acceptable to him. Then the Lord will be pleased with us and take our offering; smelling the sweet scent of the pure whole-offering of our heart he will send the fire of his Spirit and consume our sacrificial offerings, raising up our mind with them in the flames to heaven, and we shall see the Lord, our delight, without perishing, as the stillness of his revelation falls upon us, and the hidden things of his knowledge are depicted in us. The spiritual joy settles in our heart, together with hidden mysteries which cannot readily be described in words for the simple. In this way we should make our bodies a living, holy and acceptable sacrifice that is pleasing to do in our rational service. [206]

There is not space in this book to write more fully of the healing of wounds, and their becoming part of the river from the side of Christ, save to note that this divine healing is not as we think of healing in an ordinary sense when the wound becomes imperceptible, or covered with heavy scar tissue.

Rather the divine healing of wounds preserves them *as wounds*, and the healing consists in these wounds being merged into Christ's wounds so that the healing that pours from his pours from ours as he increasingly dwells in us. He also enters by the way of these wounds, through which we have been emptied of our desperate efforts at self-sufficiency and illusions of power.

A book could be written about each of the symbols of tears and fire, but here we have room to discuss briefly only two before going on to look at tears as baptism. The first will be salt, the second, oil.

Salted with Fire

In his *Religious Symbolism of Salt*,[207] James Latham has discovered a surprising number of references, the most important of which, for the purposes of this discussion, are of the Word of God, table-fellowship and, therefore, covenant. Some of the other meanings are: permanence, immortality, wisdom, fidelity. It is sometimes an agent of exorcism.

Of particular interest is Latham's chapter on the parable of salt in Mark. He is concerned with the saying, "Everyone must be salted with fire" (Mark 9:49) and the end of the poem, "Have salt within you and live in peace with one another." (Mark 9:50)

The grammatical construction requires that the text be translated: 'Have salt in yourselves and *thus* live in peace with one another'. If this expression does not refer to the well-known 'salt of friendship,' then Mark misled his audience. They certainly must have had thoughts relevant to the 'covenant of salt.'[208]

He goes on to mention the relationship between salt and fire, both complementary and contrary, and also notes that water is a symbol both of death (the deluge) and life and that these symbols are used together in the Pauline understanding of baptism. Here we must insert the covenant of tears from Chapter V, because these tears perhaps fill in the missing link, the puzzle Latham is trying to solve.

He regards the saying that everyone shall be salted with fire as obscure, and notes that many commentators refuse to tackle the problem.[209] From his point of view the difficulty lies in the richness of the symbol.

> Indeed, symbolism so pervades the words 'Everyone shall be salted by fire' that the expression can be appreciated in its fulness only after reflecting with an open mind that is aware of the history of the salt and fire symbols.[210]

He comes closest, however, to the still-point of ignition at the bottom of tears when he concludes:

> It is a rule of life to pass through trial in order to arrive at the Good—*per aspera ad astra*. Communion with God is attained by the holocaust and the salted sacrifice, but especially by *dying to self* [italics mine]. . . . There are thus two poles, which belong to most sacred substances, the *pessimum* and *optimum*. A symbol can be dangerous as well as salvific; a notion corresponding to the double aspect of the sacred: fear and divine aid. This is particularly true of such dynamic vehicles as fire and salt, both of which produce change.[211]

In passing, it also should be noted that salt is itself a form of fire, oxidizing other substances with which it comes in contact, preserving them by burning them.

Latham relates salt to constancy:

> In this day of questioning and sincere doubt, what is more important for a catechumen, about to embark on the great religious decision of his life, than the need to remain faithful to that choice? Faith has been described as a 'leap into the dark,' and once that leap has been made, he who perseveres to the end will be saved. . . .[212]

There is an echo here in Ephrem:

> Glory be to Him on high, who mixed His salt in our minds. His heaven in our souls. His Body became Bread, to quicken our deadness.[213]

This brief summary hardly does justice to Latham's painstaking and thoughtful discussion, but it illuminates several of the ongoing themes of this book: the necessary holding of polarities in the heart; the relationship between *kenosis* and our place in the Body, and most of all the connection of the "covenant of salt" with the "covenant of tears". Some practicalities of the way of tears in terms of everyday life and interrelationships will be explored in Chapter IX.

The Meeting of Oil and Water

Another symbol that is rich in polarity is oil. It is both balm and fuel for fire. It is used for anointing catechumens, and the sick. It is a pledge of the resurrection from the dead. It is a priestly and messianic symbol, and is associated with a monarch assuming a throne. Its natural history illuminates its importance:

> One must have lived near the Mediterranean to feel the deep significance of oil. It is pressed with hard labour from the bitter, inedible olive fruit of a wild tree which has been drastically pruned. It is plunged into deep water to be purified, and when it rises to the surface clear and greenish-gold it becomes a staple food and fuel for light. It is not for nothing that kings are anointed with oil, for it is a symbol of spiritual transformation.[214]

Additionally, the water into which the olives are plunged is *salted* water, making oil's significance even richer.

In his *The Holy Spirit in Syrian Baptismal Tradition*, Sebastian Brock has made some interesting observations about the significance of oil.

> Olive oil is very closely associated with the Holy Spirit in Syriac literature, but this is because oil was considered as the ideal 'conductor' for the power of the Spirit, rather than as an actual symbol of the Spirit. As Ephrem puts it:

> This oil is the dear friend of the Holy Spirit, it serves him following him like a disciple. (H. Virg. 7.6.1–2)

> Thanks to the play on words available in Syriac, the olive oil (*meshha*) is much more commonly understood as a symbol of Christ (*Mshiha* 'the anointed'). As Ephrem puts it later on in the same poem:

> From whatever angle I look at the oil, Christ looks out at me from it. (H. Virg. 7.14.6)

> Characteristically the Syriac commentators prefer to see the myron [oil of anointing, no longer pure olive oil] as symbolizing Christ, rather than the Holy Spirit.[215]

Just as plain, natural olive oil disappeared as rites became more elaborate, so did a quality even more important. The conferring of royal priesthood on the baptized

> . . . is definitely charismatic in nature, and tends to be pushed into the background once baptism begins to become more formalized from the end of the 4th century onwards.[216]

The reason for this, he has already told us:

> For baptism proper it is Christ's own baptism, with its public proclamation of Sonship, that provided the dominant model from the beginning; here the emphasis at first was just on re-birth, and at this early stage there is little hint of the Pauline teaching of baptism as a death and resurrection. It was only

towards the end of the 4th century that the Pauline view of baptism begins to catch on in the Antiochene area.[217]

There is no question that today we are suffering from the loss of the early Syriac understanding of the significance of anointing with pure oil and the royal priesthood it bestows, just as we suffer from the loss of their understanding of virginity. It is interesting that as the rite became more formalized, the olive oil became "impure" or more complex in composition. It could be said that it was an expression of greater piety, but like much added-on ritual, more is lost than is gained.

It also is indicative that the more formal the rites became, the more out of touch the liturgists were with the naturally powerful— and therefore in some ways more appropriate—symbol of the pure olive oil as de Castelleja has so graphically described.

So out of touch are we with our own earth, so divorced has religion become from creation, so trivially does our secular culture regard the need for consecration in life, that these symbols are in danger of losing what little significance remains.

The Baptism of Tears

At first the idea of tears not only being a baptism in themselves but perhaps also in some way being the "real" baptism, or that the baptism of tears is in some way more "valuable", may be shocking. But Isaac the Syrian, John Climacus, and Symeon the New Theologian state categorically that the baptism of tears is the "authentic" baptism.

Isaac the Syrian says:

> Repentance is given to man as grace after grace, for repentance is a second regeneration by God. That of which we have received an earnest by baptism, we receive as a gift by means of repentance . . .[218]

John Climacus:

> The tears that come after baptism are greater than baptism itself, though it may seem rash to say so. Baptism washes off those evils that were previously within us, whereas the sins com-

mitted after baptism are washed away by tears. The baptism received by us as children we have all defiled, but we cleanse it anew with our tears. If God in His love for the human race had not given us tears, those being saved would be few indeed and hard to find.[219]

Symeon the New Theologian:

> In the first baptism water is the symbol of tears, and the oil of unction prefigures the interior unction of the Spirit, but the second baptism is no longer in figures of the truth, but truth itself.[220]

Isaac the Syrian and John Climacus are more or less contemporaries, although there is no evidence that they knew of each other's writings. All three writers devote an entire chapter to the subject of tears, insisting that tears are absolutely essential to growth into God. Isaac's published writing on tears is supplemented in the second book of his works, which has only recently been found by Sebastian Brock in the Bodleian Library, Oxford, and is currently being translated (see Appendix III).

John Climacus devotes Chapter 7 of the *Ladder* to tears, and Symeon Chapter 4 of *The Discourses*.

Other authors refer to tears as baptism. Gregory Nazianzen speaks of the "fifth baptism", and John Chrysostom says, "You can make your own baptism flow from yourself, and you will be purified."[221]

Why do these authors place such emphasis on tears, exalting the baptism of tears even above the sacrament itself? While in some traditions baptism is delayed until adulthood, or even until just before death, the norm has been infant or childhood baptism. Promises are made for the person being baptized. There has always been controversy, which continues today, over the best way to help a young adult become aware of the significance of these promises, and reaffirm them from his or her heart.

Contemporary knowledge points to one way tears link our bodies and our interior movements. Long before modern psychoanalysis, it was known that bringing the memory of sins to consciousness *and weeping over them* wrought a particularly efficacious cleansing. Even today, it has occasionally been noted that only when we have wept over certain sins or fears do they lose their power over us. One intriguing connexion may be that weeping not only excretes toxic proteins but also releases endorphins, pain-killing substances in the brain. While the relationship between tears and a certain psychological stillness may seem obvious, the long-term healing which often occurs has not yet been explored.

But let us return to the Fathers. Baptism is putting on Christ. Ephrem's writings refer to this putting on of Christ as a robe. We have already seen at least one of his poems in this genre. He is worth quoting again:

> John whitened the stains of sins with ordinary water, so that bodies might be rendered suitable for the robe of the Spirit that is given through Our Lord. Because the Spirit was with the Son, the Son came to John in order to receive baptism from him, so that He might mix with the visible water the Spirit who cannot be seen, so that those whose visible bodies perceive the wetness of the water might perceive in their minds the gift of the Spirit.

and

> Our body was Your clothing,
> Your Spirit was our robe.[222]

Sebastian Brock continues:

> Christ's baptism, and the sanctification of the Jordan waters, provide the occasion for the recovery of the lost robe of glory in Christian baptism. Already in St Paul we have clothing imagery of "putting on Christ" at baptism, and this is directly reflected in one of the hymns against Heresies (17:5).

> Body and soul together exalt You,
> for they have been baptized in You
> and have put You on.[223]

No room here for hatred of the body or creation!

At another point Dr Brock explores Ephrem's understanding of the value of the body, and its role:

> The Body gives thanks to you
> because You created it as an abode for Yourself,
> the soul worships You
> because you betrothed it at Your coming.[224]

And again, the relationship between the divinity as fire and the creation:

> Blessed are you, my brethren, for the Fire of Mercy has come down utterly devouring your sins and purifying and sanctifying your bodies.[225]

To summarize, there are two early traditions of the significance of the waters of baptism: one is Pauline, that is, that baptism is a passage through death and life. The other tradition regards water as womb, and sees baptism as the bestowal of new life, priesthood, and virginity.[226]

The baptismal robe is also seen as a wedding garment. Dr Brock comments on Ephrem's hymn on the parable of Matthew 22:1–14:

> . . . Ephrem, with deliberate paradox, identifies the wedding garment of the parable, not with the baptismal robe of glory (as his readers might have expected), but with the actual bodies of the wedding guests, which are to correspond to the radiance and glory of Christ's body, that is, the garment that the Heavenly Bridegroom Himself put on.[227]

Ephrem's doctrine of the bodies of the baptized being radiant with the light of the indwelling Christ is crucial, for those who are baptized into Christ are to be bearers of the Spirit.

Thus when we think of baptism as putting on the "mind" of Christ, we mean more than mere intellect. We mean quite literally that the light of Christ becomes physically indwelling, and that the "mind" of Christ becomes ours, that is, the kenotic mind.

Many authors have mentioned the light that seems to radiate from the bodies of those in whom Christ lives with particular intensity by reason of their having made room for him by their tears.

> These tears are poured onto the whole face while the mind is in stillness. The body receives from them as it were suste-

nance, and joy is diffused over the face. Whosoever has had experience of these two transformations will understand.[228]

But Isaac is perhaps hinting at something more than joy. Many
of the ancients speak of a physical radiance coming from those who
have been baptized by tears, who wear the "shirt of flame". Ephrem
says:

> If you wish to wash your face, wash it, flood it with tears
> so that it may shine with glory before God and his holy angels.
> A face bathed with tears has an undying beauty.[229]

But this phenomenon is not confined to a dim historical past.
It is well documented that the 19th century Russian saint, Seraphim
of Sarov, radiated this light, and in this century Malcolm Mugger-
idge writes of the mysterious light documented on film in Mother
Teresa's Home for the Dying in Calcutta.
Symeon the New Theologian also knew this light. He developed an elaborate theology and methodology of tears too complex
to explore in the present book, but his eloquence rarely has been
surpassed:

> All these things the divine fire of compunction effects with
> tears, or rather by means of them. Apart from tears, as we have
> said, not one of these things has ever come to pass, nor will come
> to pass either in our own case or that of others. No one will ever
> prove from the divine Scriptures that any person ever was
> cleansed without tears and constant compunction. No one ever
> became holy or received the Holy Spirit, or had the vision of
> God or experienced His dwelling within himself, or ever had
> Him dwelling in his heart, without previous repentance and
> compunction and constant tears ever flowing as from a fountain.
> Such tears flood and wash out the house of the soul; they mois-
> ten and refresh the soul that has been possessed and enflamed
> by the unapproachable fire.[230]

The radiance of the body is more than a sign of the indwelling
Christ. It is also a promise of the transfiguration of the entire creation which takes place through humanity, and in which redemptive
process each of us has a role and a responsibility.

However, it must be emphasized that this task is accomplished by *Christ's work within* us and that without that indwelling, without our willing powerlessness so that God's power may be at work and not our worldly power; without our being willing to be emptied in whatever way God deems necessary, and which emptying occurs out of our sight, our efforts are not only in vain but often contribute to great chaos and suffering.

In the West there is a lot of misunderstanding about *kenosis* that stems from having forgotten this indwelling, and in Eastern Christianity there has often been an external, too-literal, often individualistic self-abasing. This is not to denigrate the prophetic witness of the Holy Fool; I am speaking of the ordinary Christian vocation.

In the West the idea of self-emptying has tended more to be identified with personal holiness and *imitation* of Christ—imitation that insists on denigrating the gifts God has given to a person and abusing the body. This imitation too has often been entirely self-oriented, arising from a misunderstanding of what both the ascetical way and *kenosis* are all about.

Rightly understood, *kenosis*, willing powerlessness, arises from union with God and acknowledgment of the indwelling Christ *by virtue of baptism into the community* and this powerlessness has little to do with artificial acts of humility or giving away all of one's money.

It does not mean being a doormat, or abandoning either justice or mercy. Rather it has to do with the way we live our lives fully with a constantly listening and attentive ear—to God, each other, and our selves. The early Church knew this virtue as *nepsis* or vigilance, and while it is often used in a sense of constant self-examination for faults or tendencies to sin—and still must be, as we attempt to allow God to replace our greed for power, status, and security, with God's mercy—it must also be understood as a vigilance for God. A poem of Ephrem's earlier in this chapter refers to the Watchers, which is suggestive not so much of self-examination but waiting for the appearance of the Lord, the Bridegroom.[231]

Thus the baptism of tears signifies the interpenetration of the kingdom into the here and now.

> The same tension between the robe of glory put on 'now'
> at baptism, and its wearing at the eschatological banquet is to be

found in many other related contexts of Ephrem's thought: thus the Church herself represents both Paradise on earth and the eschatological Paradise (in Ephrem's thought Paradise and the Kingdom are more or less synonymous). Similarly, Christ Himself represents the Tree of Life, of whose fruits the baptized already partake in this life at the Eucharist. Eschatological Paradise, with the robe of glory and the Tree of Life, is thus potentially present already in historical time, but it will only be fully realized at the eschaton, outside historical time. For Ephrem the sacramental life, fully lived, is the anticipation of the eschatological Paradise here on earth: how far this eschatological Paradise can be realized and experienced by the Christian will depend on each individual's openness to the sense of wonder, and his or her possession of the luminous inner eye of faith.[232]

It is important to remember this task of ours and that the purpose of our *theosis* is not merely vertical but influences the development of the community in time even as time is lifted into eternity. The contemporary author, Annie Dillard, has this same vision as she looks out her window at the fields and the sea by Puget Sound.

> Christ is being baptized. The one who is Christ is there, and the one who is John, and the dim other people standing on cobbles or sitting on beach logs back from the bay. These are ordinary people—if I am one now, if those are ordinary sheep singing a song in the pasture.
> The two men are bare to the waist. The one walks him into the water, and holds him under. His hand is on his neck. Christ is coiled and white under the water, standing on stones.
> He lifts from the water. Water beads on his shoulders. I see the water in balls as heavy as planets, a billion beads of water as weighty as worlds, and he lifts them up on his back as he arises. He stands wet in the water. Each one bead is transparent, and each has a world, or the same world, light and alive and apparent inside the drip: it is all there ever could be, moving at once, past and future, and all the people. I can look into any sphere and see people stream past me, and cool my eyes with colors and the sight of the world in spectacle perishing ever, and ever renewed. I deepen into a drop and see all that time contains, all the faces and deeps of the worlds and all the earth's contents, every landscape and room, everything living or made or fashioned, all past

and future stars, and especially faces, faces like the cells of every-thing, faces pouring past me talking, and going, and gone. And I am gone.

For outside it is bright. The surface of things outside the drops has fused. Christ himself and the others, and the brown warm wind, and hair, sky, the beach, the shattered water—all this has fused. It is the one glare of holiness; it is unspeakable. There is no speech nor language; there is nothing, no one thing, nor motion, nor time. There is only this everything. There is only this, and its bright and multiple noise.[233]

Why is the baptism of tears important? Because it fulfills the pledge made for us, or that we made, fulfills it continually.

What is the pledge? To allow God to empty us of all that is not God, so that we can be God's power.

Baptism is not only water and fire and light. Baptism is a constant commitment to willing powerlessness, to willingness for whatever.

Baptism is taking all that we are and have that is good, all that we are and have that is not so good, and not only ours ourselves but all that is created, bringing it into silence.

The baptism of tears is the sign of our willingness to have God take these great and terrible gifts as our offering, and as our repentance, our letting them go, our willingness to be emptied. In the singularity where our tears mingle with God's, lives this primordial silence of possibility, is salvation, is breaking out into a spacious place from the prison of our closed systems, is transfiguration and joy.

It sounds wonderful. It is wonderful, but not in the way we imagine.

It is a commitment to living in unknowing.

It is a commitment to give all that we are—like casting one's self into space where there is no up or down or sideways; and no umbilical cord. We don't have to like this freefall. But if we are to fulfill this pledge, we must say yes again and again, with tears.

What is it like to live in this silence? Isaac gives us a hint:

Delight during prayer is different from vision during prayer. The latter is more excellent than the former, as a full grown adult man differs from a small boy. It may happen that verses will grow sweet in the mouth, and that one phrase of prayer is repeated countless times, without the feeling that this suffices and that it is time to leave it and pass on to the next.

Sometimes from prayer a certain contemplation [possibly: contemplative vision or *theoria*] is born, which actually cuts off prayer from the lips; and at the sight of this he becomes as a corpse without soul, in wonder. This we call vision during prayer: it is not an image or shape that can be depicted, as the foolish say. In this contemplation during prayer, too, there are degrees and differences of gifts. But up to this point there is still prayer. For thought has not yet passed into the state where there is no prayer, but a state superior to it. For the movements of the tongue and the heart during prayer are keys: what comes after them is the entry into the treasury. Here, then, all mouths and tongues will be silent, and the heart, the treasurer of the thoughts, the intellect, the governor of the senses, the bold mind, that swift bird, and all their means and powers; and petitions will cease: for the master of the house has come. . . .

As soon as the mind has crossed this boundary of pure prayer and proceeded inwards, it possesses neither prayer, nor emotions, nor tears, nor authority, nor freedom, nor petitions, nor desire, nor longing after any of those things which are hoped for in this world or in the world to come.

Therefore after pure prayer there is no longer prayer; all prayer's movements and forms by the authority of their free will, conduct the mind thus far: for this reason struggle is involved; but beyond this limit there is wonder and no prayer. From here onwards the mind has ceased from prayer; there is sight, but the mind does not actually pray.[234]

And it is to this silent, strange, and elusive life beyond the "boundary" that we now turn.

VIII

For with you is the well of life, and in your light we see light. (Psalm 36:9 BCP)

You speak in my heart and say, 'Seek my face.' Your face, Lord, will I seek. (Psalm 27:11 BCP)

Whom have I in heaven but you? and having you I desire nothing upon earth. (Psalm 23:25 BCP)

. . . for weeping lies beyond being subject to the passions. If tears are able to wipe away from the mind of the person who mourns and weeps but for a short time the recollection of the passions, what shall we say about him who is engaged in this particular activity day and night? Who knows the benefit which comes from weeping, save those who have given themselves to it? All the saints desire this entry; and by means of weeping, a door is opened before them to enter that place of consolations, in which the footsteps of God's love are impressed by means of revelations.[235]

[If . . . this belongs to the domain of prayer], I think that, if one were to come to an exact understanding, it would prove a blasphemy if anyone among created beings were able to say that spiritual prayer can be prayed at all. For all prayer that can be prayed lies on this side of the spiritual realm. And all that is spiritual is of a class that is free from movement and from prayer.[236]

. . . The Spirit, whenever it looks out over them, will find them in prayer; and from there it will conduct them by contemplation (*theoria*), which is interpreted by spiritual sight. They do not want prolonged prayer nor the defined order of much [liturgical] office. For the recollection of God alone will be sufficient for them, and all at once they will be led off as it were captivated by love. But they do not at all neglect standing during prayer, according honour to prayer by standing on their feet at fixed times, quite apart from their continual prayer.[237]

When someone has been deemed worthy to receive this power within his soul, he has nothing left but wonder and silence, and tears all the time flowing like water; from that point on he ceases from all works.[238]

Presence perceived in an epiphanic visitation, a theophany, or the invaded solitude of a prophetic vision was 'swift-lived,' yet the acceptance of the promise it carried transformed those who received and obeyed the command. Faded presence became a memory and a hope, but it burnt into an alloy of inward certitude, which was *emunah*, 'faith.' When God no longer overwhelmed the senses of perception and concealed himself behind the adversity of historical existence, those who accepted the promise were still aware of God's nearness in the very veil of his seeming absence. For them, the center of life was a *Deus absconditus atque praesens.*[239]

The Well of Nonexperience

What lies beyond the "boundary" that Isaac is tongue-tied to describe? Many have tried to describe it and failed. Many have alluded to it knowingly, and even more writers unknowingly, especially those who in their disgust with popular religion have turned from it.

In the end we find that even the way of tears and fire is not a way except in that it is a commitment not to have one. Yet it is still the way of tears because it is a commitment to willing powerlessness, to a continual letting go of favorite images and security systems, to continual change, adaptation and transformation.

It is a commitment to let God determine the way, the means, what will be sought, and what will be left behind; to sow us with what we can receive, and, out of sight, to bring to fruition those gifts we have received and committed to God to do with what God will. By this means does God salt the earth with fire.

While it has taken many pages to talk about the way that becomes a commitment not to have a way, in the end this knowledge can be quite simple and ordinary, so ordinary as to sound banal to those who might still seek sophisticated religion as opposed to simple waiting in willing powerlessness.

"When I am spiritually awake . . . I feel attuned, in touch. I am in some kind of alignment with a higher power. This feeling springs not from *doing* anything but from letting go; when I give up the compulsions and habits that frustrate the spirit, it grows, and I change." She told me what I had heard before: that transcendent moments, when something seems almost visibly at work in your life, are not the end but the beginning, signposts pointing toward the way it might be, farther down the road, given diligence and faith.

But what kind of diligence will lead to this sense of the spirit? Inner peace is not, after all, something one can go after like a diploma or a job promotion. The best way to frustrate the spirit is to tackle it like a duty or a project to be accomplished. The most spiritual souls I know simply wait for the spirit to guide them. The waiting, however, is an active state, quiet but alert. I know people who meditate and people who pray and people who work for good causes all in a special frame of mind, the active, generous waiting for the spirit to touch them.[240]

Some oriental religions speak of the significance of the return to seeming ordinariness after enlightenment; the Ox-Herding tale is a good example. However, this book is necessarily confined to a Christian orientation, and it is my impression that the Christian way—even when no longer a way—is distinct as lived, even though in the end there may be convergence.

It should be remembered that the "return" to seeming ordinariness is not a return at all; it is one aspect of a complex process of fusion that takes place in many modes simultaneously.

Dark Nights from Eckhart to Tillich

Experience generally called "affective", and some experience which ordinarily might not be included in this category—such as what is commonly understood as the "dark night"—is not in fact wholly real or true (Isaac might say "pure") experience of God. This sort of experience, while God may be present in it, and while it may have a kernel or undergirding of reality and truth, is always tinged with illusion and fantasy.

This is true no matter how lofty the experience, and no matter how much a gift of God. The "impurity" most certainly does not invalidate the experience: it is still a person's experience, whether or not it is "pure" or not, and as a gift of God it is a source of thanksgiving and adoration.

And, like tears, experience points beyond itself.

God is certainly in experience, but often experience is confused with God's presence. To put this another way, perhaps it is only when we do not experience God that we in fact know God. And it is important to distinguish between experience and knowledge.

In the same breath it has to be said that we must not discard the affective, kataphatic way. As I have tried to show, we must not discard *anything*.

Our food is drawn from the riches of scripture, tradition, and experience: there is no forced choice between kataphatic and apophatic. The well of nonexperience lies beyond definition.

While it cannot be defined, it can possibly be described, if only indirectly. It might be useful to look briefly at a few writers by way of distinguishing dark nights from nonexperience.

In *Christian Spirituality*,[241] Rowan Williams describes Eckhart's language problem:

> Eckhart's real problem was the lack of a vocabulary. Western Catholicism by 1300 was rapidly losing the means to express theologically the basic principle of its life, the ekstasis, emptying, displacement of self in response to the self-emptying love of God, the communion of God and humanity by the presence of each in the other. It was losing the sense of Christian experience as growth in direct encounter with God, growth, therefore, in obscurity, pain and struggle; there was less realization that the roots of theology lie in such experience and that Christian speculation is properly inseparable from engagement of a personal and demanding kind with the paradoxes of cross and resurrection.[242]

Williams goes on to describe what happened to Eckhart's problem when it was taken up by Luther:

> Here Luther is, in one respect, the child of his empirically minded philosophical precursors. Knowledge is a historically conditioned affair, it is not intuitive grasp of transcendental states of affairs. But to take this seriously means equally to reject the idea of privileged authoritative propositions delivered from religious illumination. It means to grasp that any speech about God is speech about an *absence:* the world we inhabit does not present God to us as simple fact. God is made known to us in the cross, in a man's death in abandonment. So for all human beings God is to be met in what 'contradicts' or opposes him, in sin, in hell, in pain and guilt at its most extreme. *Only* here, in

what negates and mocks all human conceptions of God can God be himself. *Paradoxically, the real and absolute transcendence of God can only be understood in circumstances and experiences where there are no signs of transcendence, no religious clues.* (Itals. mine.) It is, as Luther again insists in the 'proof' of thesis 20, useless to consider the transcendence of God, 'His glory and majesty', independently of the human encounter with him in the godlessness of the cross. Here, where all theological speculation, all conceptual neatness and controlledness fall away, God is simply God. It is an experiential and historically oriented restatement of the tradition of negative theology: God himself is the great 'negative theologian', who shatters all of our images by addressing us in the cross of Jesus. If we are looking for signs of God's authentic life, activity and presence, we shall find them only in their contradictories, in our own death and hell, as in Christ's. The *theologia crucis* concerns itself only with the visible, the worldly; but it grasps and values the worldly for what it truly is, the garment of God.[243]

Then Williams comes to the crux of the matter:

What Luther (and the classical Protestant world in general up to the present century) objects to is the perversion of the contemplative approach into a 'mysticism' which imprisons God again in a set of human experiences. Eckhart's insistence that no particular, special religious experience mediates God unambiguously, that there must be no seeking after 'inwardness or peace' for its own sake, is very close to Luther's thinking. And if Luther can be read in the light of Eckhart (and of Eckhart's disciples, Suso and Tauler, whom Luther studied extensively), it is clear that the reformer cannot simply be interpreted as an enemy to contemplative theology and practice: he is, rather, an uncompromising champion of the innate iconoclasm of contemplation.[244]

Williams recalls Staretz Silouan and Olivier Clément, whom we discussed in Chapter VI, when he speaks of Luther's idea of Christian experience:

Here is the underlying structure which makes experience *Christian* experience, the *daily felt polarity between rejection and ac-*

ceptance, distance and intimacy, guilt and grace, united with the sense of God's double working in the event of the cross, the double manifestation of wrath and mercy. To know forgiveness in the midst of hell because of the cross of Christ is the criterion of true Christian faith. 'Having entered into darkness and blackness I see nothing: I live by faith, hope, and love alone and I am weak, that is, I suffer, for when I am weak, then I am strong'.[245]

This theology implies knowledge of "*Anfechtung* (dereliction, *tenatio* in its strongest sense), since God 'can manifest his power only in weakness'. . . . acceptance of the hell of self-doubt, that opens the way to grace."[246]

This willing powerlessness, acceptable because Christ has consecrated even hell itself; this lived-out daily engagement of God leads to the conclusion, so different from much practice today, that

> Christ's cross is, from one point of view, the supreme demonstration that holiness is nothing to do with mere states of mind . . . Where a human being stands in relation to God cannot in any way be deduced from his or her subjective state, any more than it can from speculative thinking.[247]

This does not obviate the need for spiritual companionship, or disinterested self-discernment, but "the 'proof' is not internal testimony, but the whole life of the believer."[248] Luther's " 'experience' is being opposed not to faith but *to reason on the one hand and specialized 'mystical' experience on the other.*"[249]

This discernment is relevant for today when, on the one hand, we are surveying in bewilderment the collapse of the idea of objectivity, and, on the other, we are fascinated by the idea of the felt experience of God.

John of the Cross in the *Ascent of Mt Carmel* and the *Dark Night of the Soul* is very close to Luther's theology of the Cross, as Williams points out, and he is harsh not only with people who would "seek their own gratification in Christ", but also with those who misdirect them.[250] The passive night of the Spirit is God's work, and in it

> . . . *to experience* what God is doing in the soul *with any degree of directness* [itals. mine] involves an acute sense of rejection, humiliation and worthlessness, a sort of dissolution of the sense

of *self*, and this is evidently something harsher than the aridity and vacancy of the active night, however painful that may be.[251]

All of these writers lived in a time when religion was an integrated factor of life. But, as we have noted, with the coming of the shift of belief toward reason and objectivity, with the coming of industry and technology, religion and personal seeking of God began to be radically questioned.

There is thus a change of concentration from describing the activity of God in transforming the person, to a defense for the idea of God. The idea of indwelling seems to be lost in this changed focus. While the support of religion has been in some way stripped away by Eckhart, Luther, and John, it is still sacramentally integrated into their lives. In more modern theologians, sacramentality, along with a sense of stewardship for creation, becomes increasingly difficult to find.

"Modern" theology, however—and we are in a post-modern age—not only sought to fight for the idea of God but, in a desperate and perhaps tragic move, also sought to use the tools of science and reason to the exclusion of other kinds of knowledge, thus again reducing God to containment in human ideas. The move toward a more empirical approach was appropriate. The problem was that the pendulum swung too far.

Often these theologians denounce "mysticism", but is it a true idea of "mysticism"? Williams quotes Ruth Burrows, who ". . . warns us against supposing that what is in question is a dramatic interior 'mystical' thing":

> What is the essence of your grief, when all is said and done? Isn't it two things; a sense that you lack God, call it absence, call it abandonment, and at the same time a devastating awareness of your own wretchedness? Oh, I know, not in the least like what John of the Cross writes about, that is what you are hastening to tell me, nothing grandiose like that, just drab petty meanness and utter ungodliness. Yes, but that is what he is talking about.[252]

I would like to suggest that Tillich, for one, did not have this in mind when he denounced "mysticism", and as we shall see, despite his seemingly opposite—subject-object—approach to what we have been talking about in this book, he comes very close to pointing to what I shall call nonexperience.

One of the aspects of the shift that ostensibly occurs in modern theology is a turning toward "the world" with the charge that this concern is what the so-called monastic writers seem to lack. But we need to remind our selves again that monastic writers are also struggling with the demons of "the world" in the same way as everyone else, though they may not express themselves in secular language. They may seem to talk about it less, they may not be visibly involved in social issues, but the battle is the same.

As Louf has shown us, monasticism is as subject to worldly temptation as any other way of life. Thus the divorce between "mystical" theology on the one hand, and "modern" theology on the other is not as great as might seem.

Dismissals of "mysticism" are often red herrings. The "mystics" themselves would wholeheartedly agree with Tillich's criticism.

Samuel Terrien describes the experiential distinction:

> It has been maintained that the Hebraic spirit was not "mystical." The word "mysticism" usually describes the religious attitude which loses subject-object awareness, overcomes the differences between the human and the divine, negates the boundary between finiteness and infinity, claims to reach in trance or in ecstasy an awareness of identification with the Godhead, and fuses the proximate with the ultimate. As a consequence of such an attitude, the human self is absorbed into divinity. Defined along these lines, the word "mysticism" is not appropriate for describing Hebraic faith in general, or the inner life of the psalmists in particular.
>
> The insistence of Mosaic faith on making a radical distinction between God and man reflected a reaction against the fascination which the ancient Near Eastern cults exercised on Israel. The storytellers of the epic age and the great prophets during the monarchy waged an uncompromising polemic against practices which tended to promote a mystical union with the numinous forces of nature. . . .
>
> When some scholars speak of the mysticism of the prophets and of the psalmists, they refer not to the *unio mystica* reached in a sexual or sublimated form but to a sense of elusive communion with Yahweh. Communion does not lead to the fusion of divine

and human identities. Whenever the psalmists used poetic metaphors to evoke the immediacy of communion, they also referred, contextually, to its relativity. Even when they used a
vocabulary which was later appropriated by Jewish and Christian mystics, *they alluded, in effect, to spiritual longings which re-
mained unfulfilled.*[253]

Schleiermacher, the "father of modern theology", seems
acutely aware not only of Christianity's embattled position vis-à-vis
empiricism, but also of the dangers of emotionalism. Even more significant, while recognizing the need to come to terms with empiricism, he also insists on the non-empirical "feeling of absolute
dependence" which is at the heart of his theology. In his search for
balance he echoes Luther's probing for a Christianity that lies between reason on the one hand and specialized "mystical" experience
on the other.

In the century that followed, Schleiermacher's notion of the
"feeling of absolute dependence" as such fell into disrepute, although it turns up in other forms in Tillich and Bonhoeffer, to name
just two of Schleiermacher's theological children.[254]

But the irony is that hard science has proved him correct: there
is no such thing as absolute objectivity: the moment observation begins, the matrix and activity of what is being observed change.

One of the implications of this discovery is that the assumption
of a separation between finite, in the sense of created, subject-object
is called into question. It is impossible to make a final distinction
between them. And herein lies the difficulty underlying much of
20th century theology.

There seems to be a two-fold, almost contradictory thrust. Not
only did modern theologians attempt to become empirical and "scientific"; at the same time they insisted on "experience"—as if there
were an empiricism of experience. Thus while attempting to adopt
a somewhat cold-blooded approach to theology as a science, they
simultaneously attempted to approach religious experience in a similarly "objective" manner. Commonality or convergence might be a
more useful way of looking at religious experience. The possibility
of an empirical approach is illusory.

The Protestant theologians of the first three-quarters of the
20th century seem also to have developed a confusion between the

experience of religion and the experience of engagement with God, while insisting that religion and theology were separate entities. Additionally, they seemed to confuse experience with knowledge.

We know now that even though absolutist distinctions—either/or—simply do not correspond to reality, we can nonetheless still use the words "empirical" and "objective" because it is not their goal that is called into question, i.e., the desire to see without human perceptive distortion, but rather the assumption that this is in fact entirely possible.

We have to revise our understanding of what we mean by these words while retaining the intention: we must somehow attempt to be as objective as possible about our perceptions, while realizing we can never be entirely separate from what we are observing. This pertains to whatever field of endeavor in which we are engaged.

And it calls for humility before the facts. No longer can we declare that we can grasp any problem and solve it by technology. Slowly our fingers are being pried open from our grasp on knowledge and we are beginning to have to admit our powerlessness and limitation.

And if this is the case, how, then, can we speak of God, who cannot be understood as object without blaspheming; how can we speak of God in terms of being and non-being, in terms of existence and nonexistence? This does not negate intellectual endeavour; it does call into question whether we can regard intellectual endeavor, at least in theology, as being ultimately anything but symbolic. This may seem a truism, but our divisions show that we have acted on a different assumption.

And these questions give rise to other questions: if this God who has pulled aside the skirts of divine glory to make a place for creation; if this God who cannot be object is constantly self-emptying to bridge the abyss; if this God is more intimately present to us than the particles and forces holding together our material selves, how can we then speak of chaos and nonbeing?

This is not pantheism, we must remember; it is pan*en*theism, the love of a kenotic God sustaining and suffering with creation, whose tears burst forth from every creature in apophatic fire. God is neither subject nor object but—if we must use a grammatical analogy—Verb who became object for our sake.

Beyond the difficulties which, intended or not, Tillich's approach causes in a moral and cultural sphere, he builds on a subject-object dialectic. His "courage to be" seems not a willing powerlessness, but a very unwilling powerlessness, in the face of which one must have courage. He has called this "Stoic courage", but whether or not such courage can be called Christian is an open question.

Yet at the same time we have to ask, how much has he revealed of what he really felt? How much was he constrained by the need to be intellectually respectable? Writing in a time when religion and theology were laughed at on the one hand, and reacting to a Roman Catholic resurgence, often of a very counter-Reformation stripe, on the other, how pressured was he to find a strait way that betrayed neither academic philosophical integrity nor his own private belief?

We cannot know what that belief was, but a curious passage at the end of *The Courage to Be* allows us a glimpse, a glimpse of a vision not unlike that of Eckhart, Luther, and John of the Cross:

> Absolute faith, or the state of being grasped by the God beyond God, is not a state which appears beside other states of the mind. It never is something separated and definite, an event which could be isolated and described. *It is always a movement in, with, and under other states of mind* [itals. mine]. It is the situation on the boundary of man's possibilities. It *is* this boundary. Therefore it is both the courage of despair and the courage in and above every courage. It is not a place where one can live, it is without the safety of words and concepts, it is without a name, a church, a cult, a theology. But it is moving in the depth of them. It is the power of being, in which they participate and of which they are fragmentary expressions.
>
> One can become aware of it in the anxiety of fate and death when the traditional symbols, which enable men to stand the vicissitudes of fate and the horror of death have lost their power. When "providence" has become a superstition and "immortality" something imaginary, that which once was the power in these symbols can still be present and create the courage to be in spite of the experience of a chaotic world and a finite existence. The Stoic courage returns, but not as the faith in universal reason. It returns as the absolute faith which says Yes to being without seeing anything concrete which could conquer the non-being in fate and death.[255]

What Tillich is really saying here is a source of speculation, but it echoes much of what Bonhoeffer said about religionless Christianity, although Bonhoeffer was by both choice and circumstance committed to a greater exterior physical experiential reality, and in his language and thought eventually diverges from Tillich. Both are concerned that religion not be an abandonment of Christianity. Both are struggling against a "magical", closed system of slogans and fatalism, in which God is invoked when there is no other explanation.

Bonhoeffer particularly speaks of Christ who

> . . . is no longer an object of religion, but something quite different, really the Lord of the world. But what does that mean? What is the place of worship and prayer in a religionless situation? Does the secret discipline, or alternatively the difference . . . between penultimate and ultimate, take on a new importance here? . . .
>
> I often ask myself why a 'Christian instinct' often draws me more to the religionless people than to the religious, by which I don't in the least mean with any evangelizing intention, but, I might almost say, 'in brotherhood'. While I'm often reluctant to mention God by name to religious people—because that name somehow seems to me here not to ring true, and I feel myself to be slightly dishonest (it's particularly bad when others start to talk in religious jargon; I then dry up almost completely and feel awkward and uncomfortable)—to people with no religion I can on occasion mention him by name quite calmly and as a matter of course. Religious people speak of God when human knowledge (perhaps simply because they are too lazy to think) has come to an end, or when human resources fail—in fact it is always the *deus ex machina* that they bring on the scene, either for the apparent solution of insoluble problems, or as strength in human failure—always, that is to say, exploiting human weakness or human boundaries. Of necessity, that can go on only till people can by their own strength push these boundaries somewhat further out, so that God becomes superfluous as a *deus ex machina*. I've come to be doubtful of talking about any human boundaries (is even death, which people now hardly fear, and is sin, which they now hardly understand, still a genuine boundary today?). It always seems to me that we are trying anxiously in this

way to reserve some space for God; I should like to speak of God not on the boundaries but at the centre, not in weakness but in strength; and therefore not in death and guilt but in man's life and goodness. As to the boundaries, it seems to me better to be silent and leave the insoluble unsolved. Belief in the resurrection is *not* the 'solution' of the problem of death. God's 'beyond' is not the beyond of our cognitive faculties.[256]

The later Bonhoeffer was a critic of Tillich, although he did not live to read *The Courage to Be*. Bonhoeffer comes very close to the heart of the idea of God's *kenosis*, which at the same time does not exclude humans from taking responsibility:

> . . . the only way is that of Matt. 18:3, i.e., through repentance, through *ultimate* honesty. . . .
>
> So our coming of age leads us to a true recognition of our situation before God. God would have us know that we must live as men who manage our lives without him. The God who is with us is the God who forsakes us (Mark 15:34). The God who lets us live in the world without the working hypothesis of God is the God before whom we stand continually. Before God and with God we live without God. God lets himself be pushed out of the world on to the cross. He is weak and powerless in the world, and that is precisely the way, the only way, in which he is with us and helps us . . .
>
> Here is the decisive difference between Christianity and all religions. Man's religiosity makes him look in his distress to the power of God in the world: God is the *deus ex machina*. The Bible directs man to God's powerlessness and suffering; only the suffering God can help. To that extent we may say that the development towards the world's coming of age outlined above, which has done away with a false conception of God, opens up a way of seeing the God of the Bible, who wins power and space in the world by his weakness.[257]

Bonhoeffer follows this line of thinking to its only conclusion:

> To be a Christian does not mean to be religious in a particular way, to make something of oneself (a sinner, a penitent, or a saint) on the basis of some method or other, but to be a man— not a type of man, *but the man that Christ creates in us. It is not the*

*religious act that makes the Christian, but participation in the sufferings
of God in the secular life. That is metanoia: not in the first place thinking
about one's own needs, problems, sins, and fears, but allowing oneself to
be caught up into the way of Jesus Christ, into the messianic event. . . .*

But what does this life look like, this participation in the
powerlessness of God in the world?. . . . When we speak of God
in a 'non-religious' way, *we must speak of him in such a way that the
godlessness of the world is not in some way concealed, but rather revealed,
and thus exposed to an unexpected light.* The world that has come of
age is more godless, and perhaps for that very reason nearer to
God, than the world before its coming of age.[258]

Williams gives a helpful summing up:

The relation between 'worldly holiness' and the 'secret discipline' of faith in Bonhoeffer's prison writings is a clear echo of
Luther's understanding of the hiddenness of the springs of
Christian living; and the living before God as those who can live
'without God' which Bonhoeffer recommends is a characteris-
tically Luther-like paradox. Bonhoeffer is one of the great inter-
preters to this century of the meaning of *Anfechtung*. He found
himself in a lonely and trackless place of the spirit, oppressed
with conflict and ambiguity, and made of that place a response
to God, in trust and action.[259]

The point of this brief survey is to try to suggest that there are
common characteristics running through the thought and experience of these very different people, characteristics that bear a fam-
ilial resemblance. Families can have very divergent members: a
hyrax (rock badger or coney in the Bible) is about the size of a hare;
its nearest biological relative is an elephant.

Here are some criteria I have used for discerning convergence
in these theologians:

1) God is understood apart from religion and religious language.

2) God is in some way experienced. (There seems often to be
a confusion between experience and knowledge.)

3) God is in some way known.

4) God is object to be described and perceived, even when described as beyond word and thought, or as knowledge not reducible
to language.

5) God is the goal of unfulfilled longing.

6) There is "affliction" in the experience, in the gap between the longing and what is longed for.

7) There is a seeking after some "solution" to remedy this longing, to find "union", whether in "absorption" mysticism, or the mysticism of the created longing for the Creator inherent in the Judeo-Christian tradition. (It should be noticed that the distinction between the created self and self-image is often not clear in these writers.)

It is significant that such diverse characters as Isaac the Syrian and Tillich talk about a boundary, a boundary to be lived on, a boundary to be crossed. It is significant that all of these writers end in some kind of "darkness," whether they construe it as "passive purification" or "faith".

There is a sense that their experience is of God's absence, and that in this very absence is presence, a kind of experience. They all seem to struggle with the simultaneous inward-outward movement, as impossible to describe as the simultaneous position and speed of a particle (Heisenberg's principle).

Additionally, the later theologians seem to dissociate theology and prayer, which may be one source of confusion to the reader. If we reverse the usual approach and understand Isaac's words in the sense of theology, and Tillich's in a sense of prayer, we begin to see even more convergence. The divorce between theology and prayer, or engagement with God, has done most damage to those who at the same time have sought both the elusive presence and obedience in the context of human structures.

Kenneth Leech expresses their dilemma:

> This is why pure faith can often seem dangerously close to atheism, for faith rejects false piety. To enter the desert is to leave behind the false trappings of religion in so far as they keep us from facing reality. And that separation can be very painful, for the trappings will be associated with people, whose friendship and support we have come to value, but who, often without knowing it, are helping to preserve us in immaturity. . . .[260]

The Problem of Experience

There is the additional problem of what we mean by "experience". The meaning of the word has changed from having a nuance of testing or discerning what is presented, to a passive "being acted on", often without discernment.

St Paul knew the perils of reactions to experience:

> For the wound which is borne in God's way brings a change of heart too salutary to regret; but the hurt which is borne in the world's way brings death. (II Cor. 7:10 NEB)

This is an age when reflecting on one's experience of God in an affective way is very fashionable. On one level this is wonderful because for too many years we could not talk about spiritual experience at all. On another level it is not so good, because people often confuse their reflections with their experience of God; and their experience of God is mistaken for God. Even the language we use today is suspect: "centering" prayer, for example, cuts just a little too close to "self-centering", and too often has turned to narcissism, the very sort of navel-gazing which has given prayer a bad name.

This latter kind of experience is dangerously prevalent, and often is paired with the additional assumption that we can know what someone else is talking about when they describe religious experience.

This mistaken impression is heightened by the fact that often there is some kind of convergence. Isaac speaks of a particular phenomenon in prayer:

> So, when there is no prayer, can this ineffable gift be designated by the name of prayer? The reason, we say, is thus: it is at the time of prayer that this gift is granted to those who are worthy; and it takes its starting point from prayer, seeing that this glorious gift cannot be granted except at this time, according to the testimony of the Fathers. Therefore it is called by the name of prayer, because the intellect is conducted from prayer towards that blessed state, and because prayer is its starting-point and it does not occur on any other occasion, according to the testimony of Mar Evagrius and others. And we see also that

with many of the saints their histories say that *their intellect was snatched* while they were standing in prayer.[261]

I have referred to this elsewhere as "the divine embrace",[262] and other writers have other names for it. It is an extremely common experience that happens often very early in a person's exploration of prayer. It is every bit as wonderful as Isaac and others describe.

One knows it has occurred only in retrospect, but it is known by its fruits in one's life and relationships with others, and it cannot be grasped or induced or manipulated. It is one of the first experiences of what happens when we are willing to be willing, when we are completely at God's disposal. We cannot even want God or this particular experience, because that is the sure way *to prevent* this gift's being given. It is, as Ignatius of Loyola says, "without cause".

Nor is this experience confined to a context specifically labeled "prayer" or "religion":

> But occasionally, without being asked, time neither stops nor passes—it drops out of mind with such simplicity and secrecy that not until later do you understand the enormous gift you have received. . . .
> As I walk by my rather dishevelled garden in the country, I kneel to pull up a weed. I am called to lunch, and reply that I'll be there in a minute. The shadows begin to pour around my feet, and the earth grows cool under my hands. A voice rings out from the house: "It's suppertime!"[263]

The first step on this way that is not a way is to discard *all* images we might have about "the spiritual life", *particularly* images of those saints we admire and *most particularly* our images of our selves, or of what we think others are talking about in terms of spiritual experiences and goals. If we are not freed from these images we will invariably end in illusion, become trapped, or worse.

Additionally, there are very special problems attached to the writers who are popular today, and whose experience seekers covet.

John of the Cross is an example. His history is not as clearcut as might seem. It may be that his family had a Jewish background.[264] He was writing for a specialized interest group, which, like all special interest groups, had its own in-group language, heavily nuanced. Further, here was someone writing at the height of the

Inquisition about a sort of mysticism almost certainly influenced by both *devotio moderna* and Sufism, thus doubly suspect. In addition he was regarded with hostility by many in his order because he was a founder of the Reform.

Add to this popular legend. Most people think of the famous, "nada, nada, nada" when they hear St John's name, and have a mental image of what "nada" is. Few know of his interest in engineering and architecture, or that he taught his novices to learn to see God in nature and the created world, spending much time with them out of doors.

If this weren't enough, there is the problem that we cannot get inside someone else's head beyond a certain point. As Andrew Louth has written of Michael Polanyi:

> At the heart of Polanyi's insight here is his recognition of what one might call the mysteriousness of our engagement with the outside world. The kind of empiricism that often underpins the scientific or experimental method assumes that our perception of the external world is relatively straightforward and unproblematic: that we simply register impressions from the external world and organize them by a process of interpretation. Polanyi's point is that in much of our perception of the external world, what we perceive is often unspecifiable in detail. We recognize one another's faces, yet are quite unable to specify what it is that we are recognizing: but that does not, of course, cast doubt on our ability to recognize one another. In some mysterious manner the details we are aware of—the shape of the nose, the look of the eyes, the way a person carries himself, and so on—are fused by us into a form, a *Gestalt*, that is for us unique and instantly recognizable. If we attempt to attend to the detail we often miss the more elusive total impression that we discern but cannot explain.[265]

Louth points to other examples: the well-known mystery of the art of medical diagnosis. Or: "We select, organize and integrate what lies in our visual field. Two people see the same bird: one simply sees a bird, the other sees what sort of bird it is."

There is the additional problem of development. You cannot tell 20-year-olds what it feels like to be 40; you cannot expect them, even if they can have a grasp of what the older person is saying, even if they have read everything a 40-year-old has, to have had the intangible wealth of "experience of life" which has distilled this reading.

The same is true of the journey into God, with the difference that necessary experience and development is often entirely unrelated to age.

If knowledge in the external world is this complex, then it would seem that to insist upon rigid systematization of the way that is not a way is absurd, especially given the fact that each person is a unique creation of and therefore uniquely related to God.

This must immediately be qualified by saying that while a certain generic spirituality—Carmelite or Ignatian, for example—may be useful for people whose journey follows certain landmarks of that particular way, it is not the only way, it is not a universal way, and it is too often glibly assumed that the image we have of John's dark night of the soul is accurate, when, in fact, we may have only a glimmering, or even be entirely wrong, unwilling to let go the idol we have made.

> The process of intellectualization takes on a life of its own, and is mistaken for the experience itself: theology is trapped in circumlocution. When the experience is forgotten and negated in this way, the Truth is dead and what is talked about is a lifeless shadow.
>
> Theologies proliferate. The number of theologies equals the number of theologians, and every man is his own theologian. The mind splits, unable to come to rest; the mind is paralyzed before its own creations and cannot stop. The fission of the modern mind is characteristic of the religious and theological mind as of any other mind. The result is the proliferation of idols called concepts of God [or spiritual experience MR]—theology as thethanatology. In the hands of Christians, theological interpretation has become the means of suicide for Christianity: the evagination of the Gospel.
>
> For how many years did Thomas Merton exist this way in his monastic life, until he came in desperation to this unheard of truth: "The contemplative is . . . simply he who has risked his mind in the desert beyond language and beyond ideas . . . in order no longer to clench our mind in a cramp upon ourselves, as if thinking made us exist."[266]

Or as if reflecting on our spiritual experience made us "spiritual", or holiness, holy; as if our reading on tears were our weeping.

It seems equally absurd to insist on "progress", or stages. There is a sense of movement and change, a sense of transition, and often we think we can see psychological integration or regression occurring. But to insist on an absolute correlation between spiritual and psychological growth, to name just one area, or that we can "progress" along some absolute scale of holiness strikes me as being the height of arrogance, or, as Ephrem would say, blasphemy.

To be sure we need discernment; we need to be able to recognize such gifts as the evidently very common gift of God which Isaac describes as the mind's being "snatched" if only to be able to reassure one another. And we need to know at least what we are *not* talking about. But to assume, as so many of us do, that we know what is going on within another's mind, much less his or her soul is very dangerous indeed.

The Problem of Affective Language

Within the problem of "experience" lies that of religious language. Earlier in this book André Louf spoke of the danger of contamination between the way of the pharisee and the way of the publican, that describing Christian experience ". . . will constantly have recourse to the vocabulary of humanistic perfection, the only one available."

The writers cited above testify to the truth of this statement. Yet there is a paradox here: if it is necessary to let go our favorite images and securities, why do we use language that signifies the very appetites we must allow to be transformed? And, is this vocabulary of acquisitiveness, of spiritual hedonism, of perfectionism indeed the only one available? Few writers—with the possible exception of Eckhart—have attempted to avoid it; perhaps the problem rarely has been recognized.

Affective language has been used to describe relatedness with God almost exclusively, *even when describing those passages of the spiritual life for which its use is entirely inappropriate.*

Why is this a problem?

Affectivity in general might be said to be an awareness of another reality impinging on one's self, exteriorly or interiorly, with a pronounced or obscure sense of attempting to attach to it, either by analytical thinking, emotional merging, or a complex of affects. "Faith"—an assent to this reality beyond a rational level also seeks to attach. This sort of affectivity assumes that there is an *object*—and we are back into the subject-object dilemma. There is a definite self-reflective interest in the life of the subject in what is going on in the relation to the object, the significance to the self, even though this sense may be oblique.

While this sort of affectivity is entirely appropriate to certain passages of life in God, to cling to it, to be unwilling to give up "attachment to a satisfying image"* when one is invited to move on, or, to put this more bluntly, to insist on a safe and subtly-controlled and controlling idolatry is to give up one's freedom and once again to be subject to "law" and the consequent constricting tunnel-vision of a life of servitude to fear.

Earlier I suggested that perhaps one way of stating the goal of life in God is to be so found in God that self-reflection is no longer necessary. Here note the distinction between the created self and an image of self that is a result of self-reflection, a distorted mirror image of a mirror image. If affective language is by definition self-reflective, then the problem would seem self-evident.

At this point it might be useful to ask why such language is employed even when it is inappropriate to what the writer is trying to communicate. What are possible motives for using affective language?

1. *Affective language is the language of praise.*

Writers often write in a white heat of inspiration as they reflect on the goodness of God, especially as they try to communicate realms of knowledge beyond concept and speech. It is often also a language of thanksgiving.

2. *Poetic/affective language is essentially non-discursive.* The "things of the New World" are not accessible to empirical analysis.

3. *Many writers of spiritual theology are writing in a literary and/or philosophical tradition.* Thus the text and use of certain words may be heavily allusive.

4. *Affective language attempts to communicate "deep to deep".* In her

*c.f. Ann Dummett's *A Portrait of English Racism.* I am indebted to Rowan Williams' unpublished lectures on detachment for part of this discussion.

or his longing to communicate from one heart to another, a writer may plunge ahead at the risk of being misunderstood on a conceptual level.

Thus the reader may use what the writer says poetically as an excuse to "attach to a satisfying image" *even when what is being referred to is a reality that impinges on but refuses to attach to the "other end" of experience*, and thus what is being talked about by the writer in affective language is essentially non-self-reflective. Language militates against being able to communicate this sort of nonexperience.

5. *Affective language invites the reader to continue the journey in spite of pain and difficulty.*

Even at the risk of inciting the very sort of spiritual materialism that must be let go, and of encouraging the reader to mistake experience for knowledge, some writers feel it necessary to arouse the desire for God on the part of the reader, even if it hints of "reward", suggesting a similiar relationship/experience is possible. Perhaps the thought behind this is that the necessary struggle for interior unity will both make itself evident, and also expose the fallacy of attachment to images and the dangers of comparing one's self to and competing with others.

This is a most dangerous assumption, justified though it may be. It tempts us to precisely what we must avoid: to mistake appearance for reality; to apply technique and technology to wrest our divine likeness to our selves, not for love of God but for pride, for greed, and for satisfaction of our longing.

We become enslaved to our seemingly holy fantasies, leading us away from the density of glory into the insubstantial and shadowy world of the disincarnate.

There is a kind of exclusiveness that goes along with this mentality: in the interest of not "cheapening" Christianity, Bonhoeffer talks about a secret discipline, which comes very close to being mystique. John of the Cross claims that very few reach the passive purification of the spirit. And Tillich's description implies that few are willing to have the courage to be.

While there is a legitimate side to this attitude it can be misleading. It tends to imply that other experience, if it does not match, is somehow inauthentic.

No one can share the *exact* experience. But that does not mean that each person's own experience is not equally authentic. It is, after all, their own, personal, unique experience. It would seem, additionally, that generic experience such as presence-in-absence is much more common than has been thought in the past. It certainly appears in many more instances and under many more guises than much writing might lead us to believe. It is not some kind of secret teaching but a meeting of the *kenosis* of willingness and the *kenosis* of grace.

Perhaps John's idea that few people reach the passive night of purification refers to the relatively few numbers of people *in his experience* who were willing to give up the more pleasant, if illusory, "experiences" and images to which they were attached.

Yet we need every faculty at our disposal to become willing: we need every sense, interior and exterior, tuned and educated to the highest possible degree. We need all forms of prayer: verbal, silent, discursive, meditative, imaging, liturgical, as well as the understanding that there come times—perhaps even a long and unending time—when these are subsumed into Christ praying the whole of our life.

We need to have a reverence and humility for this Christ who is found in the most unexpected places, a willingness to learn from every source, no matter how unlikely. Bonhoeffer points to the numbers of non-religious people amongst whom it seems to be common. And today's popular press prints story after story of encounters with God by otherwise nonreligious people. Anne Barry continues:

> Despite this story, most of the time I now lead an ordinary life. I am no mystic or seer, and frankly I don't spend much time thinking about my spiritual nature. But every so often some event will take me by surprise—a death, or a loving gesture I don't expect, or a pigeon's wing turned iridescent in the sunlight, which blinds me with beauty—and then I run smack up against that part of me that shifts and grows and questions, and rarely speaks out when other people can hear. This is the self that talks to God, or tries to, or perhaps only stumbles toward a nameless Something Other—well, our culture has no simple word for what I mean. No matter how abstract this self might seem to be or how often I push it aside and try not to notice it, it matters more than all the rest. It glues me together. Its job is to make sense out of my life.

These days, there are a lot of people like me, fumbling along on an often only half-acknowledged spiritual quest. The shape of this spiritual life does not necessarily conform to specific doctrines and creeds offered by churches and temples. . . .[267]

While this is an incomplete description, there are elements of nonexperience in it. There is a shying away from what would define and close; a necessary poverty of ritual expression; a hesitancy about the entire endeavour, and yet a knowledge of having been set upon a way from which there is no turning aside.

If one basic problem is the subtle greed, achievement, and competition inherent in the language of spiritual theology, what model can we point to as a remedy?

Wilderness and Jubilee

There is a tradition in the Midrash that the only unconditional covenant God made was with the nomadic bedouin tribes. All other covenants are conditional.

It happened once that one said [mockingly]: 'Today there is a sacrifice for the sons of the water-drinkers!' And a heavenly voice came forth from the Holy of Holies and called out: 'He who received their offerings in the desert, He will also receive their offerings now.'

R. Nathan says: The covenant with Jonadab the son of Rechab was greater than the one made with David. For the covenant made with David was only conditional, as it is said, 'If thy children keep my covenant,' etc. (Ps. 123:12), and if not: 'Then will I visit their transgression with the rod' (Ps. 89:33). But the covenant with Jonadab the son of Rechab was made without any condition. For it is said: 'Therefore thus saith the Lord of hosts, the God of Israel: There shall not be cut off unto Jonadab the son of Rechab a man to stand before Me for ever' (Jer. 35:19).[268]

There is in the story of the people a note of longing—God's longing for them to know divine relationship in ways other than sacrifices of sheep and goats, the questionable security of cities, and the set rituals of the Temple. This yearning of God's is poignantly voiced by Hosea:

I am going to lure her
and lead her out into the wilderness
and speak to her heart.
There she will respond to me as she did when she was young,
as she did when she came out of the land of Egypt.[269]

There is a sense here of lovers: God's wooing of a completely vulnerable and newly awakened beloved, teaching her everything she needs to know to yield in relaxation, a single focus, and consummation.

The need to woo her to the wilderness implies that the beloved has become hardened in her maturity, her responses (and excuses) automatic, set; her magnificent structures giving the illusion of invulnerability, and the pomp of her ceremonies conveying tired tradition.

The journey, the love-making, the awakening, were never meant to end, especially not surrounded by walls of stone, and frozen images. These were meant as stages on the way, temporary concessions God made to weakness, concessions which have somehow become permanent.

The people were meant, beginning and end, to live in the complete trust that can exist only in the wilderness, guarded by the weight of glory in the continuum between the seeming polarities of fire and cloud. The jubilee years were established to reassert this dependence and the radical insecurity to which God had called them and to which God would return them.

This is not merely the cautionary tale of a modern state but rather the story of *each one of us* as we respond to God or not; as we understand the message to keep going, or refuse it. We are invited to have the willingness not to deny the mental processes and affective experiences that have led us to God, but to leave them behind and ever evolve toward a life in God that denies nothing but at the same time renders complexity into simplicity and vulnerability.

This is Abram's journey from Ur; Israel's into Egypt; the people's exodus; and the whole biblical history. This is the journey recapitulated in Christian life, especially in baptism and eucharist, as well as the infinite number of sacraments which are the theophanies of everyday life.

So Moses, who eagerly seeks to behold God, is now taught how he can behold Him: to follow God wherever he might lead is to behold God. . . .

. . . the true sight of God consists in this, that the one who looks up to God never ceases in that desire . . . the Divine is by its nature life-giving, yet the characteristic of the divine nature is to transcend all characteristics. Therefore he who thinks God is something to be known does not have life, because he has turned from true Being to what he considers by sense perception to have being. True being is true life. This Being is inaccessible to knowledge.[270]

Earlier in this chapter Dietrich Bonhoeffer mentioned the 18th chapter of Matthew in the context of repentance and "ultimate honesty".

At that time the disciples came to Jesus and asked, 'Who is the greatest in the kingdom of Heaven?' He called a child, set him in front of them, and said, 'I tell you this: unless you turn round and become like children, you will never enter the kingdom of Heaven. Let a man humble himself till he is like this child, and he will be the greatest in the kingdom of Heaven. Who receives one such child in my name receives me. But if a man is a cause of stumbling to one of these little ones who have faith in me, it would be better for him to have a millstone hung round his neck and be drowned in the depths of the sea. Alas for the world that such causes of stumbling arise! Come they must, but woe betide the man through whom they come.

'If your hand or your foot is your undoing, cut it off and fling it away; it is better for you to enter into life maimed or lame, than to keep two hands or two feet and be thrown into the eternal fire. If it is your eye that is your undoing, tear it out and fling it away; it is better to enter into life with one eye than to keep both eyes and be thrown into the fires of hell.

'Never despise one of these little ones; I tell you, they have their guardian angels in heaven, who look continually on the face of my heavenly Father.' (Mt. 18:1–10 NEB)

Bonhoeffer is not the only person for whom this is a key scriptural passage. In his biography, Archimandrite Sophrony says that it is the passage that gave him courage to pray, to know that God would not despise him in his then utterly secular state.

We have already looked at the child, and what the child's receptivity is; we have said that the only sin of which we must repent is turning from gazing on the Face of God.

God gives us this vision at the moment of our creation. As we become more and more willing, we become more and more aware of this vision until it is all we can see. And some who have become utterly willing seem to glimpse the Uncreated Light.

In letting go experience we come closer and closer to *knowing*, in the deepest, most intimate biblical sense of that verb, that we gaze on the Face of God. The "angel" is a euphemism for seeing God: we see God magnified through our tears. Sin is to look away; sin is to distract another. If we are looking on God through our tears it does not matter what we are doing or where we are. The sight of God impels us, pours God's love through us, and our tears light fires on the earth.

It is in nonexperience—and in what nonexperience becomes (but of which no one can speak)—that we receive this knowledge.

The Nonexperience of Nonexperience

Although nonexperience is by definition indescribable, I would like to attempt to point to a few characteristics of people who live in it.

It is not a dark night. There is no "sense", no "feeling", no "experience". Words like "presence" and "absence" and "affliction" are meaningless. Nonexperience is not Polanyi's "personal knowledge", although if someone has known it there are perhaps enough common landmarks in what follows that they will recognize what I am talking about and be comforted.

These people feel trapped by the surety others express, and are put off by group discussion of prayer. A lot of them cannot meditate and never have been able to, either in the discursive form or the still-prayer form, though they may at one time have practiced it and continue to go through the form of practicing it as they know they must for survival.

Others may have practiced meditation of some type and continue to, but feel they are in a vacuum. Most have an intimate (in the Hebraic sense) knowledge of God: they are known by, grasped by God.

What do we mean by the knowledge given in nonexperience? This word is used in different ways. Gregory of Nyssa says "Being is inaccessible to knowledge", meaning knowledge equivalent to conceptual knowledge. But I mean knowledge that is pre-conceptual. It is something other than what is commonly understood as "contemplation" in contemplation's many forms. Contemplation, too, is experience.

This knowledge is not "experience", not even of "absence", not even of the "hum" of the universe. And this knowledge cannot, unlike some kinds of contemplative knowledge, be "translated" into concept. It cannot be grasped even to that extent.

The only analogy that comes to mind is to liken this knowledge to the experiments that take place under the mountains in Switzerland at CERN. Here subatomic particles are smashed together, and the results of their collisions leave "tracks" that can be sensed and partially displayed by computer graphics.

Perhaps we could say that this knowledge, too, leaves "tracks" but tracks that are so oblique that the description even of them is impossible. Here we move into a lived-out apophatic, because people with this knowledge are also hesitant about saying it is there or not: indeed, it is not "there": it is part of being. Or perhaps Being indwelling.

The non-experience that surrounds this knowledge is equally oblique, yet it renders what is commonly referred to as "experience" in spiritual theology, something to be regarded with impatience. At the same time their appreciation of sense-experience increases.

People who have been moved into nonexperience—which is not a "higher" or "lower" state—are often initially troubled because no one seems ever to have heard of—or perhaps dares to say—that he or she, too, has no "experience" of God, at least not the sort one reads about in articles, or hears about in shared prayer sessions.

The people who may live in nonexperience are not people who have necessarily concentrated on an apophatic way or any other way. They may regard themselves as agnostics or even atheists. They are perhaps Thomas Christians in the best sense.

I have a great regard for the Apostle Thomas. Long maligned as "the doubter" he is in fact one of the most singlehearted of the believers in the group of disciples. He is determined to keep the integrity of Jesus' message.

When Jesus speaks of his own and not Lazarus' death, Thomas alone instantly understands and is ready to die with him. At the Last Supper when he asks about the "way", Thomas wants to follow his master's way and no other. He wants to make sure he has understood the truth as Jesus meant it, not as he, Thomas, might want it to be.

As for his doubt of the resurrection—well, after being so long with those thick, bumbling, contentious companions, he had every right to be skeptical of their report of the final outcome of the hideous days in Jerusalem. He wanted only the one Way, not something his friends had concocted.

When he saw the risen Jesus, it wasn't necessary to fulfill the invitation to put his hand in the Lord's side. The mysterious way was made plain, and Thomas threw himself into it. Thomas is a lesson in stubborn loyalty, not to a peer group's pressure, but to the truth of the Lord he served.

It is the peer group's pressure that is perhaps most discouraging to these people who live in nonexperience, the pressure to "believe", to be locked into a system that more and more seems like a prison; whose devotion and theology seem like idols. But devotion and theology are important, and the people who perhaps will recognize nonexperience still immerse themselves in good liturgy, while being increasingly put off by bad. Devotionalism, or any -ism can make their flesh crawl.

In fact, they don't really like talking about "God", or religion, or "spirituality". Most books seem insipid. Scripture, however, is almost unbearable. Often it seems to penetrate to the point of physical pain, although these people take little notice of how they feel without, however, abusing the creation or depriving themselves, out of a false sense of "asceticism", of the tools they need to help them grow into God.

They are confused when people talk about "progress" or "higher" or "lower" or "states", ways that are "right" or "wrong" or especially that "work".

They feel a bit—when they bother to notice, which isn't often, and never more than a fleeting glance—like something pulled inside out—a sleeve, for example; or something that was once concave that is now convex, one side being constantly pulled through to the other. This "feeling" is not really a feeling: it is too other-oriented.

This "feeling" is rather like background radiation, everywhere penetrating everything. It is an organpoint—or nonorganpoint, since it is not really noticed—to the ordinary joys and sorrows of life, what such a person might have once called "affective". These joys and sorrows continue and become even more acute because they are everywhere interpenetrated by . . . by: by what it is impossible for such a person to say. Such events once might have been significant in what they once would have called "spiritual life" but are no longer.

They are significant as life events, but life's significance is now focussed elsewhere, and interest is continually drawn toward this nonexistent point which is everywhere. They are exposed, and feel no compulsion to protect themselves or control those about them.

The affective perception of God has ceased.

These people seem more alive in every faculty than the general population, but this aliveness is focussed away from itself.

Thus someone in this passage might say, "I have no spiritual life, as that is commonly understood. It is dead. Thanks be to God."

The transition into this passage can be extremely painful and difficult, especially if the affective life has been rich. The transition resembles the "dark nights" discussed earlier in this chapter and can last for a long time. Sometimes, though, it happens relatively quickly. Sometimes it can hardly be perceived. To move from the transition to the passage can be very confusing; few people have been willing to recognize it.

In the transition, "experience" of God is cut off or gradually disappears. The temptation comes to lose willingness, to abandon the no-where one is not being led, and either to distract one's self with outer experience, or to wish for a return to an affective spirituality which is not only repugnant but also no longer possible.

As Williams has put it, the temptation is to stay with the light coming through the prism in all its many colours, no matter how dark and painful, shunning the unknown where the light behind the prism is shining, even if it is no longer light or experience.

As the nonexperience of nonexperience becomes more dominant the nature of the pain associated with its transition changes, and even the willingness to be done to by God somehow seems to

come from the "direction"—except that there is no direction—
toward which one is being drawn. While some might call this pain
"spiritual suffering", no one who is in this passage would name it
thus.

It has to be emphasized again: this is *not* darkness or aridity or
even, in ordinary terms, pain. These named are all experiences, and
while it is impossible to say that those who are alive do not experience, in this passage there is virtually no self-reflection in terms of
reflecting on experience in a valuative way. What "light" there is is
so pre-conceptual that it cannot be sought after or grasped, and is
so obscure that one would not know how or what to seek or desire.

Complete self-forgetfulness is not possible in this life, nor is the
nonexperience of nonexperience a "state". But there is an increasing
shift from interest in the processes concerning the self to a kind of
detached observation when absolutely necessary. But even this
takes on a different character: there is no longer any measurement
or achievement or failure, nor is there affective reaction to what is
found. Compunction itself has taken on a different character.

Coinhered with this nonexperience, "ordinary" life continues,
though at the same time life is no longer "ordinary" or "extraordinary" but has taken on an entirely different and itself indescribable
character. Occasionally there may be a time of "experience", as, by
analogy, time becomes "stretched" for a highly skilled athlete for
whom a split second becomes an increasingly attenuated, even lei-
surely, moment for decision. Time changes. The effects of nonexperience on experience have no affective character: there is nothing
to which to attach.

Additionally, what Gerald May has called "unitive experience"
disappears. It may be that this sort of experience is sublimated into
something else, or goes unnoticed, although the people in this passage are very wide-awake. They share with Nicholas of Cusa and
others the ancient knowledge that "God is a circle whose circumference is nowhere and whose centre is everywhere."

Beauty becomes more beautiful; sorrow more sorrowful. The
incarnation, compassion and interrelatedness, the glory of creation
and its intense shimmering with the love of God are more and more
ineffable. Such people are increasingly aware of the Heart of Fire
that animates creation. Perception of what is "real" changes.

In this changing perception of reality much of what formerly seemed clearly "good" or "evil" no longer seems so. This is not to say that there is no sense of evil, or that it is subsumed into Buddhist "ignorance". Their sense of evil becomes much more acute, if less easily defined.

But some aspects of life that might previously have been named evil are increasingly seen otherwise, perhaps as chaos struggling for order. What may formerly have seemed chaos no longer does. Dualism is seen increasingly as continuum.

These people cannot say, for example, where affectivity merges with nonexperience, any more than one can determine the precise moment when evening comes, or the night, or night fades into dawn, or dawn into day. Paradox becomes a cause for rejoicing, and even a way of worship.

Attitudes toward asceticism change. On one level asceticism becomes a tool of personal survival in the face of new knowledge of a reality which more and more forces choice between asceticism— in the sense of maintaining willingness, however that is appropriate—and anaesthesia. The one leads to ongoing death of self-image; the other leads to mortal death.

This has been the choice all along, but in this way of life "doing" takes on less importance. Asceticism ceases being a voluntary game of external forms which one hopes will help to give an internal focus: instead the interior response of willingness that now is willed by God dictates what the outer life must be. Sometimes what this outer life must be will scandalize those with more stereotyped ideas of holiness and asceticism. Chastity and charity have merged.[271] Morality springs from this fusion, and is no longer confused with cultural convention.

The pelagian phase of asceticism is long past. Asceticism is now a way of lessening the pressure caused by "slippage" between inner and outer life. There is a new kind of stripping, and the need to listen without distraction becomes paramount.

On the other hand, increased vulnerability provides significant hazards, and there is proportionally increasing peril of self-deception and revolts of a subtle kind. But it also appears that as acute as such crises may become, there is at the same time a drawing, an attraction toward, a commitment to nonexperience that will not be gainsaid, and which will bring the wanderer back from forays and cul-de-sacs—but with the sense that there is no "back" just as there is now no "home".

What I have just described may seem cold and frightening—both affective adjectives that simply do not apply. But to respond in kind: at heart there is an unspeakable joy which nothing and no one can destroy.

There are a few more marks of discernment: one is the very hesitancy that comes with this passage. A common response is "that sounds so very familiar, but my life is such that I would hardly dare say it could apply to me."

Another mark is that a person in this passage has no sense of being "afflicted", no matter what is going on outside or inside him or her. Affliction implies a certain kind of self-observation, and this person's focus is elsewhere.

Nonexperience is longing that no longer seeks fulfillment. Even longing itself is being continually let go, and tears mark its passing even as they magnify the Face of God.

Nonexperience is the passage to dwelling in the Silence that interpenetrates every cell and particle; the well of Silence, of Living Water where we find the waters of eternal life, possibility, salvation, which satisfy our thirst for ever (Jn. 4:14).

We know God in nonexperience, even as we know dark matter, dark light, dark energy compose most of the reality of the universe, though we have not been able yet to "find" them.

Nonexperience is the prayer of the abyss, living in the silence of the primordial moment, stretched by Christ, with Christ indwelling, across the abyss, making up by being poured-out-through what is lacking, what remains to be done, in the reconciliation and transfiguration of all things.

IX

He mounted on cherubim and flew; he swooped on the wings of the wind. (Psalm 18:11 BCP)

. . . in stillness and in staying quiet, there lies your strength . . . the Lord is waiting to show you his favour, yet he yearns to have pity on you . . .(Is. 30:15,18 NEB)

Be still before the Lord and wait patiently for him. (Psalm 37:7 BCP)

'Be still, then, and know that I am God.' (Psalm 46:11 BCP)

For God alone my soul in silence waits; truly, my hope is in him.
He alone is my rock and my salvation, my stronghold, so that I shall not be shaken. (Psalm 62:6–7 BCP)

. . . and there is that Leviathan, which you have made for the sport of it. (Psalm 104:27 BCP)

When he established the heavens, I [Wisdom] was there, . . .
when he marked out the foundations of the earth,
then I was beside him, like a little child;
and I was daily his delight,
rejoicing before him always,
rejoicing in his inhabited world
and delighting in the sons of men.[272]

His mother said to the servants, 'Do whatever he tells you.' (Jn. 3:5 NEB)

I have told you all this so that in me you may find peace. In the world you will have trouble. But courage! The victory is mine; I have overcome the world. (Jn. 16:33 NEB and RSV)

Make no mistake about this: if there is anyone among you who fancies himself wise—wise, I mean, by the standards of this passing age—he must become a fool to gain true wisdom. For the wisdom of this world is folly in God's sight. (1 Cor. 3:18–19 NEB)

It is now my happiness to suffer for you. This is my way of helping to complete, in my poor human flesh, the full tale of Christ's afflictions still to be endured, for the sake of his body which is the church . . . to deliver his message in full; to announce the secret hidden for long ages and through many generations, but now disclosed to God's people, to whom it was his will to make it known—to make known how rich and glorious it is among all nations. The secret is this: Christ in you, the hope of a glory to come. (Col. 1:24–27 NEB)

True wisdom is gazing at God. Gazing at God is silence of the thoughts. Stillness of mind is tranquillity which comes from discernment.[273]

Let this be for you a luminous sign of the serenity of your soul: when, as you examine yourself, you find yourself full of mercy for all humanity, and your heart is afflicted by pity for them, burning as though with fire, without making distinction of individuals,—when, by the continual presence of these things, the image of the Father in heaven becomes visible in you, then you can recognize the measure of your mode of life, not from your various labours, but from the transformations which your understanding receives. The body is then wont to swim in tears, as the intellect gazes at spiritual things, as these tears stream from the eyes as if from torrents, moistening the cheeks, involuntarily and without being forced.[274]

The man wearing blessed, God-given mourning like a wedding garment gets to know the spiritual laughter of the soul.[275]

God does not demand or desire that someone should mourn out of sorrow of heart, but rather that out of love for Him he should rejoice with laughter of the soul. . . .
As I ponder the true nature of compunction, I find myself

amazed by the way in which inward joy and gladness mingle
with what we call mourning and grief, like honey in a comb.[276]

> Alone to sacrifice thou goest, Lord,
>   Giving thyself to death whom thou hast slain.
> For us thy wretched folk is any word,
>   Who know that for our sins this is thy pain?
>
> For they are ours, O Lord, our deeds, our deeds,
>   Why must thou suffer torture for our sin?
> Let our hearts suffer for thy passion, Lord,
>   That sheer compassion may thy mercy win.
>
> This is that night of tears, the three days' space,
>   Sorrow abiding of the eventide,
> Until the day break with the risen Christ,
>   And hearts that sorrowed shall be satisfied.
>
> So may our hearts have pity on thee, Lord,
>   That they may sharers of thy glory be:
> Heavy with weeping may the three days pass,
>   To win the laughter of thine Easter Day.[277]

"If you believe in the existence of a loving and merciful
God, then life is a comedy."[278]

The Pillar of Cloud and Fire

Tears bring us to silence, and silence is the foundation of relatedness.

The prayer of the abyss is our living in this silence of the first spark and the single drop; the listening of creation as it is called into being; the obedience of creation as it is called into transfiguration.

The work of God is both serious and merry; so it is intended we should be. God's kenotic acts are entirely gratuitous: there is no need for God to create; there is no need for God to redeem. It is for sheer love that God does both; and for no purpose. God is at play.

Thus it is too with the way of tears: the holding of two things in the heart is both knowledge of the human tragedy and our insecure, perilous freedom, and at the same time the lightness, delightedness of life lived in the security of the redeeming, playful love of God. As Rahner points out, the human person thus sees

> . . . through visible things and perceives the inexpressible that lies beyond. When he looks upon the cross of his Lord, then, behind the tortured foolishness of what he beholds, there opens to him the wide and shining vista of security in God's grace and redemption. . . .
> . . . he has but to plunge into this abyss and that in doing so he will never lose himself; he knows that he may be childlike and even foolish. For the fundamental rule of this divine game is: 'He who loses, wins'. . . .[279]

There is an icon of Michael the Archangel holding a transparent ball that, as the viewer regards the painting, magnifies the folds of the angel's robes. The globe looks like a great teardrop; it is imprinted with the initials of Christ and crowned with his cross; and

291

it is through God's tears mingled with ours that we see, magnified, God's face; it is through tears we know that beyond sorrow, laughter plunges to even greater depths in the abyss, and that the creation is too great a delight to God, too deep an expression of God's wisdom to be, in the end, anything but what God will delight in perfectly.

The story of God is the story of gratuitous, kenotic, playful relationship: God within God in the three Persons of the blessed Trinity; God absenting God in a moment of silence as if God were holding God's breath so that the creation might exist; God pouring out creative, committed, compassionate love.

If we are to mirror this God, if we are to fulfill our vocation as co-creators, if Christ is to indwell and his kenotic love pour through us, then we must live out of the knowledge of this silence and this laughter even as we live and relate to one another. We must be intent in the silence, and ready to glimpse the incongruent reality that makes us laugh. We must be ready to see not only the beauty and glory of what God's gifts to us enable us to create, but also the absurdity, the ridiculousness, of taking our selves too seriously in the light of the divine perspective, or despairing when our hearts are in hell.

Good relationships come not from the domination of one personality over another but from the meeting of two solitudes; the listening of one heart to another. At times of talk and laughter, this silence is present—indeed, it is from its presence that the laughter is born.

We may weep alone, but when we laugh we are engaged with another who has—through idea or print or conversation or picture or being—shown us the laughter that lies at the heart of all things. Or in a moment of awareness of divine play we may laugh "without cause" as we pray, knowing its source does not lie with our selves.

To engage this silence and to live out of it requires the willing powerlessness, the personal *kenosis* that mirrors the divine *kenosis*, which has been the subject of this book. As we have seen, this does not mean self-sacrifice that is an abuse of the creation, or an artificially imposed self-abasement, but rather a letting go of the construction of the house of cards we build to hide in, letting them slip, collapse, and finally be blown away by our breath exhaled with God's in merriment.

It is worth listening to Isaac again to remind our selves of what is meant by "the world".

> These are: love of riches; the gathering of possessions; fattening up the body, giving rise to the tendency toward carnal desire; love of honour, which is the source of envy; the exercise of position of power; pride and the trappings of authority; outward elegance; glory among men, which is the cause of resentment; fear for the body.[280]

As long as we are desperately striving to maintain the sort of world Isaac describes we are in slavery; our grim purpose does not leave us free to play and laugh with God.

If we are listening, if we dwell in God's silence, we are engaged with the Other; we are looking toward the creation; we are looking away from protecting our selves; we are exposed and poised. We have been stopped in our tracks by astonishment and have let fall the rags we clutch about our selves.

As we have seen this dwelling in God's silence, God's silence indwelling, is not contingent on prayer in a monastic cell or even conditions of exterior tranquillity. It is precisely in those moments when tranquillity has been shattered that this listening, this silence—if it is God's—has the most power to heal and transform relationships, whether it is the relationship with God that brings personal *kenosis;* the listening in this relationship to another, which heals a one-on-one rift; the presence that perceives the true network of interrelatedness in an office; or the halting of hostilities between warring nations.

This is not a way of suggesting "how to" patch up the world. That would imply a self-generated activity that imposes power of some kind.

Only God can know the healing of the nations. We must learn to listen for that healing.

But we can ask how: how can we live in a non-self-aggrandizing way; how can we live without controlling others; how can we enable the silence and laughter necessary to the world's healing? This is not a question that applies to others so much as our selves, our own creative self-restraint, our own kenotic attitude that enables God.

Two simple analogies can give us clues: games and parties.

If one is engaged in a game there is an unspoken process at work that involves deep listening to the others and focusses away from the kinds of self-aggrandizement of which Isaac speaks. Serious game-players are not so much interested in winning as in the game itself.

Even in highly competitive games it is the love of the sport as much as the drive to win that attracts its participants.

But whether we are talking about team or individual games, there is an agreement to listen one to the other, to the opponents, and, in spontaneous play, for the Player.

The best kind of game in which to observe this balance of listening and response is to watch two children playing a game they are making up as they go along. Each is listening for the next new step of the game to emerge from him or her self. Both are listening not only for the ideas that emerge from the other but testing that idea against some larger but undisclosed game that is unfolding from the silence.

This equality does not imply equality of skills but equality of right to contribute. One child may be stronger; the other may be more inventive. One may be clumsy with hands; the other able to make delicate moves. But if the inherent equality of right to contribute to the play—even if this right is not exercised—is violated, the game comes to an end.

To return to Gutierrez for a moment, each child's right "to count" must be respected, whether that child is leader or follower.

To count means that the creativity of the other is not quashed; that ideas are listened to even if it is subsequently jointly agreed that this or that one will be discarded. To count is to value the inherent worth of the other person, whether physically or psychically weaker or stronger. If one child constantly controls the other's movements or tries to manipulate ideas, or exploits there will invariably be a squabble.

There is also a mutual listening for when the game should be broken off—to be ended, or continued another time.

What is true of games is also true of parties. Spontaneous parties arise from wonder as the Spirit springs from intense listening, dwelling in silence, in the most ordinary noisy circumstances.

A good organized party stems from careful preparation, the creation of an environment, and an ability on the part of both hosts and guests to listen not only to individual guests but also to the tenor of the whole.

Each of us is a host at every moment.

This process begins with the planning of the party: a theme or environment is decided upon; details—especially those that will cause relaxation, surprise and delight—emerge and are effected; the guest list is thought through not only with an idea to creating the possibility of beloved friends meeting one another, but also encounter of disparate characters who may delight in each other.

Note this is not control: the host is creating possibility. If the guests accept the invitation, knowing that the host gives parties for sheer delight, for purposeless play and not for exploitation, they willingly contribute their own gift of possibility to the environment created.

Every good host or hostess will say that the most important thing about giving a party is to have the work done ahead of time— a solitary process—so that on the day itself she or he can come to the party out of rest, bringing a clear and listening heart. The party-giver must come to the proceedings with true *apatheia*, ready to engage and disengage: to weep with those who weep; to laugh with those who laugh; to disengage and engage another.

The party-giver carries within the *nexus* not only of silence but also of the vastness of divine wisdom and laughter which, if the party is a success, enlarges the hearts of all who come and sends them away refreshed with new hope and peace.

The party-giver is like the woman who lights the Sabbath candles, creating a circle of radiance in which divine hilarity can reassert its primacy in the lives of those who enter.

But the guests also have responsibility: they too are hosts for one another. They must be willing, even if not at their best, to be drawn out of themselves; they must be willing, at least, to be enabled. Their listening must be attuned. There must be trust that the hostess, who in reality is divine Wisdom, and the other guests will be vigilant, watching for any little needs of others, knowing what will make people more comfortable and free; helping the shy ones find people who will draw them out; rejoicing when there is a new and unexpected meeting of hearts.

At a party such as this people will be taken out of themselves, grow a little, risk a little, make confessions, become vulnerable, receive healing. Guests will serve one another: a word of affirmation; a personal concern; attentiveness to eatables and drinkables; a sense of when the conversation has lapsed again into the silence of wonderment, and move on.

At most parties there are a few who cannot fully participate. Even so, they are still a part of the merriment, and discreetly aided to do what is appropriate: drunks get put to bed; crashers are included if they behave, quietly asked to leave if they don't; disagreements reconciled or the participants distracted. The splashy guests are not allowed to dominate little ones; and the little ones are given the loving attention they often do not have under other, more contemptuous, circumstances, which makes them bloom with astonishing profusion, and reveal the depth, talent, and grace which other people may have concluded are simply not there.

Then it comes time for the party to end, often at a peak moment. Perhaps a few people stay on because they are too engrossed to notice that the party is breaking up, and often there is a mellow winding-down. There is no sense of time, but there is a silent, agreed-upon moment when someone makes a move to leave, and all disperse with a sense of thanksgiving, of goodness, and regret that the tangible party must end.

Parties create freedom. Parties are a mirror of co-creation: no one knows or is able to pre-determine what will happen at a party. Like sparks in the stubble we catch fire from one another even as we listen. Play is a commitment not to know, to wait on revelation.

And it is joy not to know, to rejoice in the expansiveness of the unseen field of God's love, the quantum field where the lilies of love spin and do not worry, and the grass bows its head under the weight of grain that will be ground and made Bread, Body. The sparrows free-fall, feathers all counted, notes pouring from their throats.

There are those who think parties are unseemly, but Jesus himself went to parties, made his first miracle at a party, made water wine to show that earth already is married to heaven.

And he was enabled by his Mother, who was the first of our race to put on wholly her Son's kenotic mind, the mind of God listening and knowing and laughing as Love reaches across the abyss. All through her life she listened: Ephrem points to the fact that Jesus' conception took place through her ear, a "quaint" notion, says

Dr Brock, yet Ephrem has captured exactly the sense of play, as does the Christmas antiphon:

> When all things were in quiet silence, and night was in the midst of her swift course; thine almighty Word leapt down out of thy royal throne, Alleluia!

She gave all, became willing as no one had before: willing to give up all that was precious in the eyes of her culture; willing to give up reputation; willing to have a sword pierce her. Without other than the angel's promise, she was taken into this wilderness, knowing only that the Word would become incarnate, and not counting the cost.

And she delights that her Child is borne to the world; delights that we are reborn in his resurrection. The gratuity of her obedience, and her delight mirror the play of God's *kenosis*.

In Luke's gospel we hear of Mary's silence; we see her intent listening; we are told she treasures her unspeakable joys and sorrows and ponders them in her heart, and the desert dwellers point to her weeping.

We do not hear of her laughter, but surely a wry smile twitched about her lips at Cana? And what but the laughter of Easter was her soul leaping toward her God?

So do we need to have the silence that is sabbath, that is God's rejoicing at the completion and beginning of creation. We need to weep our way into this willingness, into the self-forgetfulness of play, so that we may delight in the next act of creation that springs from our tears mingled with God's.

We rest in this silence, like the ark of the biosphere floating on the sea of God's tears, surrounded by, yet far from the noise and confusion of sin, which is being quieted and ordered and cleansed by these tears. And if we are looking at God through our tears, and laughing at God's play, we cannot be part of this sin, but only part of its reconciliation.

This mingling of tears and laughter is the fulcrum, the silence in which we dwell in equipoise, in freedom and possibility.

And what is subversive about all this?

It counters every cynical assumption and materialistic ideal of the ages, past and present. It is the mind of Christ the Serpent in the Beatitudes held up to counter the poison of the serpent's wisdom. It undermines the phony idealism that hides the exploitative nature of institutions. Aspects of human nature may not change; and we need institutions. But institutions and societies do not have to be dominated by what is worst in us.

The casting off of slavery to fear, slavery to the world, slavery to self-destruction; the healing of our selves, our society, the nations will come through weeping, silence, and laughter.

We must learn the ultimate honesty of self-knowledge that no longer seeks to blame others, or looks solely at self-aggrandizement, but which has been cleansed by tears that carry us through despair, and magnify the face of God in those we call enemy. In the mingling of tears for each tragedy of chance or human making we will begin to touch reality. We need to come to the knowledge of being God's nation of priests in which each person, each nation, is both offerer and offering, mirroring God's *kenosis*, and co-creating with it.

It is only in the silence at the bottom of these tears that new possibility will arise: in so many of our works—relief of hunger, establishment of human dignity, efforts toward equality of exodus and jubilee, working for world peace—we have exhausted the possibility of our own thoughts and ways. From the silence of the first spark and the first drop of the abyss, from the primordial silence of creation; from hearts hushed in the dark flame of the tears of God who is Silence comes the possibility we seek, and without which we will die.

And the vision of reality that emerges from this silence brings us to laughter: blessed laughter that reveals; laughter that heals; laughter that appreciates; laughter that rejoices in barriers broken; laughter that adores; laughter with tears that leaves us willingly helpless to do aught but be drawn into the abyss of God's joy.

Postlude

The Furnace

The city lies cradled between two rivers which meet just below its heart. They are flung wide above its head, and great swaths of meadow and wood follow their courses to allow the city to breathe.

Its streets grumble with traffic, and its broad pavements are not wide enough to contain the people who jostle in its markets at the noon of day.

My solitude is on the broadest avenue, where two roads part, just above the confluence of these rivers. The only springs here are my tears. The cry of the owl in the canyon is now the cry of the poor at night on the street outside the stone walls that surround me.

The small hours see me wake in the radiance of two sanctuary lamps in the chapel below my roost. I dress, drink coffee, and let the dark impress me.

With the coming of pale dawn through tall windows, my priedieu and books appear; one by one worshippers slip in below me to pray.

There are psalms and the breaking of bread.

Then there is silence.

Sometimes I venture forth to walk beside one of the rivers.

On such a day I cross the great meadow, and look back to the city's spires, for once clearly visible in the ever-present haze that settles on it in the circle of surrounding hills. They seem to reach for the half-light.

The sun lies low on the horizon: the city is far north; it is the day of longest night.

I walk slowly up the towpath, stunned by any light at all after days of dull grey skies.

I am not alone.

Toward me comes a tall lady, bent with age, indomitable in her grace, supported by her walking stick. Her winter-apple cheeks are crowned by eyes that sparkle with the cold, and with good humour. Her pace is stately, and as she approaches I hear from beyond her a familiar, haunting cry as a wild goose calls to its mate.

She nods, and I stammer a greeting.

She turns, declaring it time to begin her journey home, and we match steps, hers firm as she steadies herself; mine hesitant, as I feel her years and her wisdom.

Around the bend in the river we came to a flock of wild geese so great it blocks the river's channel and spills on to the bank beyond. "They come here," my companion says above the noise of the birds' nervous muttering, "to rest on the way. Look, they are not afraid."

A rower comes down the river. The flock parts, one wave coming toward us, one swarming up the bank. Behind the rower their ranks close again. I am dumbstruck, transfixed by the hundreds of huge, elegant, black-wimpled brown-and-white birds.

Some are watchful; others dip into the water, or snatch the sere grass. Their conversation rises and falls as people stroll past on the bank, or a large jet flies low overhead.

And when I turn, my companion is gone.

Already the light is dying, and I, too, turn slow steps toward my resting place in one of the darkening shapes of the city. Home I cannot call it, for I too am on the way, and do not know where I am led.

As I cross the river by the pleasure-boat yard, where masts and hulls wait wrapped in shrouds, I hear to my left a sound that makes me whirl and grasp the bridge's rail: the geese are calling, calling, the regular cadenced belling that stirs their heavy bodies to urgency. Then I hear one hurling itself aloft, sending the others to the air like flames.

The leaders circle, circle again. More and more geese are calling now; more and more rising into the dusk. With their ascending their voices cry louder and louder.

The great flock turns in a single movement, their clamour floating in their wake.

They head east toward the dark and toward the morning, the morning that burns somewhere beyond the longest night, and heralds the unending day.

Appendix I

**Liber Graduum
or
Book of Steps
(Anon c 400)
Translated by Sebastian Brock**

On the Tears of Prayer

1. Understand [grasp] what I am going to say, my child: There are tears that arise from sorrow and there are tears that arise from joy, just as our Lord said: "You shall weep, lament, and sorrow, but the world will rejoice; but after a time your tears will be turned to joy." (Jn. 16:20) Someone may weep because of his sins—and he does well to do so, as it is written: "Sorrow that is because of God is compunction which turns one to salvation/life". (2 Cor. 7:10) Others may have conquered sin and moved away from sinful acts to perform good deeds, and they weep for/in joy, out of their love for their Lord who performed a great [act of] grace for them, delivering them from the slavery of death, and making them free; for [these people] have humbled themselves and kept His commandments, just as David said, "This is the day that the Lord has made; come, let us dance with joy at it. O Lord, deliver us, O Lord, rescue us!" (Ps. 118:24–25) Let us dance with joy on this day of our salvation!

And when someone has been delivered from servitude to death, he serves the Lord in joy, and not in sorrow, as David explained: "Serve the Lord in joy and enter his presence with praise" (Ps. 100:1); and again he said, "Serve the Lord in awe and take hold of him with trepidation. Kiss the son lest he be angry and you [all] perish from his way; for in a little [shortly] his anger [wrath] will burn, and all the wicked will be burnt up. However, blessed are those who trust him" (Ps. 2) from this world: he will deliver them and then they shall leave it and be perfected in the Love of our Lord Jesus; they will be glorified with him on the great and awesome day.

2. On the subject of tears, which I mentioned: a person may weep for his friend, because he loves him and he is distant from him. If, then, someone far away weeps for his friend, it may be either out of his love or out of his sorrow; but once he actually sees his dear friend, he will weep when they happen to meet face to face, and his tears will pour out over his [friend's] neck, in the sight of anyone who happens to be nearby. It is obvious to everyone that these are tears of joy; for when such a person sees this dear friend whom he had not been expecting to see, he will weep and sob with an abundance of tears.

It is the same with people who sin and so are distanced from our Lord and his righteousness: they weep with sorrow, just as someone weeps when he is far from his friend and feels sorrow concerning him. Such people feel sorrow for their sins, since they fear the judgement of our Lord, and they weep, so that God may have compassion on them and forgive them.

If they then turn away from their sins and are justified, they can draw close to our Lord and their tears turn to ones of joy. And when they become sinless [without any sins] and are delivered from sin, they weep with joy as they encounter our Lord, just like the person who sees his dear friend he had not expected to see, and he falls on his neck, weeping over him with sobs and tears of joy.

So in our case we should be eager to try to become without any sins, asking our Lord to deliver us from sin, just as Paul said: "What a wretched person I am! Who can save me from this body of death, apart from the grace of God which is in our Lord Jesus Christ" (Rom. 7:24).

3. Accordingly let us leave behind everything that is visible, seeing that it is transient, and pass over from external sins; then, once we have cut off those of our sins that are visible, we can stand up in the fight/contest against the sin that dwells right inside us— those evil thoughts which sin forges within our heart; and we can run towards the contest which awaits us and carry it out in prayer,

just as our Lord did before us: (Paul) showed us that Jesus "offered supplication with a mighty groan and many tears to Him who delivers him from death" (Heb. 5:7–9)—and he was heard and was perfected.

Our Lord teaches us the same thing: when we come to a state where we are without any outward sins, we should approach the contest of prayer, just as our Lord both said and did.

Paul said to the brethren in the Lord: "Epaphra performs a contest for your sakes in his prayer" (Col. 4:12). This is [the prayer] which our Lord groaned out forcefully when "he was in anguish in prayer, and his sweat was like drops of blood" (Lk. 22:43) and he shed many tears,—in order to show us that when we no longer have any external sins and outward faults, we should offer up supplication and prayer.

For until we find ourselves in anguish in prayer just as he did, and we [too] shed tears just as he shed them, groaning forcefully just as he groaned,—not until then will we be delivered from the sin which dwells in the heart, or from the evil thoughts it devises from within/inside us.

Thus it is appropriate for "men who are in Christ to raise up their hands in every place, without anger and without any evil thoughts" (I Tim. 2:8) they should shed tears in their love and yearning for our Lord, [waiting] for when they shall come and see him face to face, as it is written: "Blessed are the pure in heart for they shall see God." (Mt. 5:8) In this world, as Paul said: "as though in a mirror in the eyes of our hearts we behold our Lord; but in that world, face to face" (1 Cor. 13:12).

4. The heart does not become pure, then, unless hidden sin has disappeared/ceased from it, and any evil thoughts that had been hidden away in it through the strength of the sin that dwells there, have come to a complete end. Neither will this sin be eradicated from our heart, nor will the evil thoughts and the sin's other fruits disappear unless we pray just as our Lord and all his preachers prayed.

Then, once we have prayed to the Lord in our heart, we shall be full of joy from our lips inwards: for we will rejoice inwardly when our heart no [longer] reproves us of sin and when we have become open faced in the presence of our Lord, having kept all his commandments.

We will rejoice in the way that David said: "My heart will rejoice in you, Lord, and in those who reverence your name. I will give thanks to you, my Lord and my God, with all my heart; and I will praise your name for ever, for your grace has been abundant upon me, and you have rescued my soul from the lowest Sheol" (Ps. 86:11–13).

You can see how God delivered our fathers from the hand/grasp of Sheol, and how their hearts rejoiced in the Lord and those who reverence his name—just as Mary said: "My soul magnifies the Lord, and my spirit has rejoiced in God my Saviour, for he has looked upon the lowliness of his maidservant" (Lk. 1:4–6, 8)—you can see how she was rejoicing in her spirit inwardly, and exulting in her mind, having found grace and mercy in the presence of the Lord.

5. Let it be a law for ourselves, then, that we should run after perfection. Once we hear the word of truth and of mercy, let us be "good soil/earth" (Mt. 13:1–9) for it, and let it put forth in us rootlets/ shoots, striking root in our soul, and sprouting so as to give fruit, thirtyfold, sixtyfold, and a hundredfold. Do not let us prove to be "thorny ground", choking/stifling the seed of truth—with the result that we are choked of life on that day of judgment of our Lord. Nor let us be the poor earth on the roadway, which does not allow anyone to hide the good seed, but the birds come along and peck it up, so that it never sprouts.

Thus we should not be hard ground, otherwise the word of life will not enter us and strike root in us, but instead the evil one will snatch the good seed from our "earth".

Nor should our minds be far distant from awareness [knowledge], like thin soil in which seed withers and does not sprout, owing to the rays of the sun.

Let us [rather] be diligent in providing fruit, lest, when there spring up children who perform the acceptable and perfect will of our Lord, we ourselves actually wither under the new Sun of Justice, that Sun of Mercy "in whose wings is healing" (Mt. 13:3–9, 19–33).

So once we have heard the Word which summons us to the way of life of our Lord and of his heralds/preachers, let us come and allow ourselves to be perfected; let us set as a law for ourselves to imitate them, saying, "Why not become like them, seeing that they themselves were like us" (Phil. 3:17). Let us listen to Paul who says, "I have despised all that is visible, and I consider as dung all the gain that will remain here [when we die], and not accompany me to that world of truth/reality and of glory. Become like me, for I too was like you" (Phil. 3:17).

You see that, if we want, we shall become like Paul.

Appendix II

John the Solitary *On Prayer*
Translated by Sebastian Brock
(c 425)

1. Do not imagine, brother, that prayer consists solely of words, or that it can be learnt by means of words. No, the truth of the matter, you should understand, is that spiritual prayer does not reach fullness as a result of either learning or the repetition of words. For it is not to a man that you are praying, before whom you can repeat a well-composed speech: it is to Him who is Spirit that you are directing the movements of your prayer. You should pray therefore in spirit, seeing that He is Spirit.

2. No special place is required for someone who prays in fullness to God. Our Lord said "The hour is coming when you will not be worshipping the Father in this mountain or in Jerusalem"; and again, to show that no special place was required, he also taught that those who worship the Father should "worship him in spirit and in truth"; and in the course of his instructing us why we should pray thus he said "For God is a Spirit," and He should be praised spiritually, in the spirit. Paul too tells us about this spiritual prayer and psalmody which we should employ: "What then shall I do?," he says, "I will pray in spirit and pray in my mind; I will sing in the spirit and I will sing in my mind." It is in spirit and in mind, then, that he says that one should pray and sing to God; he does not say anything at all about the tongue. The reason is that this spiritual prayer is more interior than the tongue, more deeply interiorized than anything on the lips, more interiorized than any words or vocal song. When someone prays this kind of prayer he has sunk deeper

309

than all speech, and he stands where spiritual beings and angels are to be found; like them, he utters "holy" without any words. But if he cease from this kind of prayer and re-commences the prayer of vocal song, then he is outside the region of the angels and he becomes an ordinary man again.

3. Whoever sings using his tongue and body, and perseveres in this worship both night and day, such a person is one of the "just". But the person who has been held worthy to enter deeper than this, singing in mind and spirit, such a person is a "spiritual being". A "spiritual being" is more exalted than the "just", but one becomes a "spiritual being" after being "just". For until a man has worshipped for a considerable time in this exterior manner, employing fasting, using the voice for psalmody, with long periods on the knees, constant vigils, recitation of the psalms, arduous labours, supplication, abstinence, paucity of food, and all such things, his soul continuously being filled with the remembrance of God, full of due fear and trembling at his name, humble before all men, considering everyone better than himself even when he sees a man's actions: should he see a debauched person, or an adulterer, or someone grasping, or a drunkard, he still acts humbly before them and in his hidden innermost thoughts really considers them better than himself, not just making an outward pretence, but, seeing someone amidst all these evil things, he goes up to him and acts in a humble way before him, begging him, "pray for me, for I am a sinner before God, I am guilty of many things, for not one of which I have paid the price". Only when someone achieves all this—and greater things than those I have mentioned—will he arrive at singing to God in the psalmody which spiritual beings use to praise Him.

4. For God is silence, and in silence is he sung by means of that psalmody which is worthy of Him. I am not speaking of the silence of the tongue, for if someone merely keeps his tongue silent, without knowing how to sing in mind and spirit, then he is simply unoccupied and becomes filled with evil thoughts: he is just keeping an exterior silence and he does not know how to sing in an interior way seeing that the tongue of his "hidden man" has not yet learnt to stretch itself out even to babble. You should look on the spiritual infant that is within you in the same way as you do on an ordinary child or infant: just as the tongue placed in an infant's mouth is still because it does not yet know speech or the right movements for

speaking, so it is with that interior tongue of the mind; it will be still from all speech and from all thought: it will simply be placed there, ready to learn the first babblings of spiritual utterance.

5. Thus there is a silence of the tongue, there is a silence of the whole body, there is the silence of the soul, there is the silence of the mind, and there is the silence of the spirit. The silence of the tongue is merely when it is not incited to evil speech; the silence of the entire body is when all its senses are unoccupied; the silence of the soul is when there are no ugly thoughts bursting forth within it; the silence of the mind is when it is not reflecting on any harmful knowledge or wisdom; the silence of the spirit is when the mind ceases even from stirrings caused by created spiritual beings and all its movements are stirred solely by Being, at the wondrous awe of the silence which surrounds Being.

6. These are the degrees and measures to be found in speech and silence. But if you have not reached these and find yourself still far away from them, remain where you are and sing to God using the voice and the tongue in love and awe. Sing with application, toil in your service until you arrive at love. Stand in awe of God, as is only right, and thus you will be held worthy to love Him with a natural love—Him who was given to us at our renewal.

7. And when you recite the words of the prayer that I have written for you, be careful not just to repeat them, but let your very self *become* these words. For there is no advantage in the reciting unless the word actually becomes embodied in you and becomes a deed, with the result that you arc scen in the world to be a man of God—to whom glory, honor and exaltation is fitting, for eternal ages, amen.

This translation was originally published in the *Journal of Theological Studies*, N.S., Vol. XXX, Pt. 1, April 1979, and is reprinted by permission. The entire article and notes should be read to appreciate the full significance of John's extraordinary text.

Appendix III

From the Second Book of Isaac the Syrian

Unpublished Bodleian manuscript discovered by Sebastian Brock; translated by Dana Miller and Sebastian Brock

[On the Succession of Those Things Through Which the Intellect
Is Steered Towards the Glorious Things of God]

From the intellect's constant reflection and musing on things
pertaining to the divine nature, and from buffetings and exertions
in spiritual conflicts and struggles, a certain power is perceptibly
born which joins with the intellect. This power, then, generates
continual joy in the intellect; through joy a man draws nigh to simple purity of thoughts (that state which is called the pure realm of
nature); and through purity he is deemed worthy of the operation
of the Holy Spirit; being at first made pure, he is afterwards made
holy. Sometimes it happens that amid the reflections of his engagement,* a man experiences a certain limpid impulse that transcends
the flesh, and he acquires interior stillness that is of God, in a resemblance of the things to come, in continual and ineffable rest in
God.

---

*i.e., in prayer, reading, etc.

[From Whence is Constant Weeping Born,/That State Concerning which It is Recorded of Some of the Saints that They Wept Without Ceasing?]
[152a]

A constant flow of tears comes about in a man for three causes: [firstly,] from awestruck wonder arising from insights continually revealed to the intellect and replete with mysteries, tears spill forth involuntarily and painlessly. For with the vision of the intellect a man considers these insights, being held fast with wonder at the knowledge of things spiritually revealed to the intellect through the same insights and, [at the same time] tears flow effortlessly by themselves because of the strength of the sweetness that confines the intellect to gazing at the insights. The Fathers call such tears the type of the Manna that the sons of Israel ate, and the outpouring of water from the rock, "for that rock was Christ",* that is to say, insights both mystic and spiritual. Or else, constant weeping arises from the fervent love of God that consumes the soul, and because of its sweetness and delightfulness a man cannot endure not to weep continually. Or [thirdly], constant weeping comes from great humility of heart.

Now humility of heart comes about in a man for two causes: either from precise knowledge of his sins, or from recollection of the humility of our Lord, nay rather, from the recollection of the greatness of God. I mean, how exceedingly the greatness of the Lord of all lowered itself, so that in such ways as these He might converse with and admonish men. He humbled Himself even so far as to assume a human body, wherewith, even with His own body, He endured men and associated with them, and showed Himself so despised in the world, He Who possesses ineffable glory above with God the Father, and at Whose sight the angels are struck with awe, and the glory of Whose countenance shines throughout their orders. [152b] In this aspect of humility He appeared to us, such that men, because of His ordinary [human] appearance, laid hands on Him as He spoke and suspended Him from the wood [of the Cross].

Wherefore, if someone does not possess this flow of tears, it

---

*I Cor. 10:4.

does not mean that he is simply without tears, but that he is bereft of the cause of tears and does not possess in his soul the roots that generate them. That is, he has never experienced the taste of the love of God; reflection upon divine mysteries has not been aroused in him through long continuance with God; and he does not have humility of heart, though he should think concerning himself that he has humility. Do not bring me the example of those who are humble by nature saying "Lo, there are many such who, although their nature bears witness that they are humble, yet they do not possess tears." Do not bring nature into the question, for these men have suppressed emotions* that are rendered mild and are cooled from their fervour and vehemence, but they do not possess the humility of discerning men, humility that consists of lowly thoughts, the painstaking reflection of discernment, a man's consciousness of his own insignificance, a contrite heart, a flow of tears from compunction of mind, and prudence of the will. But if you wish, ask them, for they have not even one of these or a compunctionate rumination or concern over their conscience. They do not reflect upon the humility of our Lord, they do not have intense grief that transfixes them on account of the knowledge of their sins, they do not possess burning fervour that consumes their heart at the memory of the good things to come, together with the rest of the beneficial thoughts that are usually set astir in the heart by vigilance of mind. Well, then, place also the sucklings, who [153a] live in this world without any thoughts at all, in the stage of the humble! But if you include those who are innocently pure and mild by nature in the stage of those who are consciously and voluntarily humble, then you must likewise call virgins those who are born eunuchs from their mothers' wombs and place them in the ranks of the virgins and the saints, though not their volition, but nature, withheld them from wedlock and caused them to abide in virginity.

Thus, in the case of those who are by nature innocently pure and humble, it is nature itself that numbs their emotions, not the power of the will. Further, they neither taste nor perceive at all that sweetness and the consolations of the bestowals of grace which those who are humble for our Lord's sake taste. For this reason they have

---

*or 'impulses'.

not received the gift of continual, comforting tears, those which the Fathers, say, as it were in a figure, are received in the land of promise: "When you enter there, you will have no fear of war." Consolation is promised to the afflicted of heart. Howbeit, those who have no hope while they mourn will not be sent consolations; and those who do not thirst while earnestly desiring will not be refreshed by the watercourse of the Spirit. If together with what is of nature men possess a voluntary exercise of discernment [discernment of the will], call such as these blessed, for they have been accounted worthy to have in their excellent volition an aid to nature itself, such that without violent struggle they can perform their virtuous deeds. Hence they also receive the consolation that follows a good volition. But if men only possess qualities derived from nature, do not envy them, even as you would not praise irrational creatures and call them blessed.

And so, you [153b] do not have humility of heart, or the sweet and flaming compunction of the love of God, which things are the roots of tears that instill delectable consolation into the heart. Do not take as an excuse the deformities of nature and men whose hearts are naturally gross and whose inner members—which arouse in the soul the stored up power of rationality—are impaired, so that you [do] not feel even a little sorrow over your failings! It is evident that those who possess, together with natural innocence and gentleness, illumined and discerning intuitions, also have tears. For wherever there is discerning humility of heart, it is not possible for a man to see himself and not weep. And this occurs even if he does not wish to do so, for involuntarily the heart causes these things to leap up, and causes weeping to pour forth continually on account of the flaming compunction and contrition of heart that irresistibly [stirs] within him.

From stillness a man can gain possession of the three [causes of tears]; love of God, awestruck wonder at His mysteries, and humility of heart. Without these it is unthinkable that a man should be accounted worthy to taste of the wellspring of flaming compunction arising from the love of God. There is no passion so fervent as the love of God. O Lord, deem me worthy to taste of this wellspring! Therefore, if a man does not have stillness, he will not be acquainted with even one of these, though he performs many virtuous deeds. He cannot know what the love of God is, nor spiritual knowledge, nor can he possess true humility of heart. He will not know these three virtues, or rather, these three glorious gifts. He will be astonished when he hears of certain men that they possess constant weeping, for he will suppose that they weep at will, or that they force themselves to this, and consequently he will think the thing incredible.

Fragments from the Second Book of Isaac the Syrian
Translated by Sebastian Brock

The gift of God and the awareness of Him is not the cause for [does not result in] commotion and shouting; it is entirely filled with peace, being where the Spirit resides, together with love and humility.

And this is the sign of the coming of the Spirit, for by these things the person whom the Spirit has overshadowed is made perfect.

Someone who has [actually] tasted truth is not contentious for truth. Someone who is considered among men to be zealous for the truth has not yet learnt what truth is really like: once he has truly learnt it, he will cease from zealousness on its behalf . . . (Kephalia 77)

If zeal had been appropriate for putting humanity right why did God the Word clothe Himself in the body in order to bring back the world to His Father by means of gentleness and humble manners; and [why] was He stretched out on the Cross for the sake of sinners, handing over [His] sacred body to suffering on behalf of the world?

I myself say that God did all this for no other reason, but only in order to make known to the world the love that He has, His aim being that, as a result of our greater love arising out of an awareness of this, we might be captivated by His love [or into love of Him], when He provided the occasion of [this manifestation] of the kingdom of heaven's great potency—which consists in love—by means of the death of His Son.

The whole purpose of our Lord's death was not to deliver us from sins, or for any other reason, but solely in order that the world might perceive/become aware of the love God had for creation. Had all this astounding affair taken place solely for the purpose of the forgiveness of sins, it would have been sufficient to deliver/redeem [us] by some other means. For who would have made an objection if He had done what he did by means of an ordinary death? But He did not make His death at all ordinary—in order that you might realise the nature of this mystery. Rather, He tasted death in the cruel suffering of the Cross. What was the need for the outrage done to Him and the spitting? Just death and in particular *His* death, without any of these other things which took place, would have sufficed for our salvation/redemption. What wisdom, filled with life, is God's! Now you understand and realise why the coming of our Lord took place, and all the events that followed it, even to the extent of His relating the purpose quite clearly out of His own holy mouth: "To such an extent did God love the world/ that he gave His Only begotten son"—referring to the Economy brought about by His renovation. (Kephalia 78)

The reasons for the coming into being of the world and for the advent of Christ are one and the same: an indication to the world of the immense love of God who brought about both events. . . . (Kephalia 79)

†   †   †

When you seek but fail to find close at hand, beware of losing faith, otherwise something which you are not seeking and of which you are unaware will be born [find birth] in you: for lack of faith receives a punishment. Do not say "I have laboured for so long and failed to find" or that "the reality of the matter does not correspond to the greatness of the description". Beware of thinking like this, for punishment is close at hand for lack of faith, and a heart that has no faith stands condemned. In what does this punishment consist? As a result of the sense of abandonment brought by your lack of faith you will fall into giving up hope and giving up hope will hand you over to despondency, and despondency will pass you out to laxity, and laxity will keep you away from the object of your hope. And no greater evil than this can befall you. . . .

†   †   †

When you pray attach the following to your prayer:

O God, make me worthy to become aware of that hope which is reserved for the righteous at your Coming, when you come in our body to make known your glory to the worlds.

O God, who brought your love into the world when it knew you not, who were revealed to the righteous in divers manners throughout all generations through revelatory hints, resurrect the deadness of my senses so that I may become aware of you, and as a result make haste to travel in your direction, not pausing till the hour when death imposes a limit to my voyage in the harbour of silence.

O Christ, the Harbour of Compassion, who revealed Yourself in a sinful generation, for whom the righteous had waited in their own generations, who was revealed for the joy of all creation, grant to me other eyes, other hearing, another heart, so that, instead of the world, I may see, hear and perceive the things you have reserved for the race of Christians at the revelation of your glory as they make use of [benefit from] a different kind of sense perception. . . .

† † †

Apart from the illumination which is born in the soul as a result of them, what profit is there in laws and rules, but for the fact that every time someone goes astray in the darkness he can be put on his way by their means, that is by means of appointed times of prayer and the fixed Office. It is like the case of someone who has lost his way, and has then gone back to his starting point: he starts out again and arrives at where he wants to go. Rules and laws similarly put right someone who has gone astray in darkness: once he approaches them, they put him back on the path from which he had strayed. . . .

† † †

A person who is afraid of sin, will not be afraid of Satan. Everyone who longs for God's gift will have no fear of trials. Anyone who firmly believes that the Creator's concern controls the entire creation, will not be put into confusion by anything. . . .

† † †

Notes

[1]The spiritual homilies of Isaac the Syrian. These selections newly translated from the Syriac for this book by Dr Sebastian Brock, Oriental Institute, Oxford University. See also *The Ascetical Homilies of Saint Isaac the Syrian*, tr. Holy Transfiguration Monastery, Boston, 1984, p. 297. Hereafter cited as *A.H.* The translation by Wensinck may be more readily available: *Mystic Treatises by Isaac of Nineveh*, tr. A J Wensinck, Nieuwe Reeks, Deel XXIII, No. 1, Wiesbaden, 1969. Hereafter cited as Wensinck. References are by *Bedjan's page numbers* in margin of Wensinck's translation. This passage is Wensinck, p. 430.

[2]*The Elusive Presence* by Samuel Terrien, Harper and Row, New York 1978, p. 461.

[3]H. Eccl. 36.2–4 in *The Holy Spirit in the Syrian Baptismal Tradition* by Sebastian Brock, Poona 1979, p. 130. Hereafter cited as *Holy Spirit*.

[4]Nativity 11:6–8 in *The Luminous Eye*, by Sebastian Brock, Rome 1985, p. 12.

[5]Nativity 12–16; 21–24 in *The Harp of the Spirit*, by Sebastian Brock, London 1983, pp. 52–63.

[6]Isaac the Syrian, tr. S Brock; *A.H.*, p. 297–298; Wensinck, p. 430.

[7]*The Suffering of God* by Terence E Fretheim, Philadelphia 1984, p. xiii.

[8]*The Sayings of the Desert Fathers* tr. Benedicta Ward, Cistercian, Kalamazoo 1983, p. 184.

[9]Dom André Louf to author.

I. The Fractured Rock

[10]Isaac the Syrian, tr. S. Brock; *A.H.*, p. 34; Wensinck, p. 49.

[11]Symeon the New Theologian quoted in *The Mystic of Fire and Light* by George Maloney, Dimension Books, Denville 1975, p. 134.

[12]For a detailed discussion see *Grief and Growth* by R Scott Sullender, Paulist Press, Ramsey 1985.

319

[13]*Ibid.*, p. 40.

[14]*Will and Spirit* by Gerald May, Harper and Row, San Francisco 1982, p. 20.

[15]*Grief and Growth*, p. 72.

[16]*Soloveitchik On Repentance* by Pinchas H Peli, Paulist Press, Ramsey 1984, p. 261.

[17]*Ibid.*, p. 36.

[18]*Revelations of Divine Love* by Julian of Norwich, Paulist Press, Ramsey 1978, Chapter 27 (Long Text), p. 225.

[19]*Soloveitchik On Repentance*, p. 261.

[20]*Holiness* by Donald Nicholl, Seabury Press, New York 1981, pp. 43–44.

[21]*Crime and Punishment* by Fyodor Dostoyevsky, tr. Constance Garnett, Airmont, New York 1967, pp. 26–27.

[22]*The Suffering of God, op. cit.*

[23]*The Prophets* by A J Heschel, Harper and Row, New York 1962.

[24]*Soloveitchik on Repentance*, p. 38.

[25]See *The Fire of Your Life* by Maggie Ross, Paulist Press, Ramsey 1983, pp. 57ff.

[26]"The Assault on Freud" by John Ryle, *London Times*, December 22, 1985.

[27]Unpublished lecture, "Emotion and Feeling" by Rowan Williams, typescript IV:4–5.

[28]*Ibid.*, IV:8.

[29]See also *The Contemplation of Otherness* by Richard Wentz, Mercer, Macon 1984.

[30]*Microcosm and Mediator, The Theological Anthropology of Maximus the Confessor* by Lars Thunberg, Acta Seminarii Novetestamentici Upsaliensis XXV, C W K Gleep, Lund and Einar Munksgaard, Copenhagen 1965. See also the condensed version of this vast work by the same author, *Man and Cosmos*, SVS Press, Crestwood 1985.

[31]*The Brothers Karamazov* by Fyodor Dostoyevsky, tr. Constance Garnett, Everyman, London 1912, p. 451.

[32]*Penthos* by Irénée Hausherr, Cistercian, Kalamazoo 1982, p. 87.

[33]*The Brothers Karamazov* tr. Constance Garnett, Everyman, London 1927, Vol. I, p. 45.

II. The Hidden Source

[34]*The English Hymnal*, Oxford 1933, #42.

[35]*Liturgy of the Hours*, Catholic Book, New York 1976, pp. 596–597.

[36]*The Elusive Presence*, p. 476.

[37]*Luminous Eye*, pp. 10–11.

[38]*Ibid.*, p. 48. See also Fretheim's excellent discussion in Chapter 1 of *The Suffering of God, op. cit.*

[39]*The Elusive Presence*, p. 476.

[40]*Ibid.*, p. 460, itals. mine.

[41]Unpublished poem by the Right Reverend John V. Taylor, Oxford, December, 1985.

[42]"Can We Know Spiritual Reality?" by Donald Evans, *Commonweal*, 13 July 1984, p. 394, itals. mine.

[43]*The Courage to Be* by Paul Tillich, Yale University Press, New Haven 1952, pp. 178, 180, itals. mine.

[44]*The Denial of Death* by Ernest Becker, Free Press, New York 1973, pp. 279–280, itals. mine.

[45]Review of *Habits of the Heart* by Robert Andersen in *National Catholic Reporter*, October 11, 1985.

[46]*The Sayings of the Desert Fathers*, pp. 167–168.

[47]tr. S Brock; *A. H.*, p. 15; Wensinck, pp. 18–19.

III. The Polluted Spring

[48]*The English Hymnal*, #98.

[49]*The March of Folly* by Barbara Tuchman, Knopf, New York 1984, p. 383.

[50]*Ibid.*, p. 282.

[51]*The Road Less Travelled* by M Scott Peck, MD, Simon and Schuster, New York 1978, p. 278.

[52]*People of the Lie* by M Scott Peck, MD, Simon and Schuster, New York 1983, p. 75.

[53]*Ibid.*, p. 78.

[54]*Ibid.*, p. 215.

[55]"Repentance and Experience of God" by André Louf, *Monastic Studies* #9, Mount Saviour Monastery, Pine City, New York, Autumn, 1972, pp. 28–29.

[56]*The March of Folly*, p. 387.

[57]*People of the Lie*, p. 195.

[58]"Salvation: Do We Run After Or Wait For It?" by Kenneth Briggs, *National Catholic Reporter*, December 27, 1985.

[59]*People of the Lie*, p. 74, footnote, itals. mine.

[60]"Repentance and Experience of God", p. 38.

[61]"St Anthony of Egypt: the Man and the Myth" by Diarmuid 'O Murchú, *Cistercian Studies*, Vol. XX, 1985:2, p. 93.

[62]*Luminous Eye*, pp. 107ff.

[63]"Repentance and Experience of God", p. 39.

[64]*Ibid.*, p. 38.

[65]*Ibid.*, p. 29.

[66]"My Innate Sense of Being Powerless" by Anne Fauvell, *Sisters Today*, Vol. 56, No. 10, June/July, 1985, pp. 613–614.

[67]*People of the Lie*, p. 209.

[68]From an unpublished sermon by the Rev Harry Reynolds Smythe, Priest Librarian, Pusey House, Oxford.

IV. Clearing the Watercourse

[69]Anon, "Book of Steps" in *Liber Graduum* (c 400), unpublished translation by Sebastian Brock. For complete text of this section, see Appendix I.

[70]Gregory the Great, *Moralia* 31, 93 in *The Animals of St Gregory* by Brian O'Malley, Paulinus Press, Rhandirmwyn 1981, p. 76.

[71]Isaac the Syrian, tr. S Brock; Wensinck, p. 253; *A.H.*, pp. 178–179.

[72]*Early Irish Lyrics* ed. Gerard Murphy, Oxford 1956, pp. 63–65, kindness of Esther de Waal.

[73]Symeon the New Theologian quoted in *Inward Stillness* by George Maloney, Dimension Books, Denville 1976, p. 115.

[74]"Love" by George Herbert in *The Temple*, Paulist Press, Ramsey 1981, p. 316.

[75]"Time Essay" by Roger Rosenblatt in *Time*, December 17, 1984, discussing the Bhopal tragedy in the light of John Donne.

[76]*The English Hymnal*, #42, v. 2.

[77]*Dorotheos of Gaza*, tr. Eric P Wheeler, Cistercian, Kalamazoo 1977, pp. 95ff.

[78]*Ibid.*, pp. 149ff.

[79]*Ibid.*, p. 151.

[80]*Ibid.*, p. 154.

[81]Frederick Buechner in *Wishful Thinking*, Harper and Row, New York 1974.

[82]*Crying, the Mystery of Tears* by William H Frey, II, PhD, Winston Press, Minneapolis 1985.

[83]*The Jonah Complex* by André Lacocque and Pierre-Emmanuel Lacocque, John Knox Press, Atlanta 1981, p. 79.

[84]*Crying*, pp. 84ff.

[85]tr. S Brock; *A.H.*, p. 82; Wensinck, p. 125.

[86]Quoted in *Here I Stand* by Roland Bainton, Lion Publishing, Tring 1983, pp. 82–83.

[87]"Humility and Obedience in Monastic Tradition" by André Louf, *Cistercian Studies*, Vol. XVIII, 1983:4, pp. 261–282, itals. mine.

[88]"St Anthony of Egypt: The Man and the Myth," p. 92.

V. The Mirror in the Pool

[89]*The English Hymnal*, #42, v. 3.

[90]"Our Fragile Brothers" by Jim Nieckarz, *Commonweal*, July 12, 1985, pp. 405–406.

[91]*America*, September 28, 1985, p. 146.

[92]*The Lord of the Rings* by J R R Tolkien, Allen and Unwin, London 1966, p. 232.

[93]*Crying*, p. 103.

[94]*Ibid.*, p. 112.

[95]Gregory the Great quoted in *Inward Stillness*, p. 112.

[96]*Penthos*, p. 130.

[97]Isaac the Syrian, tr. S Brock; Wensinck, p. 252; *A.H.*, p. 178.

[98]*Penthos*, pp. 125–126.

[99]For a study of laughter as healing see Norman Cousins' *Anatomy of an Illness*, W.W. Norton, New York 1979.

[100]Isaac the Syrian, tr. S Brock; Wensinck, p. 507–508; *A.H.*, p. 345.

[101]*Ibid.*, *A.H.*, p. 383; Wensinck, p. 577.

[102]*John Climacus* tr. Colin Luibheid and Norman Russell, Paulist Press, Ramsey 1982, pp. 138–139.

[103]Aeschylus, *Agamemnon*, Bk. I, line 177.

[104]tr. S Brock; *A.H.*, pp. 241–242; Wensinck, pp. 339–340. Note, however, that there are some occasions of desire for prolonged sleep that endanger health. While some psychologists advocate treating depression with extended periods of sleep, this is not a universal cure, and in some people pathological amounts of sleeping can be dangerous if not life-threatening.

[105]tr. S Brock; Wensinck, p. 492; *A.H.*, pp. 392–393.

[106]Art Hoppe quoted in "The Marital Arts" by Mary Kay Blakely, *The New York Times Book Review*, September 22, 1985, p. 20.

[107]*Inward Stillness*, p. 109.

[108]*Penthos*, pp. 8–9.

[109]*Soloveitchik on Repentance*, p. 231. Abraham Isaac Kook also discusses repentance in his book, *The Lights of Penitence*, tr. Ben Zion Bokser, Paulist Press, Ramsey 1978. Kook's treatment is profound and very beautiful, but has come into my study too late to treat properly in this volume. He needs a study of his own.

[110]"The Holy Spirit and Monasticism Today" by Olivier Clément, *Cistercian Studies*, Vol. XIV:4, p. 325.

[111]*Penthos*, p. 19.

[112]*Soloveitchik on Repentance*, p. 38.

[113]*Ibid.*, p. 263.

[114]*John Climacus*, p. 137.

[115]*Ibid.*, p. 143.

[116]*The Sayings of the Desert Fathers*, p. 117.

[117]Isaac the Syrian, tr. S Brock; *A.H.*, p. 174; Wensinck, p. 245.

[118]*Ibid.; A.H.*, p. 116; Wensinck, p. 165.

[119]"Monks and Tears: A Twelfth-Century Change" by Brian Patrick McGuire, Medieval Institute, University of Copenhagen. The passage he refers to is from *In Epiphania Sermo* 3,8. *Opera Bernardi* IV, ed. J Leclercq and H Rochais Rome 1976, p. 30. Nec parum distat inter has lacrimas devotionis et aetatis utique iam virilis, atque eas quas primaeva aetas inter infantiae vagitus emisit, lacrimas utique paenitentiae et confusionis. Verumtamen longe amplius utrisque praecellunt aliae quaedam lacrimae, quibus et infunditur sapor vini. Illas enim lacrimas vere in vinum mutari dixerim, quae fraternae compassionis affectu in fervore prodeunt caritatis, pro qua, etiam ad horam, tui ipsius immemor esse sobria quadam ebrietate videris.

There is not so much difference between these tears of devotion shed by an adult and the tears which babies shed amidst their childish wailings, both being tears of penitence and confusion. However, far above these there stands out another kind of tears, those to which the savour of wine is added. For indeed one could speak of them as being changed into wine, since, arising from the affection of brotherly compassion, they come forth in the ardour of love, as a result of which one seems for that moment to lose one's self-awareness in a kind of "sober drunkenness". Translation kindness of Helen Brock.

[120]*The Love of Learning and the Desire for God* by Jean Leclercq, OSB, Fordham University Press, New York 1982, p. 59.

[121]Quoted in *Teach Us To Pray* by André Louf, DLT, London 1974, p. 106.

[122]*Ibid.*, pp. 38ff.

[123]"Biblical Antiquities of Philo: David and Jonathan LXII" (Pseudo Philo) in *Library of Biblical Studies*, tr. M R James, KTAV, New York 1971, p. 237.

[124]*The Jerome Comentary*, ed. R E Brown, J A Fitzmyer, R E Murphy, Geoffrey Chapman, Englewood Cliffs 1968, article on John, pp. 445ff.

[125]*Ibid.*, article on Luke, pp. 147ff.

[126]*Ibid.*, p. 153.

[127]See II Kings 6:17.

VI. Tapping the Fountain

[128]Isaac the Syrian, tr. S Brock; *Ascetical Homilies*, pp. 82–83. See also *Pilgrimage of the Heart* ed. George Maloney, pp. 162–163, and *Philokalia: Early Fathers*, tr. Kadloubovsky and Palmer, pp. 251–252, and Wensinck, p. 85. The whole point of tears is that they bring the person into sacred time, which not only means timelessness but even a reversal of events in time as we know it. The "new world" is now, not merely an apolcalyptic moment. See Sebastian Brock, *The Holy Spirit in Syrian Baptismal Tradition*.

[129]*The English Hymnal*, #42.

[130]*John Climacus*, p. 140.

[131]*Ibid.*, p. 141, brackets mine.

[132]Isaac the Syrian, tr. S Brock; *A.H.*, p. 174; Wensinck, p. 245.

[133]*Ibid.; A.H.*, pp. 14–15; Wensinck, p. 18.

[134]*John Climacus*, p. 144.

[135]*Ibid.*, p. 145.

[136]*Ibid.*, p. 143.

[137]*Ibid.*, p. 141.

[138]*Ibid.*, p. 143.

[139]tr. S Brock; *A.H.*, p. 178; Wensinck, p. 253.

[140]*The River of Light*, by Lawrence Kushner, Harper and Row, San Francisco 1981.

[141]*Will and Spirit*, p. 350, note 11.

[142]Isaac the Syrian, Book II, unpublished Bodleian manuscript, tr. Dana Miller and Sebastian Brock.

[143]*The Work of Craft* by Carla Needleman, Knopf, New York 1979.

[144]"Does the Writer Exist?" by Joyce Carol Oates, *New York Times Book Review*, April 22, 1984.

[145]"Strange Fish" by Lee Anne Schreiber, *New York Times Book Review*, July 3, 1983.

[146]"Art, Life and T.S. Eliot" by Irvin Ehrenpreis, *New York Review*, June 28, 1984, itals. mine.

[147]tr. S Brock; *A.H.*, pp. 390–391; Wensinck, p. 489.

[148]*Ibid.; A.H.*, p. 392; Wensinck, p. 492.

[149]"Talk of the Town" in *The New Yorker*, August 25, 1985, pp. 19–20.

[150]*A Celebration of Faith* by Austin Farrer, Hodder and Stoughton, London 1970, pp. 72–73.

[151]c.f. *The Suffering of God*.

[152]Unpublished lectures on detachment by Rowan Williams.

[153]*The Sorrow of God and the Pain of Christ*, pp. 74ff.

[154]Isaac the Syrian, tr. S Brock, Book II, Kephalia IV:78.

[155]*The Risk of Love*, by W.H. Vanstone, Oxford 1978.

[156]*Holy the Firm*, by Annie Dillard, Harper and Row, New York 1977, pp. 71–72.

[157]"Making the Darkness Conscious" by Sister Paula Hirschboeck, OP, *Sisters Today*, Vol. 55, #1, August/September, 1983, p. 20.

[158]"The Holy Spirit and Monasticism Today", p. 323.

[159]*People of the Lie*, p. 171.

[160]"Can We Know Spiritual Reality?", p. 395.

[161]"The Holy Spirit and Monasticism Today", pp. 318, 321.

[162]*The World of Silence*, by Max Picard, Gateway, South Bend 1982, p. 71.

[163]Isaac the Syrian, tr. S Brock; *A.H.*, p. 177; Wensinck p. 251.

[164]*Ibid.*; *A.H.*, p. 83; Wensinck, p. 126.

[165]*Ibid.*; *A.H.*, p. 96; Wensinck, pp. 127–128.

[166]"*John the Solitary, On Prayer*," by Sebastian Brock, *Journal of Theological Studies*, New Series, Vol. XXX, Part 1, 1979, pp. 97–98. For full text see Appendix II.

[167]Isaac the Syrian, Book II, tr. Dana Miller.

[168]"The Beast at the Center of the Galaxy" by Derral Mulholland, *Science '85*, September, 1985, p. 52.

[169]Isaac the Syrian, tr. Sebastian Brock, in "Divine Call and Human Response", p. 73; *A.H.*, p. 120; Wensinck, p. 172.

[170]"Purification by Atheism" by Olivier Clément, *Orthodoxy and the Death of God* ed. A M Allchin, Supplements to Sobornost #1, 1971, p. 243.

[171]*Holy the Firm*, p. 76.

[172]c.f., "Holy Days", by Liz Harris, *The New Yorker*, September 16, 1985, p. 98. She draws on Sholem, but the phraseology of her distinction between this panentheism and pure spiritual hedonism, or pantheism, is nicely drawn.

[173]Visions, apparitions, locutions and the like. These, if they have occurred, usually happen very early on, and by now have long ceased to have significance except possibly as distractions, if they occur at all. Their occurrence is more questionable than validating. Most people do not have them, and, if they are wise, do not want, and above all, do not need to have them.

[174]*Microcosm and Mediator. Man and the Cosmos* is a distilled version of this work.

[175]Isaac the Syrian in "Divine Call and Human Response", p. 507; *A.H.*, pp. 344–345; Wensinck, p. 507.

[176]T.S. Eliot, *The Complete Poems and Plays*, Faber and Faber, London 1969, p. 196.

VII. The Fountain Is the Furnace

[177] *The Book of Lights* by Chaim Potok, Penguin, London 1983.

[178] *Kabbalah*, by Gershom Scholem, NAL, New York 1978.

[179] *T.S. Eliot*, p. 198.

[180] *Climacus*, p. 127.

[181] "The Blessing of Water in the Oriental Liturgies" by Gabriele Winkler, *Concilium* Series, "Blessing and Power" p. 58.

[182] Isaac the Syrian, tr. S Brock; *A.H.*, p. 178; Wensinck, p. 252.

[183] *Pilgermann*, by Russell Hoban, Picador, London 1984, pp. 87–88.

[184] *Luminous Eye*, p. 89.

[185] "Hymn on Christ as Light in Mary and in the Jordan", tr. S Brock, *Eastern Churches Review*, Vol. VIII:2, 1975, p. 138.

[186] *Harp of the Spirit*, pp. 62–63.

[187] "A Hymn of St Ephrem to Christ on the Incarnation, the Holy Spirit and the Sacraments" tr. Robert Murray, *Eastern Churches Review*, 3, pp. 142–150.

[188] Symeon the New Theologian, in *Inward Stillness*, p. 117.

[189] *Luminous Eye*, p. 83.

[190] *Ibid.*, p. 73.

[191] *Holy Spirit*, p. 12.

[192] Isaac the Syrian, tr. S Brock; *A.H.*, p. 269; Wensinck, p. 384.

[193] Isaac the Syrian, tr. S Brock, in "Divine Call and Human Response", p. 74.

[194] *Holy Spirit*, p. 86.

[195] *The Elusive Presence*, p. 352.

[196] *Luminous Eye*, p. 44.

[197] *Ibid.*, p. 45.

[198] "The Thrice-Holy Hymn in the Liturgy", in *Sobornost*, 7:2, 1985, p. 27.

[199] *Luminous Eye*, p. 81.

[200] *Holy Spirit*, p. 13.

[201] *Ibid.*, p. 11.

[202] Nicetas Stethatos quoted in *Inward Stillness*, p. 110.

[203] "Cane of Galilee" in *The Brothers Karamazov* tr. David Magarshack, Penguin, Vol. II, pp. 426–427.

[204] c.f. *Fire*, "Lightning in the East".

[205] *Luminous Eye*, p. 64.

[206] Sahadona, quoted in *Holy Spirit*, p. 14.

[207] *The Religious Symbolism of Salt* by James Latham, Théologie Historique #64, Éditions Beauchesne, Paris 1982.

[208] *Ibid.*, p. 227.

[209]*Ibid.*, p. 232.

[210]*Ibid.*, p. 240.

[211]*Idem.*

[212]*Ibid.*, p. 242.

[213]*Selected Works of St Ephrem the Syrian* tr. J B Morris, Oxford 1847, p. 12.

[214]*Knowing Woman* by Irene Claremont de Castelleja, Harper and Row, New York 1974, pp. 56–57.

[215]*Holy Spirit*, pp. 16–17.

[216]*Ibid.*, p. 38.

[217]*Ibid.*, p. 37.

[218]tr. S Brock; *A.H.*, p. 223; Wensinck, p. 315. See also *Penthos*, p. 131.

[219]*Climacus*, p. 137.

[220]Symeon the New Theologian, quoted in "Symeon the New Theologian and the Way of Tears" by Sister Sylvia Mary, CSMV in *One Yet Two* ed. M Basil Pennington, OCSO, Cistercian, Kalamazoo 1976, p. 118.

[221]*Penthos*, p. 131.

[222]*Luminous Eye*, p. 72.

[223]*Ibid.*, p. 73.

[224]*Ibid.*, p. 24.

[225]*Idem.*

[226]See Winkler, *op.cit.*

[227]*Luminous Eye*, pp. 74–75.

[228]tr. S Brock; Wensinck, p. 246, *A.H.* p. 175.

[229]*Penthos*, p. 55.

[230]*Symeon the New Theologian*, tr. C J de Catanzaro, Paulist, Ramsey 1980, p. 82.

[231]I am indebted to Pamela Lee Cranston, who brought some aspects of the *kenosis* problem to my attention.

[232]*Luminous Eye*, p. 76.

[233]*Holy the Firm*, pp. 66–68.

[234]Isaac the Syrian, tr. S Brock; Wensinck, pp. 164–166; *A.H.*, pp. 115–116.

VIII. The Well of Nonexperience

[235]*Ibid.;* Wensinck, p. 253; *A.H.*, p. 178.

[236]*Ibid.;* *A.H.*, p. 118; Wensinck, p. 168.

[237]*Ibid.;* *A.H.*, p. 183; Wensinck, p. 260.

[238]*Ibid.;* *A.H.*, p. 391; Wensinck, p. 489.

[239]*The Elusive Presence*, p. 470.

[240]"In Search of the Spirit" by Anne Barry, *New Woman*, October, 1985, p. 126.

[241]*Christian Spirituality* by Rowan Williams, John Knox, Atlanta 1980.

[242]*Ibid.*, p. 137.

[243]*Ibid.*, pp. 146–147.

[244]*Ibid.*, pp. 147–148.

[245]*Ibid.*, p. 149, itals. mine.

[246]*Idem.*

[247]*Ibid.*, p. 150.

[248]*Idem.*

[249]*Ibid.*, pp. 150–151.

[250]*Ibid.*, p. 167.

[251]*Ibid.*, p. 174.

[252]*Ibid.*, p. 175.

[253]*The Elusive Presence*, pp. 304–305, itals. mine.

[254]For an introduction to Schleiermacher's thought, see *Friedrich Schleiermacher*, by C W Christian, Word Books, Waco 1970; *A Prince of the Church*, by B A Gerrish, SCM, London 1984.

[255]*The Courage To Be*, p. 179.

[256]Dietrich Bonhoeffer, *Letters and Papers from Prison*, SCM, 1971, pp. 281–282.

[257]*Ibid.*, pp. 360–361.

[258]*Ibid.*, pp. 361–362, itals. mine.

[259]*Christian Spirituality*, p. 156.

[260]*True God* by Kenneth Leech, Sheldon Press, London 1985, p. 155.

[261]tr. S Brock; Wensinck, p. 171; *A.H.*, pp. 119–120.

[262]c.f., *Fire.*

[263]"Talk of the Town", *The New Yorker*, November 11, 1985, p. 36.

[264]Teresa certainly did: c.f., for example, Gerald Brenan's *St John of the Cross: His Life and Poetry*, Cambridge 1973; or the more recent and complementary *St John of the Cross* by Alain Cugno, Burns and Oates, London 1982.

[265]*Discerning the Mystery* by Andrew Louth, Oxford 1983, p. 59.

[266]"Merton Rimpoche: A Stranger in an Iron Cage" by Charles K Kinzie, *Contemplative Review*, Autumn, 1985, p. 6.

[267]"In Search of the Spirit", p. 124.

[268]*Mekhilta de Rabbi Ishmael*, tr. Jacob Z Lauterback, Vol. II, Philadelphia, 1949, pp. 185–191.

[269]Roman Catholic Lectionary, Monday 14th Week, Year 2.

[270]*Life of Moses* by Gregory of Nyssa, tr. A J Malherbe and E Ferguson, Paulist Press, Ramsey 1978, p. 119; pp. 232–235.

[271]cf. the chapter on "Chastity" in *The Fire of Your Life, op. cit.*

IX. The Pillar of Cloud and Fire

[272]Prov. 8:73, tr. Hugo Rahner in *Man At Play*, Herder and Herder, New York 1967.

[273]Isaac the Syrian, tr. S Brock; *A.H.*, p. 305; Wensinck, p. 444.

[274]*Ibid.; A.H.*, p. 392; Wensinck, p. 492.

[275]*Climacus*, p. 140.

[276]*Ibid.*, p. 141.

[277]"Good Friday, the Third Nocturn" by Peter Abelard, tr. Helen Waddell in *Medieval Latin Lyrics*, Penguin, London 1962.

[278]Garrison Keillor quoted in *Time*, November 4, 1985, p. 71.

[279]*Man At Play*, pp. 54, 56.

[280]tr. S Brock; *A.H.*, p. 15; Wensinck, p. 18.

Bibliography

Works Cited in This Volume

Articles

America, September 28, 1985, p. 146, untitled anonymous editorial.

"Habits of the Heart" by Robert Andersen in *National Catholic Reporter*, October 11, 1985.

"Talk of the Town" by Anon, *The New Yorker*, August 25, 1985.

"Talk of the Town" by Anon, *The New Yorker*, November 11, 1985.

Article on Garrison Keillor, *Time*, November 4, 1985, p. 71.

"In Search of the Spirit" by Anne Barry, *New Woman*, October, 1985.

"The Marital Arts" by Mary Kay Blakely, *The New York Times Book Review*, September 22, 1985.

"Salvation: Do We Run After Or Wait For It?" by Kenneth Briggs, *National Catholic Reporter*, December 27, 1985.

"Divine Call and Human Response" by Sebastian Brock, *The Way*, January, 1981.

"Hymn on Christ as Light in Mary and in the Jordan" tr. S Brock, *Eastern Churches Review*, Vol. VIII:2, 1975.

"John the Solitary, *On Prayer*" by Sebastian Brock, *Journal of Theological Studies*, New Series, Vol. XXX, Part 1, 1979.

"The Thrice-Holy Hymn in the Liturgy" by Sebastian Brock, *Sobornost* 7:2, 1985.

"The Holy Spirit and Monasticism Today" by Olivier Clément, *Cistercian Studies*, Vol. XIV, #4.

"Purification by Atheism" by Olivier Clément, in *Orthodoxy and the Death of God*, ed. A M Allchin, Supplement to *Sobornost*, Vol. 1, 1971.

"Art, Life and T.S. Eliot" by Irvin Ehrenpreis, *New York Review of Books*, June 28, 1984.

"Can We Know Spiritual Reality?" by Donald Evans, *Commonweal*, 13 July, 1984.

"My Innate Sense of Being Powerless" by Anne Fauvell, *Sisters Today*, Vol. 56, No. 10, June/July, 1985.

"Holy Days" by Liz Harris, *The New Yorker*, September 16, 1985.

"Making the Darkness Conscious" by Sister Paula Hirschboeck, OP, *Sisters Today*, Vol. 55, #1, August/September, 1983.

"Merton Rimpoche: A Stranger in an Iron Cage" by Charles K Kinzie, *Contemplative Review*, Autumn, 1985.

"Humility and Obedience in Monastic Tradition" by André Louf, *Cistercian Studies*, Vol. XVIII, 1983:4.

"Repentance and Experience of God" by André Louf, *Monastic Studies*, #9, Mount Saviour Monastery, Pine City New York, Autumn, 1972.

"The Beast at the Center of the Galaxy" by Derral Mulholland, *Science '85*, September, 1985.

"A Hymn of St Ephrem to Christ on the Incarnation, the Holy Spirit and the Sacraments" tr. Robert Murray, *Eastern Church Review*, 3.

"Our Fragile Brothers" by Jim Nieckarz, *Commonweal*, July 12, 1985.

"Does the Writer Exist?" by Joyce Carol Oates, *New York Times Book Review*, April 22, 1984.

"St Anthony of Egypt: the Man and the Myth" by Diarmuid 'O Murchú, *Cistercian Studies*, Vol. XX, 1985:2.

"Biblical Antiquities of Philo: David and Jonathan LXII" (Pseudo Philo) in *Library of Biblical Studies*, tr. M R James, KTAV, New York 1971.

"The Assault on Freud" by John Ryle, *The London Times*, December 22, 1985.

"Time Essay" by Roger Rosenblatt, *Time*, December 17, 1984.

"Strange Fish" by Lee Anne Schreiber, *New York Times Book Review*, July 3, 1983.

"Symeon the New Theologian and the Way of Tears" by Sister Sylvia Mary, CSMV in *One Yet Two* ed. M Basil Pennington, OCSO, Cistercian, Kalamazoo 1976.

"Emotion and Feeling" by Rowan Williams. Unpublished lecture, 1985.

"The Blessing of Water in the Oriental Liturgies" by Gabriele Winkler, *Concilium* Series, "Blessing and Power", 178 T & T Clark, Edinburgh 1985.

Books

Aeschylus, *Agamemnon*, Bk. I, line 177. See *Bartlett's Familiar Quotations*.

Anon., "Book of Steps" in *Liber Graduum* (c. 400), unpublished translation by Sebastian Brock.

Bainton, Roland, *Here I Stand*, Lion Publishing, Tring 1983.

Becker, Ernest, *The Denial of Death*, Free Press, New York 1973.

Bonhoeffer, Dietrich, *Letters and Papers from Prison*, SCM, London 1971.

Brenan, Gerald, *St John of the Cross: His Life and Poetry*, Cambridge 1973.

Brown, R E, Fitzmyer, J A, Murphy, R F., eds., *The Jerome Commentary*, Geoffrey Chapman, Englewood Cliffs 1968.

Brock, Sebastian
—*The Luminous Eye*, C.I.I.S, Rome, 1985.
—*The Harp of the Spirit*, *Sobornost* Supplement #4, London 1983.
—*The Holy Spirit in the Syrian Baptismal Tradition*, Jacob Vellian, Poona 1979.

Buechner, Frederick, *Wishful Thinking*, Harper and Row, New York 1973.

de Castelleja, Irene Claremont, *Knowing Woman*, Harper and Row, New York 1974.

de Catanzaro, C J, tr., *Symeon the New Theologian*, Paulist, Ramsey 1980.

Christian, C W, *Friedrich Schleiermacher*, Word Books, Waco 1970.

Colledge, O S A, Edmund, and Walsh, S J, James, tr. *Julian of Norwich: Showings*, Paulist Press, Ramsey 1978.

Cousins, Norman, *Anatomy of an Illness*, W.W. Norton, New York 1979.

Cugno, Alain, *St John of the Cross*, Burns and Oates, London 1982.

Dillard, Annie, *Holy the Firm*, Harper and Row, New York 1977.

Dostoyevsky, Fyodor
—*Crime and Punishment*, tr. Constance Garnett, Airmont, New York 1967.
—*The Brothers Karamazov*, tr. Constance Garnett, Everyman, London 1912.
—*The Brothers Karamazov*, tr. Constance Garnett, 2 Vols., Everyman, London 1927.
—*The Brothers Karamazov*, tr. David Magarshack, Penguin, London 1976.

Dummett, Ann, *A Portrait of English Racism*, Pelican, Harmondsworth 1973.

Eliot, T S, *Four Quartets*, Faber and Faber, London 1969.

The English Hymnal, Oxford 1933.

Erickson, Milton, E L Rossi, ed.
—*Hypnotherapy, An Exploratory Casebook*, Irvington, New York 1979.
—*The Collected Papers of Milton H Erickson*, 4 vols., Irvington, New York 1980.

Farrar, Austin, *A Celebration of Faith*, Hodder and Stoughton, London 1970, pp. 72–73.

Fretheim, Terence E, *The Suffering of God*, Fortress Press, Philadelphia 1984.

Frey, William H II, PhD, *Crying, the Mystery of Tears*, Winston Press, Minneapolis 1985.

Gerrish, B A, *A Prince of the Church*, SCM, London 1984.

Hausherr, Irénée, *Penthos*, Cistercian, Kalamazoo 1982.

Heschel, A J, *The Prophets*, Harper and Row, New York 1962.

Herbert, George, *The Temple*, Paulist Press, Ramsey 1981.

Hoban, Russell, *Pilgermann*, Picador, London 1984.

Isaac of Nineveh
—*The Ascetical Homilies of Isaac the Syrian*, tr. Holy Transfiguration Monastery, Boston, 1984.
—Book II, unpublished Bodleian manuscript, tr. Dana Miller and Sebastian Brock.
—*Mystic Treatises by Isaac of Nineveh*, tr. A J Wensinck, Nieuwe Reeks, Deel XXIII, No. 1, Wiesbaden, 1969.

Kadloubovsky, E and Palmer, G E H, *Early Fathers from the Philokalia*, Faber and Faber, London 1959.

Kook, Abraham Isaac, *The Lights of Penitence*, tr. Ben Zion Bokser, Paulist Press, Ramsey 1978.

Kushner, Lawrence, *The River of Light*, Harper and Row, San Francisco 1981.

Lacocque, André and Pierre-Emmanuel, *The Jonah Complex*, John Knox Press, Atlanta 1981.

Latham, James, *The Religious Symbolism of Salt*, Théologie Historique #64, Éditions Beauchesne, Paris 1982.

Lauterback, Jacob Z. tr., *Mekhilta de Rabbi Ishmael*, Vol. II, Philadelphia, 1949.

Leclercq, Jean, OSB, *The Love of Learning and the Desire for God*, Fordham University Press, New York 1982.

Leech, Kenneth, *True God*, Sheldon Press, London 1985.

Liturgy of the Hours, Catholic Book, New York 1976.

Louf, André, *Teach Us To Pray*, DLT, London 1974.

Louth, Andrew, *Discerning the Mystery*, Oxford 1983.

Luibheid, Colin, and Russell, Norman, trs., *John Climacus*, Paulist Press, Ramsey 1982.

Malherbe, A J, and Ferguson, E, tr., *Life of Moses*, by Gregory of Nyssa, Paulist Press, Ramsey 1978.

Maloney, George
    —*Inward Stillness*, Dimension Books, Denville 1976.
    —*The Mystic of Fire and Light*, Dimension Books, Denville 1975.

May, Gerald, *Will and Spirit*, Harper and Row, San Francisco 1982.

Murphy, Gerard, ed., *Early Irish Lyrics*, Oxford 1956.

Needleman, Carla, *The Work of Craft*, Knopf, New York 1979.

Nicholl, Donald, *Holiness*, Seabury Press, New York 1982.

O'Malley, Brian, *The Animals of St Gregory*, Paulinus Press, Rhandirmwyn 1981.

Panikkar, Raimundo, *Blessed Simplicity*, Seabury, New York 1982.

Peck, M Scott, MD
    —*People of the Lie*, Simon and Schuster, New York 1983.
    —*The Road Less Traveled*, Simon and Schuster, New York 1978.

Peli, Pinchas H., *Soloveitchik On Repentance*, Paulist Press, Ramsey 1984.

Picard, Max, *The World of Silence*, Gateway, South Bend 1982.

Potok, Chaim, *The Book of Lights*, Penguin, London, 1983.

Rahner, Hugo, *Man At Play*, Herder and Herder, New York 1967.

Ross, Maggie, *The Fire of Your Life*, Paulist Press, Ramsey 1983.

Scholem, Gershom, *Kabbalah*, NAL, New York 1978.

Southern, R.W., *Western Society and the Church in the Middle Ages*, Pelican, Harmondsworth 1973.

Sullender, R. Scott, *Grief and Growth*, Paulist Press, Ramsey 1985.

Terrien, Samuel, *The Elusive Presence*, Harper and Row, New York 1978.

Thunberg, Lars
    —*Microcosm and Mediator*, The Theological Anthropology of Maximus the Confessor, Acta Seminarii Novetestamentici Upsaliensis XXV, C.W.K. Gleep, Lund and Einar Munksgaard, Copenhagen 1965.
    —*Man and Cosmos*, SVS Press, Crestwood 1985.

Tillich, Paul, *The Courage To Be*, Yale University Press, New Haven 1952.

Tolkien, J R R, *The Lord of the Rings*, Allen and Unwin, London 1966, p. 232.

Tuchman, Barbara, *The March of Folly*, Knopf, New York 1984.

Vann, Gerald, OP, *The Sorrow of God and the Pain of Christ*, Acquin Press, London 1947.

Vanstone, W H
—*The Risk of Love*, Oxford, New York 1978.
—*The Stature of Waiting*, Seabury, New York 1983.

Veilleux, Armand, tr., *Pachomian Koinonia* (3 vols), Cistercian, Kalamazoo 1980.

Waddell, Helen, tr., *Medieval Latin Lyrics*, Penguin, London 1962.

Ward, Benedicta, tr., *The Sayings of the Desert Fathers*, Cistercian, Kalamazoo 1983.

Wentz, Richard, *The Contemplation of Otherness*, Mercer, Macon 1984.

Williams, Rowan, *Christian Spirituality*, John Knox, Atlanta 1980.

Wink, Walter, *Naming the Powers*, Fortress Press, Philadelphia 1984.

Books in the Background and of Related Interest

When one has been interested in a subject for a long time it is difficult to know how much reference material to include. Since I have been forced by circumstance to give away my library more than once, there are a lot of books that probably could be cited and maybe even some that should be cited, which have passed out of memory.

Additionally, the interdisciplinary seminars I attended between 1966—1972 had an astonishing bibliography attached to them, and to list all of those books would take several pages. Since the reading was done in a professional psychoanalytic context, there is no way of sorting out how much of my own insight I brought to the subjects under discussion, and how much simply sank in, bypassing conscious discursive rational processes.

Additionally, I have the possibly deplorable habit of rarely reading a book straight through. I have also been blessed with synchronicity. Many books I would not know to consult have somehow come into my hands and fallen open at the only useful—for the purposes of this book—passage they contain. This is especially true in areas (such as patristics) I have only begun to explore.

Thus there is a problem: how do I provide a helpful bibliography that might suggest other avenues of exploration to interested readers?

The solution that most readily presents itself is to divide such a bibliography into two parts: one that is a response to the question, "Who (or what) have been your major influences?"; and the second simply to list *some* of the pertinent books (from my once again divided library) I have brought abroad with me, or acquired here. This is a fairly arbitrary solution, but I can think of no other that would be workable.

The first section I must do informally, as some of the seminar books are (or were) arcane and, in those days, read in microfilm editions.

There is no question in my mind that the cadences heard early in life help form thought patterns. For me this was my father's propensity to recite poets ancient and modern, but with a marked preference for those of the 19th and early 20th century; as well as the odd bit of scripture (often as an ironical comment). There was in addition almost daily exposure in school to the liturgy of the *Book of Common Prayer*, the Coverdale translation of the psalms, and the Authorized Version of the Bible.* Our house was full of well-written books on politics and history, and my mother had kept all her children's books on ancient Greece, which caught a child's imagination.

Music has been a constant companion from birth, and sometimes a profession.

In university I was exposed to two authors whom I know to have been my most direct influences: the Jewish theologian Abraham Joshua Heschel, and the anthropologist theologian, Loren Eisley.

The seminar reading that comes to mind includes, besides classical authors: philosophy: G E Moore, Stephen Korner, Gilbert Ryle, Richard Robinson, Stephen Passmore, C S Peirce, Samuel Alexander, A N Whitehead. There was also some work in value theory. Comparative spirituality: Buddhism: *Tibetan Book of the Dead*, *Tibetan Book of Great Liberation* et. al.; Milarepa; Phadmasambava; Therevada: Buddhaghosa, Jaktaka Stories (Pali Text Society),

---

*This observation does not imply hostility to contemporary liturgies and translations.

Gradual Sayings (ditto); and Zen Buddhism; Confucius; Taoism: Lao Tzu and Chuang Tzu; Sufism: Avicenna, Ibn Al 'Arabi; Zoroastrianism: major texts and philosophical commentaries.

Christian authors (besides the four Evangelists) included such writers as Thomas Traherne along with the more commonly read Western mystics; and a smattering of biographies of interesting characters such as Cardinal Wiseman.

Psychology and medicine tended to run together, probably because we read very little in the former *per se*—we were applying it—and the latter was brought to light in the context of what was medically known—especially by the physician members of the seminar—about the people we discussed. Additionally, I read numerous volumes—particularly in physiology—on my own. We also looked at philosophical physicians such as Thomas Browne and Sir William Osler.

Ethology and ecology were emerging disciplines in that day, and our reading ranged from studies of ecological systems, to body language in humans and animals, to behaviors of specific groups of animals: elephants seemed to come up often, and I myself went through a phase of passionate devotion to herpetology, specializing in *chelonia*.

After I left New York I spent some time "in the field" in some of these areas of biological interest.

The second part of this listing can be done in the usual way, with the addition of the comment that I have acquired some of the books listed below in the course of this study but have not yet had time to read them. There are also quite a few I have heard about—but not yet got my hands on (such as Koestler's *Act of Creation*)—but one has to stop somewhere.

Ancient Christian Writers and *Classics of Western Spirituality*, both published by Paulist Press, are good introductory volumes to many authors who treat the subjects in this book. Since there are already more than 40 volumes in each series, it seems best to simply mention them and leave it to the interested reader to order the Paulist catalogue.

Ayer, A J, *Wittgenstein*, Weidenfeld, London 1985.

Barfield, Owen, *Saving the Appearances*, Harcourt Brace Jovanovich, New York 1965.

Bartholomew, D J, *God of Chance*, SCM, London 1984.

Beasley-Murray, G R, *Baptism in the New Testament*, Eerdmans, Grand Rapids 1984.

Becker, Ernest, *Escape from Evil*, The Free Press, New York 1975.

Bethge, Eberhard, *Dietrich Bonhoeffer*, Fount, London 1985.

Brock, Sebastian, *Syriac Perspectives on Late Antiquity*, Variorum Reprints, London 1984.

Brown, Raymond E, *New Testament Essays*, Paulist Press, Ramsey 1965.

Brown, David, *The Divine Trinity*, Duckworth, London 1985.

Chitty, Derwas J, *The Desert a City*, SVS, Crestwood 1966.

Clément, O, Brobrinskoy, B, Behr-Sigel, E, Lot-Borodine, M, *La Douloureuse Joie*, Spiritualité Orientale N. 14, Abbaye de Bellefontain, Bégrolles-en-Mauges 1981.

Creel, Richard E, *Divine Impassibility*, Cambridge University Press, 1986.

Dalai Lama, The
  —*A Human Approach to World Peace*, Wisdom, London 1984.
  —*Kindness, Clarity, and Insight*, Snow Lion, Ithaca 1984.

Deikman, Arthur J, M D, *The Observing Self*, Beacon Press, Boston 1982.

Eco, Umberto, *Semiotics and the Philosophy of Language*, Indiana, Bloomington 1984.

Edwards, Betty, *Drawing on the Right Side of the Brain*, Tarcher, Los Angeles 1979.

Goleman, Daniel, *Vital Lies, Simple Truths*, Simon and Schuster, New York 1985.

Greenstein, George, *Frozen Star*, Freundlich, New York 1983.

Gribbin, John, *In Search of Schrödinger's Cat*, Bantam, New York 1984.

Griffin, Susan, *Rape The Power of Consciousness*, Harper and Row, San Francisco 1979.

Harding, M Esther, *Woman's Mysteries*, Harper and Row, New York 1971.

Heschel, Abraham Joshua, *The Earth is the Lord's/The Sabbath*, World, New York 1963.

Israel, Martin, *The Pain that Heals*, Crossroad, New York 1982.

Izutsu, Toshihiko, *Sufism and Taoism*, California, Berkeley 1983.

Katz, Steven T, ed., *Mysticism and Philosophical Analysis*, Sheldon Press, London 1978.

Konner, Melvin, *The Tangled Wing*, Harper and Row, New York 1983.

Kreeft, Peter J, *Love is Stronger than Death*, Harper and Row, New York 1979.

Llewelyn, Robert, *Love Bade Me Welcome*, DLT, London 1984.

Lonergan, Bernard J F, *Insight*, Harper and Row, San Francisco 1978.

Lossky, Vladimir, *The Mystical Theology of the Eastern Church*, SVS, Crestwood, 1976.

Love, David, *The Sphinx and the Rainbow*, Bantam, New York 1984.

Louf, André, *The Cistercian Alternative*, Gill and Macmillan, London 1983.

Louth, Andrew, *The Origins of the Christian Mystical Tradition*, Oxford 1981.

MacDermot, Violet, *The Cult of the Seer in the Ancient Middle East*, California, Berkeley 1971.

Main, John, OSB, *Word Into Silence*, Paulist Press, Ramsey 1981.

May, Gerald, MD, *Care of Mind, Care of Spirit*, Harper and Row, San Francisco 1982.

Moltmann, Jürgen, *Theology and Joy*, SCM, London 1973.

Murdoch, Iris, *The Sovereignty of Good*, Ark, London 1970.

Murray, Robert, *Symbols of Church and Kingdom*, Cambridge 1977.

Neusch, Marcel, *The Sources of Modern Atheism*, Paulist Press, Ramsey 1982.

Oppenheimer, Helen, *The Hope of Happiness*, SCM, London 1983.

Page, Ruth, *Ambiguity and the Presence of God*, SCM, London 1985.

Palmer, G E H, Sherrard, Philip, Ware, Kallistos, *The Philokalia*, 3 Vols., Faber and Faber, London 1979.

Pétrement, Simone, *Simone Weil*, Mowbrays, London 1974.

Polanyi, Michael, *Personal Knowledge*, Routledge Keagan Paul, London 1978.

Poundstone, William, *The Recursive Universe*, Morrow, New York 1985.

Prigogine, Ilya, *Order Out of Chaos*, Bantam, New York 1984.

Pseudo-Denys, tr. John D Jones, *The Divine Names* and *Mystical Theology*, Marquette, Milwaukee 1980.

von Rad, Gerhard, *Wisdom in Israel*, SCM, London 1972.

Reeves, Marjorie, *Joachim of Fiore and the Prophetic Future*, SPCK, London 1976.

Saward, John, *Perfect Fools*, Oxford 1980.

Scholem, Gershom G, *Major Trends in Jewish Mysticism*, Schocken, New York 1954.

Sophrony, Archimandrite, *The Monk of Mount Athos*, Mowbrays, London 1973.

Storm, Hyemeyohsts, *Seven Arrows*, Ballantine, New York 1972.

Ulanov, Ann and Barry, *Primary Speech*, John Knox, Atlanta 1982.

Weil, Simone, *Waiting For God*, G P Putnam, New York 1951.

Williams, Rowan
—*Resurrection*, DLT, London 1982.
—*The Truce of God*, Fount, London 1983.

Wilson, A N, *How Can We Know?*, Penguin, Harmondsworth 1986.

Wolf, Fred Alan, *Taking the Quantum Leap*, Harper and Row, San Francisco 1981.

Wyman, Leland C, *Southwest Indian Drypainting*, UNM, Albuquerque 1983.